Unsolved Crimes

Unsolved Crimes

FOLLOW THE TRAIL OF THE WORLD'S MOST NOTORIOUS COLD CASES

John Wright

The Reader's Digest Association, Inc.
Pleasantville, NY/Montreal/London/Singapore

A READER'S DIGEST BOOK

Copyright © 2010 Amber Books

Produced by Amber Books Ltd
Bradley's Close
74–77 White Lion Street
London
N1 9PF
United Kingdom
www.amberbooks.co.uk

FOR AMBER BOOKS
Project Editor Michael Spilling
Design Jerry Williams
Design Manager Mark Batley
Picture Research Terry Forshaw

FOR READER'S DIGEST
U.S. Project Editor Kim Casey
Consulting Editor Debbie Parker
Manager, English Book Editorial, Reader's Digest Canada Pamela Johnson
Canadian Project Editor J. D. Gravenor
Project Designer Jennifer Tokarski
Senior Art Director George McKeon
Executive Editor, Trade Publishing Dolores York
Associate Publisher, Trade Publishing Rosanne McManus
President and Publisher, Trade Publishing Harold Clarke

Library of Congress Cataloging in Publication Data

Wright, John D., 1938-
   Unsolved crimes : follow the trail of the world's most notorious cold cases / John D. Wright.
      p. cm.
   ISBN 978-1-60652-182-3
   1. Cold cases (Criminal investigation)--Case studies. 2. Murder--Case studies. I. Title.
   HV6515.W75 2010
   364.1--dc22
                            2010004936

We are committed to both the quality of our products and the service we provide to our customers.
We value your comments, so please feel free to contact us.

      The Reader's Digest Association, Inc.
      Adult Trade Publishing
      Reader's Digest Road
      Pleasantville, NY 10570-7000

For more Reader's Digest products and information,
visit our website:
            www.rd.com (in the United States)
            www.readersdigest.ca (in Canada)
            www.readersdigest.co.uk (in the UK)
            www.rdasia.com (in Asia)

Printed in Singapore

1 3 5 7 9 10 8 6 4 2

CONTENTS

INTRODUCTION

Crime dramas on television always trap the culprit, whether by a small detail noticed by an amateur sleuth or through the accurate lab tests of a forensic scientist. However, investigators are not so lucky in real life—30 percent of murderers and 75 percent of robbers escape detection in the United States. Despite the power of DNA matches, most cases are solved by traditional police methods, such as trace evidence and the examination of a suspect's motive, their links to the victim, and the strength or lack of an alibi.

However, when unsolved crimes remain on the books for years as cold cases, DNA samples can produce enough evidence for convictions. In 2004 a DNA profile led to a man being convicted nearly 30 years after he committed two rapes in England. For this reason, more police departments are establishing cold-case divisions that may also free inmates who were wrongly imprisoned.

Baffling Cases

The 60 cases recounted here continue to baffle investigators. Some merited international coverage, such as the murder of Elizabeth Short, known as "The Black Dahlia," and the assassination of the Swedish prime minister Olof Palme. Other cases were localized mysteries such as the killing of Canadian teenager Richard Hovey and the spectacular art robbery at Britain's Waddesdon Manor. Every case remained unsolved when this book went to press.

The crimes have been chosen to highlight the different ways perpetrators avoided justice. At times police have been at fault when they failed to protect a crime scene from contamination, which happened after child beauty queen JonBénet Ramsey was murdered at home in 1996. Key suspects have walked free

Los Angleles police officers examine blood-stained clothing found in a storm drain connected to the death of Elizabeth Short in January 1947.

after the prosecution relied on circumstantial evidence, like the supposed "inside job" during a robbery of the Northern Bank of Belfast in Northern Ireland in 2004.

Sometimes solid evidence cannot be found when police are fairly sure they know who is guilty, such as the murderers of union leader Jimmy Hoffa. Even serial killers can avoid detection by randomly selecting victims without previous links to them, such as California's "Zodiac Killer" and Australia's "Mister Cruel."

Clever Criminals and Conspiracies

Foreign governments have played their part in blocking arrests: For example, it is still unknown who poisoned the former KGB agent, Alexander Litvinenko, in London in 2006. Sometimes the criminals were simply too clever: the counterfeiters of "superdollars" and D. B. Cooper, who leaped out of an airliner over Oregon with $200,000 in stolen cash, both covered their trail

Unsolved Crimes presents each case in sequence, beginning with the crime then following with a brief account of the investigation, highlighting the clues uncovered, key suspects and, if any, the trials that failed to convict. Finally, a box of "Lingering Doubts" covers ways in which the investigation may have gone astray and offers speculation about potential leads. Since many of these cases are still live, you will be better prepared to follow any news reports of their progress. At the time of going to press all these cases were unsolved, but some of these crimes, without a doubt, will be solved in the future.

Shoppers walk past a plaque marking the place where former Swedish Prime Minister Olof Palme was assassinated in Stockholm in 1986.

A forensic expert searches for trace evidence on a vehicle linked with the fatal poisoning of Alexander Litvinenko in 2006.

MURDER

Homicide has always been the most serious crime. Today's murderers still use timeless methods like knives and arsenic but they have also adopted modern ways to kill, such as radioactive substances and liquid explosives. Forensic science brings its own techology to crime scenes, but many infamous murders remain unsolved.

ROSE HARSENT

The village of Peasenhall, nestled in a valley in the county of Suffolk, England, was a tight-knit community of churchgoers at the beginning of the twentieth century. This was the point in time when Rose Harsent arrived as a servant girl at Providence House, the home of William and Georgeanna Crisp. On Sunday, June 1, 1902, Harsent's father stopped by for a visit and to leave clean linen for her. Instead, as he entered the back door, he discovered his daughter's body in the kitchen at the bottom of the staircase leading to the servants' quarters. She lay on her back in a pool of blood. The 23-year-old woman's throat was cut, and there were deep gashes on her shoulders and hands; her nightdress was burned and parts of her body were charred, as if someone had attempted to set fire to her remains. When a doctor arrived, he determined that she had been dead for four to six hours.

The Investigation and Suspect

At first the police believed Harsent had tripped down the stairs and dropped her candle and oil lamp, cutting herself and causing the burn marks. But paraffin was discovered in a broken medicine bottle near the body along with a newspaper used to set the fire, an obvious attempt to destroy evidence. They searched her room and found a lewd poem and suggestive letters.

William Gardiner. One note had been sent to Harsent to arrange a midnight meeting that Saturday. This was not signed, but officers matched the handwriting to that of William Gardiner, 35, a carpenter who lived nearby with his wife, Georgie, and their six children. He was a hardworking man and a highly respected reader, choirmaster, and Sunday school teacher in the local Primitive Methodist church. Harsent also attended the church and was a choir member.

Illicit Affair. An autopsy found that the unmarried woman was six months pregnant. Investigators quickly believed this was the result of an affair

she had conducted with Gardiner. A year earlier two young men had seen the couple enter a vacant cottage and heard their lovemaking. This information was quickly circulated, so the police alleged that Gardiner had seduced Harsent and killed her to prevent any demands or accusations she might make. On June 3, only two days after the murder was discovered, police arrested Gardiner, sending a shock wave through the pious community.

The Trials

The first trial began on November 7, 1902, at the Suffolk Assizes (superior court) in Ipswich, the county town. Gardiner testified that he never met Harsent that evening because he was at home in bed with his wife when the murder was committed, and she verified this statement. The Gardiners, however, had been at a neighbor's house during a heavy storm and did not get to bed until about 2:00 A.M. His wife did not fall asleep until about 5:00 A.M. and got up three hours later. At about 7:00 A.M. a neighbor saw Gardiner coming from his washhouse, where a large fire was seen from the boiler inside. Harsent's employer, Mrs. Crisp, testified that she had heard a thud and scream between 1:00 or 2:00 A.M. but did nothing because her husband said Rose would inform them if anything was wrong.

Hung Jury. The prosecution said the broken medicine bottle at the crime scene had been prescribed for the Gardiners' children. Blood had also been found on Gardiner's clasp knife, but he claimed it was used to cut up rabbits. Given the strong circumstantial evidence of the note and Gardiner's relationship with the woman, most of the jury did not buy his alibi. However, one juryman did. Evan Edwards held out obstinately for a verdict of not guilty against the 11 other jurors. Since a unanimous verdict was required, the hung jury forced another trial.

This letter and its envelope were allegedly sent by William Gardiner to Rose Harsent to arrange a midnight meeting. He denied in court that the love tryst had occurred.

Rose Harsent seemed to be an innocent country girl who had been seduced and made pregnant, but the police discovered intimate letters from several local men.

Retrial. The trial occurred on January 21, 1903, at the same courthouse. Public opinion was starting to support Gardiner in what was now called "the Peasenhall mystery," and this time the jury showed more sympathy for his wife's alibi. Still, they returned no verdict when ten members judged him innocent and two guilty.

Nolle Prosequi. A third trial was prepared to be heard at the town of Bury St. Edmunds, but the prosecution decided the evidence would not convict. It next entered a plea of *nolle prosequi* ("unwilling to pursue"),

REOPENING COLD CASES

DNA testing is a dream come true for innocent suspects and a nightmare for criminals. Its accuracy in identification has dominated court trials, released numerous prisoners, and reopened unsolved and nearly forgotten cases.

An extreme example of the latter is the rape and murder of Muriel Drinkwater in 1946 in Penllergaer, Wales. The 12-year-old schoolgirl was known as the little nightingale because of her habit of singing during school walks. On the day she was abducted, she was singing as she got off the school bus to begin the lonely mile walk through the woods to her family's farm. When she failed to emerge, local people searched through the night and found her body the next afternoon just off the path.

Police search for Muriel Drinkwater on July 2, 1946, the day they found her body.

The attacker had battered her head and shot her twice. Near the murder spot, police recovered the pistol, but it yielded no real clues. Detectives brought in several suspects and took thousands of statements. This produced a description of a suspicious man, about 30 years old, wearing a brown sports jacket and brown corduroy trousers, but he was never traced.

With the advent of DNA, however, the South Wales Police reopened the file in 2003, making this one the world's oldest cold cases. They believe the murderer, if alive, will be in his eighties.

The search for Muriel's DNA was not easy, because the police station in charge of the case had been closed. Detective Chief Inspector Paul Bethell finally located the girl's school raincoat in a storage space, and forensic scientists recovered the killer's DNA profile. No match was found in the national DNA database, so detectives are now trying to trace relatives of the criminal, perhaps his son or grandson. They are also looking at 40 or 50 suspects' names from the original investigation.

meaning that Gardiner became one of the few defendants tried for murder in England without a verdict ever being returned.

Aftermath

Gardiner's release was welcomed by the locals, who mostly believed that he had been framed. He moved from Suffolk to London to run a shop, keeping his name despite advice to change it. The public remained fascinated with the case, and promoters tried unsuccessfully to lure Gardiner to appear on stage. He died at the age of 72 in 1941 in virtual obscurity.

No Further Suspects. No police search was conducted for another suspect, despite many hunches. An attack by an outsider seemed less likely than the revenge of a jealous lover, whether it was Gardiner's wife or a boyfriend of the victim. In later years, village gossip revealed that Harsent had not been so innocently seduced, because she was sexual involved with several other local men. The police never pursued other potential suspects since no obvious evidence existed against any of them.

"A Most Mysterious Murder." In a BBC television program that reconstructed the case in 2005, *A Most Mysterious Murder—The Case of Rose Harsent*, the author and actor Julian Fellowes decided that Gardiner's wife had killed Harsent in a jealous rage, and he reasoned that she would have confessed if Gardiner had been convicted.

William Gardiner (center) stands outside the Suffolk assizes court in Ipswich after the retrial that judged him neither guilty nor innocent. A planned third trial was canceled.

Lingering Doubts

- Bloodstained clothes were not found at Gardiner's house. Was this what he was burning so early in the morning in his washhouse?

- Did the Crisps know about their servant's sexual habits? Why didn't they take seriously the sound of a scream in the night?

- Why didn't the police try to trace the other men who wrote to Harsent? Were officers ever suspicious of Gardiner's wife?

- How much was the second jury influenced by Gardiner's good reputation and his public support?

THE VILLISCA MURDERS

The streets of Villisca, Iowa, went dark on Sunday, June 9, 1912, when the electric company switched off the lights after a dispute with the city council. Even so, Josiah Moore, 43, and his wife, Sara, 39, took their four children to the annual Children's Day Program at their Presbyterian church. The event lasted from 8:00 P.M. until 9:30 P.M. It had been a tiring day beginning with the regular church services that morning, so the family invited two friends of their children to stay the night.

The next morning, their neighbor Mary Peckham noticed an unusual quietness at the Moores' home on the corner. Finding the door locked and receiving no response, she called Josiah's brother, Ross Moore, who had a key. In the downstairs bedroom, he found the bodies of the two visiting Stillinger sisters, Lena, 11, and Ina, 8. When Mrs. Peckham summoned the sheriff, the city marshal arrived and discovered the bodies of the entire family in their bedrooms upstairs: the parents and their children, Herman, 11; Katherine, 10; Boyd, 7; and Paul, 5. The eight victims had all been brutally murdered as they slept.

The eight victims died in this white frame house. It was privately purchased and renovated in 1994 and is open for tours. Ghost hunters have frequently spent nights there.

The Investigation

The police found all the outside doors locked and the windows closed. The crime scene was badly compromised before the local National Guard arrived at midday to cordon off the area. There are estimates of 100 people walking around the rooms to view the bodies. Some personal items were also removed by curious visitors, and someone apparently took part of the father's skull as a souvenir. This human traffic also confused bloodhounds brought in to track scents.

Time of Deaths. The coroner estimated that the slayings had occurred shortly after midnight, and the murderer had moved from bed to bed battering the skulls of each victim. According to grand jury testimony from physicians and others who viewed the crime scene, each of the children was struck only once or twice. The parents were struck multiple times. The father had received the worst attack. The victims' facial features were unrecognizable, and the killer had covered all the faces with the sheets and left Lena Stillinger in a sexual position, although she had not been raped.

Physical Evidence. The murder weapon, a bloody ax belonging to the father, was found in the visitors' bedroom and nearby on the floor was a slab of bacon. The murderer had attempted to wipe the blood from the ax and cleaned his hands on other items. On the kitchen table was a bowl containing bloody water. Investigators said the victims were struck with the ax's back end or side, although the blade was used on the mother. No readable fingerprints were found at the scene.

The Suspects

Early in the investigation, police suspected that an outsider, probably a maniac, had haphazardly killed the victims. They tried to link known killers to the town without success.

- **Henry Lee Moore, 37.** No relation to the Moore family, he had been convicted of murdering his mother and grandmother in Columbia, Missouri, six months after the Villisca deaths. The authorities interviewed him but found no connection.

- **Frank F. Jones, 57.** A private detective, James Newton Wilkinson, then focused on Jones, a state senator from Villisca. Moore had worked at Jones' farm implements store but left to set up his own rival business, taking lucrative customers with him. Rumors also said Moore had an affair with Jones' daughter-in-law. Jones had attended the local Methodist church that evening. Many locals disliked him, calling him arrogant. Wilkinson pushed the case, saying Jones had hired a man, William "Blackie" Mansfield, to carry out the killings, but a grand jury failed to indict Mansfield on July 21, 1916, because he proved he was elsewhere at the time of the murder.

- **Rev. Lyn George Jacklin Kelly, 33.** In 1917 attention turned away from Jones to the Rev. Kelly, who was visiting the Presbyterian church on the night of the murders. He signed a confession that year saying God had told him to commit the murders. "'Slay utterly' came to my mind," he wrote, "and I picked up the ax, went into the house and killed them." Kelly supposedly had taken a bloodied shirt to the cleaners, but it was never recovered. Others said he had told people about the murders before

A report of the crime in the June 13, 1912, *Villisca Review* featured a banner headline and photographs of Josiah and Sara Moore who died with the children.

Investigators focused briefly on local state senator Frank Jones, but no connection with the deaths could be established.

they were discovered. The Iowa Attorney General's office charged him with the murders, but Kelly recanted his confession before the trial.

The Trials

In the first trial beginning in September 1917, the prosecutors gathered devastating facts about Kelly's character, documented months after the murders.

Sexual Deviancy. Kelly was a voyeur known to walk through the town late at night and peek through windows. Girls reported that he lured them to his room to teach them stenography but asked them to undress, attempting to fondle them. The prosecution also pointed out that Kelly was left-handed—as the murderer was thought to be—but they had no real physical evidence against him.

Defense of Insanity. The defense argued that Kelly's confession was the result of mental problems, and his obsession with the murders had made him delusional. They added that testimony about his deviant sexual behavior did not apply to the murder case. The jurors failed to reach a verdict: eleven wanted to acquit him, and one person thought he was the murderer but should be found not guilty because of his insanity.

Acquittal. The retrial in November had the same strong defense that resulted in Kelly's acquittal. Kelly was only tried for the death of Lena Stillinger, allowing the state to continue with the other indictments if they wanted, but they opted to quit. Kelly would later spend time in mental institutions in Washington, D.C., and Long Island, New York.

Lingering Doubts

- How could the killer batter eight people to death without one of them waking?

- After the hit man, William Mansfield, was not indicted, why didn't police continue to pursue Senator Jones, who seemed to have the motive of revenge?

- Was Rev. Kelly mentally disturbed when he confessed to the crime? If so, was the one juror correct in saying he killed the victims while insane?

- Some investigators believed the killer used the slab of bacon for masturbation. Was this primarily a sexual crime? Why didn't the jurors focus more importance on Kelly's deviant habits?

REVEREND EDWARD HALL AND ELEANOR MILLS

On the cold evening of September 16, 1922, near New Brunswick, New Jersey, a young couple was walking down a local lovers' lane when they made a gruesome discovery—two corpses, a man and woman, lying on their backs. The lovers fled and called the police who arrived to find that both victims had been shot in the head. The local community was shocked when they were later identified as the Reverend Edward Hall, 41, an Episcopalian minister, and Mrs. Eleanor Mills, 34, a member of his choir and wife of the church's sexton (caretaker). It was later revealed that they had been conducting a four-year love affair.

Detective Hanlon of the New Jersey State Police prepares court exhibits of the clothing worn by Edward Hall and Eleanor Mills when they were murdered.

The Investigation

On inspection, the crime scene was bizarre. The bodies had been posed, after being brutally killed, with their feet pointing toward a crab-apple tree. Hall's right arm was touching the woman's neck, and his Panama hat covered the single bullet wound to his head. Mills's left arm had been placed on the minister's right thigh and her brown silk scarf was wrapped around her neck. Her throat had been cut and the wound was already infested with maggots indicating that she had been killed sometime before, and she had been shot three times in the head. The autopsy also discovered that her tongue had been cut out, a fact revealed four years later.

Unusual Evidence. A .32 caliber cartridge case was recovered from the scene, and, more unusual, scattered around and between the bodies were pieces of shredded paper. The paper was identified as Hall's and Mills's torn up love letters. Hall's business card had also been propped up against the heel of his left shoe. Unfortunately this piece of evidence was compromised when the police allowed spectators to pass it around to look at it.

Cold Case Reopened. The case lay dormant for four years, until the New Jersey governor reactivated it in 1926 when a newspaper reported that the minister's maid had informed Hall's wife that he and Mills were planning to elope. The maid added that Mrs. Hall and her brothers had

A portrait of
Eleanor Mills.

Workers exhume
the body of
Eleanor Mills for
an autopsy before
the trial of Frances
Hall and her two
brothers. Edward
Hall's body was
also exhumed.

gone to the lovers' lane on the night of the murder. Several other witnesses also placed them near that area.

The Suspects

The young couple that discovered the bodies, the Ku Klux Klan, and an unknown drifter were all first considered. These ideas were discounted when evidence began to point to family matters.

- **Frances Hall, 48.** Reverend Hall's wife was charged with his murder on July 28, 1926. She had been aware of her husband's affair, and when he disappeared she told several people that the couple was probably dead.

- **Henry Stevens, 52.** Frances Hall's older brother was arrested with his sister. He was respected as a gentleman and had been a professional marksman. His bloodstained handkerchief, bearing an S for Stevens, was found near the murder scene and given to the police.

- **William ("Willie") Stevens, 50.** Frances Hall's other brother was also arrested with her. He had a mental disability and spent much of his time loitering about the town's firehouse.

The morning after the murders, he told the Hall's maid, "something terrible happened last night." He also had his suit professionally cleaned the next morning to remove unidentified spots. However, no one apparently could say he had worn it the night of the murder.

- **Henry Carpender, 40.** A prominent New York stockbroker and Frances Hall's cousin, he was arrested as a prime suspect, but charges were later dropped due to lack of evidence.

- **James Mills, 45.** Eleanor Mills's husband was never seriously considered as a suspect. He was a hard-working man who, besides his church job, worked as a janitor at the local school. On the night of the murder he visited the church twice looking for his wife.

The Reverend Edward Hall poses outside his Episcopal church, St. John the Evangelist, in New Brunswick, New Jersey. Eleanor Mills was a choir singer there.

The Trial

The trial began on November 3, 1926, in Somerville, New Jersey. It lasted for a month and was covered by national newspapers and radio. The prosecution's scenario was that Frances Hall, who came from a wealthy and well-connected family, had her philandering husband killed with the help of her two brothers—William providing the gun (he owned the same type of gun as the murder weapon) and Henry firing the shots. Examination of William's gun, however, showed it had been disabled and was no longer capable of firing live rounds.

The "Pig Woman." The state's case was damaged by the inconsistent testimony of the key witness, Jane Gibson, 50, known in press reports as the Pig Woman because she raised hogs. Her story was that she saw a figure in her cornfield and thought he might be stealing her corn. Riding her mule toward him, she spied two men and two women arguing near a crab-apple tree. She heard a woman ask, "Explain these letters," then another woman scream, "Don't!" three times and "Henry" before three quick shots. However, her story changed with each retelling.

Drama in Court. Gibson's appearance proved to be a sensation. She collapsed on the first day with stomach pains, and two weeks later was carried into court on a stretcher where she identified the suspects as the people she had seen in the cornfield. She had previously been unable to identify them.

As Gibson entered on a stretcher, her mother, seated near the front of the courtroom, shouted, "She's a liar, a liar, a liar! That's what she is and what she's always been." The defense then added insult to injury by suggesting the Pig Woman herself might have committed the murder.

Calling Card. Another blow for the prosecution came after it exhibited the Reverend Hall's business card that had been found at the crime scene. Although William Hall's fingerprints were found on the card, experts testified that the prints had been

Mary Winkler waits on the stand for the jurors to return after a court recess.

THE SPOUSE DID IT?

When a murder victim is married, the police and public will often presume the spouse is guilty. If this seems improbable, detectives still normally put the spouse through intense questioning to eliminate him or her as a suspect. DNA and fingerprints are virtually useless in a marital murder, since the couple would normally have close contact with each other and often with the murder weapon.

While many husbands and wives have been convicted of this crime, others have been arrested in high-level cases and declared innocent. These include the Hollywood actor Robert Blake, who was arrested for the 2001 shooting of his wife, Bonnie, 44, as she waited for him in their car. The jury acquitted the 71-year-old star of *In Cold Blood* although two Hollywood stuntmen said he had tried to hire them for the deed. The defense said they were liars and drug addicts, and Blake went free. No other suspects have been named since. Other arrested and released husbands include Dr. Sam Sheppard (see page 37), Claus von Bülow, and O. J. Simpson.

Jurors and judges tend to be more sympathetic to accused wives, who often claim they were abused by their husbands. Among these was Mary Winkler, 33, who confessed to accidentally shooting her husband, Matthew, 31, in the back, in 2006. He was a Church of Christ minister, but she said he had punched and kicked her regularly. After killing him, she fled from Tennessee to Alabama with their three young daughters. Convicted of voluntary manslaughter in 2007, she was given a prison sentence of 210 days and, because of jail time already served between her arrest and conviction, she was released after 67 days. Most of her time was spent in a mental-health facility.

Lingering Doubts

- What was the significance of the posed bodies? Why did the murderer display Edward Hall's business card and scatter the couple's shredded love letters around their corpses?

- Since the maid said the wife and her brother's sons had gone to the crime scene, and others also saw them near it, why did it make such a difference when the Pig Woman changed her story?

- Were the jurors influenced by the prosecution's poor presentation and by fact that the Halls came from such a notable family?

compromised when the police allowed spectators to pass the card around, because the suspect's prints may have been added after the crime.

Meanwhile, Henry, who was the suspected shooter, had three witnesses to corroborate his story that he was fishing somewhere miles away on that evening. The defense had little need to add more. On December 3, 1926, after deliberating for five hours, the jury declared the three defendants not guilty.

WILLIAM DESMOND TAYLOR

One of Hollywood's most shocking murders was the shooting of the famous actor and director of silent movies William Desmond Taylor, 49. This popular man worked on more than 80 films and had served as head of the Motion Picture Directors' Association. Taylor was shot in the back on the cold night of February 1, 1922, at his bungalow in Westlake Park, an expensive Los Angeles neighborhood. At 7:45 P.M., he waved good-bye to his close friend Mabel Normand, as her chauffeur drove her away. Normand, a movie comedian, had spent an enjoyable evening with Taylor drinking cocktails, despite it being the era of Prohibition. Some 12 hours later, his butler, Henry Peavey, discovered Taylor's body. His death came as a shock to Hollywood and movie fans as details of the case slowly revealed a world of sexual liberation and drugs within the film industry. The story that transpired transformed the public's idea about the actors they had admired and looked up to as role models.

William Desmond Taylor took a break from Hollywood during World War I, serving as a lieutenant with the British army in Dunkirk, France.

A photo-diagram of Taylor's home in Los Angeles highlights the room in which he was murdered. His body is depicted lying in front of an overturned chair.

The Investigation

When police arrived, they found a crime scene with virtually no evidence. The area had not been secured, and was being overrun by Paramount Studio people who had been given access by the butler. An executive and cameraman were among those who badly compromised any existing clues, and the group even took away Taylor's personal letters in case they revealed embarrassing intimate details about him.

The Disappearing Doctor.

In the crowd was a man who said he was a doctor. He hurriedly examined the body, stating, incorrectly, that Taylor had suffered a stomach hemorrhage. By the time police arrived and discovered the wound in Taylor's back, made by a .38 caliber bullet, the mystery doctor had disappeared and was never seen again.

A "Funny Looking" Man. Police interviewed neighbors, two of whom reported hearing a bang that sounded like a car backfiring at around 8:00 P.M. They saw a dark figure on Taylor's porch that one described as a "funny looking" man who went back into the bungalow before reappearing and casually walking away.

Who Was William Desmond Taylor? Taylor was known around Hollywood as a charming gentleman. He was born William Cunningham Deane-Tanner in Ireland, and had been married to a wealthy New York society woman from 1901 to 1912. He deserted his wife and their daughter in 1908, and by 1912 he was working as an actor in Hollywood. His wife eventually found and contacted Taylor after he had made his name in Hollywood, and he made his daughter his heir.

Detectives looked at love letters written by actresses and fans, hoping to spot a hidden motive in them. They also speculated that Taylor's well-publicized campaign against illegal drugs might have provoked drug dealers to hire a hit man, but this avenue of inquiry failed to turn anything up.

The Suspects

- **Mary Miles Minter, 19.** Taylor was a mentor to this blond actress and they were also romantically involved, although he had begun to avoid Minter, because he was concerned about her infatuation with him. Police discovered three golden hairs when they examined the victim's jacket, and her love letters were found in the bungalow along with her handkerchiefs and her pink nightgown. Minter may have appeared that night with the gun she had used in an earlier unsuccessful suicide attempt. While threatening to shoot herself, it

MURDER OR ACCIDENT?

How can investigators decide if what seems to be a tragic accident is actually murder? It might not be easy if the victim was in a car crash or fell out of a window. Fatal accidents are so frequent that police will often look no further unless very suspicious circumstances exist.

One of America's longest-running conspiracy theories involves Karen Silkwood's death in her Honda on November 13, 1974. Silkwood, 28, worked at a plutonium plant near Oklahoma City and was a union activist who had complained about unsafe working conditions. On the fatal day, she was driving alone to give supporting documents to a *New York Times* reporter. Suddenly, her car swerved off the highway into a concrete wall. Strangely, no documents were found in the car. Union officials employed an independent accident investigator who inspected a dent on the Honda's rear fender and skid marks on the road. He concluded that Silkwood had been forced off the road by another car. Oklahoma's highway patrol recorded it as an accident.

Even lengthy investigations of car deaths can fail to end suspicions. After Princess Diana died in a crash in a Paris tunnel in 1997, French and British inquiries blamed the accident on the drunk chauffeur. Mohamed Al Fayed, whose son Dodi died with her, still claims they were murdered because the British establishment wanted to get rid of her.

Detectives have similar difficulties with deaths by falling. While on his honeymoon in 2005, George Smith IV fell overboard from a cruise ship between Greece and Turkey. An argument between unidentified speakers had been heard in his cabin and blood was found inside and outside of it, as well as on a canopy covering the lifeboats. His wife, Jennifer, was found passed out far from the cabin and had no recollection of what happened. No suspect has ever been named.

Karen Silkwood had complained to the Atomic Energy Commission about safety problems.

Charles Carsen, a former sea captain, claimed that while hoboing his way across California he met three men, one of whom he knew as Edward Sands, who said they were planning to "get even" with Taylor. He was considered an unreliable witness and his evidence was discounted.

Mary Miles Minter had a romantic relationship with Taylor. After his death, she made only four more movies before retiring from the Hollywood scene.

is possible she accidentally shot Taylor when he tried to stop her.

- **Charlotte Shelby, 44.** Minter's manipulative mother owned a .38 caliber pistol like the murder weapon. Soon after the murder she left the country for several years. The press speculated that that she killed Taylor to prevent her daughter from throwing away her acting career on an older man.

- **Mabel Normand, 29.** A cocaine and opium addict who had inspired Taylor's antidrug work; Normand was the last known person to have seen him alive. After the murder, police found her rummaging through Taylor's personal items—she may have had a romantic bond with the victim, but this was never proven. Although her chauffeur had previously shot one of her lovers, Normand had an alibi and was dismissed as a serious suspect.

- **Edward Sands, 27.** Taylor's ex-valet and cook had previously been imprisoned for embezzlement and had also deserted the U.S. Navy three times. Although he was born in Ohio, he pretended to be English and used several aliases. When he left Taylor, half a year

Lingering Doubts

- Why did detectives concentrate on Hollywood insiders and not seriously consider the possibility that the killer was a burglar or revenge-minded drug trader?

- Although the clues and motive pointed to the neurotic actress Mary Miles Minter or her mother, why would three district attorneys fail to act? Was there a cover-up to protect the film community?

- Even though the servant Edward Sands was a small-time crook who had successfully robbed Taylor and disappeared, why would he return to murder his former employer?

- Why did the police ignore the seemingly sincere deathbed confession of Margaret Gibson, a recent Roman Catholic convert?

before the murder, he stole his car along with around $5,000 in cash and other valuables. The police never located Sands.

- **Henry Peavey, 39.** Taylor's butler found the body and was an early suspect. Peavey was due in court on charges of lewd behavior on the day Taylor was killed. The director had put up bail money for him and was due to testify on his behalf. Hollywood gossip speculated that the two men were having a homosexual affair, but investigators found no evidence of this.

- **Margaret Gibson, 27.** A silent-movie star who had worked with Taylor on four movies, Gibson was never considered a suspect, but confessed to the murder as she was dying in 1964. Gibson had been arrested and released without charges in 1923 for being part of an extortion ring.

Harry Oakes poses with a machete while wearing a tie, indicating his two roles as a rich businessman and rugged islander.

HARRY OAKES

Sir Harry Oakes was born in Maine and prospected for gold during the Klondike Gold Rush and later in California, Australia, and New Zealand. In 1912 he struck it rich in northern Ontario, Canada, and became one of that country's wealthiest people. In 1924 he became a Canadian citizen for business reasons. He moved to the Bahamas in 1935 and became a property developer, living in a magnificent house in Nassau. He was knighted in 1939 by the king of England.

On the morning of July 8, 1943, the 68-year-old was found murdered in his bed by a houseguest, Harold Christie. Oakes had been bludgeoned to death and his body doused with gasoline and set on fire. Feathers from his pillow covered his remains.

The Investigation

Police examining the half-charred body recorded four indentations on the left side of Oakes's head, caused by a sharp, pointed instrument. Blood and fingerprints were found on a nearby Chinese screen, a single bloody handprint was on the wall next to the bed, and muddy footsteps were on the steps to the bedroom. Besides setting the body on fire, the murderer had also tried, unsuccessfully, to burn the bedroom.

Alfred de Marigny, Oakes's son-in-law, is escorted by police after his arrest. He was acquitted and then expelled from the islands.

The Meddling Duke. The Duke of Windsor, governor of the island after abdicating the British crown, was eager to have the death listed as a suicide. The duke was unpopular with many people in Britain and wanted to avoid being involved in any additional scandals. In his attempt to do this, he blocked news of the investigation and called in two Miami detectives.

Fingerprints. By the time they allowed prominent locals in to see Oakes's bedroom, the murder scene had been disturbed. The detectives later announced that a fingerprint on the Chinese screen matched that of Count Alfred ("Freddie") de Marigny, 33, the French son-in-law of Oakes and an unpopular figure on the island. Marigny was arrested and the crime scene was scrubbed of all other fingerprints, making it impossible to implicate anyone else.

Other Suspects

- **The Mafia.** Oakes had opposed legal gambling on the island, and some thought the gangsters may have taken revenge in their usual manner. "Lucky" Luciano and Meyer Lansky were among the mobsters who wanted to develop the casinos.

- **Walter Foskett, 61.** Oakes's lawyer, Foskett, was also suspected. A 1959 FBI report containing an interview with Maryland art dealer Fred Maloof stated that Foskett threatened him with a gun after

CONTAMINATING CRIME SCENES

Vital evidence can be ruined if the police do not secure a crime scene properly to keep out anyone who is not involved in the investigation. Even officials designated to be there can leave their own DNA or other trace evidence at the site or even on the victim. To avoid this contamination, investigators wear protective uniforms, masks, gloves, and plastic overshoes. The murder victim and objects within the area are not moved until the forensic scientist arrives. Any evidence is then carefully packed and labeled.

Evidence has been spoiled or compromised in many well-known cases. In the unsolved 1996 murder of the child beauty-queen JonBenét Ramsey (see page 77), police allowed family and friends to wander freely in the house. In most cases, even small details can lead to confusion. At the 2007 California trial of music producer Phil Spector for the shooting of actress Lana Clarkson, the defense argued that evidence was compromised by the type of sticky tape used to lift fibers from the victim's dress. They claimed this may have obliterated the blood-splatter evidence that showed Spector was standing too far from Clarkson to have shot her. The jury later failed to reach a verdict, and Spector was found guilty at a second trial in 2009.

Music producer Phil Spector arrives with his wife, Rachelle Short, for opening statements in his trial.

arguing over paintings that Oakes was supposedly using to help buy a Miami hotel. When Maloof informed Oakes, the millionaire claimed to know nothing about the paintings being offered. He was furious that his lawyer had swindled him and promised to "straighten him out." Oakes was murdered just days after this conversation.

- **Harold Christie, 47.** Fred Maloof also told the FBI that he believed Christie, who had discovered Oakes's body, was also involved in the killing. Christie was a property speculator and former rum-smuggler who also wanted gambling on the island.

The Trial

The court case began in the Bahamas on October 18, 1943. The prosecution produced witnesses who testified to Marigny's strained relationship with Oakes. He disliked the Frenchman for eloping with his

An assistant (left) holds plans to Marigny's house for (left to right) Chief Justice Oscar B. Haly and defense attorneys Godfrey Higgs and W. E. A. Callender.

daughter, Nancy, on her eighteenth birthday, when she became old enough to inherit his fortune. Nancy, however, could not understand her parents' antagonism toward him.

Unusual Behavior. One witness said they saw two men arguing the day before the murder. Oakes was upset that his wife had received letters from Marigny, and ordered him to stop writing to her, calling Marigny a sex maniac. Police also told the jury that Marigny had visited the police station at 7:30 A.M. on the morning of the murder looking very distressed and asking if someone could examine his car that he had transformed into a truck.

The Finger Points at Christie. The defense gained some ground when it was revealed that inspectors had confused the fingerprints in the room and initially said they were not Marigny's. Defense lawyers also pointed the finger at Christie, asking why he parked his car out of sight of the house that night. He claimed it was to save gas. The local police superintendent also testified to have seen Christie as a passenger in another car at midnight on the night of the murder, even though Christie claimed to have not left the house.

Marigny's Alibi. Marigny testified, saying that he had been entertaining guests on the night of the murder and had driven one home at 1:00 A.M., taking around 45 minutes to do so. A couple staying at his home overnight asked him why his hands, hair, and beard were singed. Marigny replied that it had happened when he lit his cigar and that he also cooked on a gas stove.

On November 12, jurors took less than two hours to find Marigny innocent by a majority vote of 9 to 3.

- De Marigny was a likely suspect because of his gold-digger reputation and the constant arguments he had with Oakes, so did the police set him up? Did they do this to draw attention away from certain powerful individuals on the island who had tried to stop Oakes from blocking the casinos?

- Is battering a victim to death and leaving muddy footprints in his bedroom the work of a professional hit man?

- How did the killer break into the house, enter Oakes's room, commit the brutal beating, and leave without waking Christie who was sleeping in the next bedroom? How could Christie have slept through the noise of the beating and the smell of the fire?

- Could Christie himself have committed the crime or been part of it? He claimed he lifted Oakes's body when he discovered it the next morning because he did not realize the victim was dead. But did he just use this to explain why his contact evidence was on the corpse?

THE BLACK DAHLIA

Elizabeth Short was a pretty, 22-year-old, unemployed waitress, known to her friends as the Black Dahlia. This was a word play on a popular movie *The Blue Dahlia,* because she dressed in black and had striking black hair. On January 15, 1947, a mother walking with her child came upon Short's mutilated body in Leimert Park, Los Angeles. Her torso had been cut in half and her face slashed from the corners of her mouth to her ears. The murderer had placed the victim's hands above her head with her elbows bent at right angles.

Short grew up in Medford, Massachusetts, before moving to California at the age of 19.

This murder has fascinated the public for more than 60 years, and inspired both book and film adaptations, including *The Black Dahlia,* starring Scarlett Johansson and Hilary Swank, which was released in 2006.

The Investigation

The corpse was identified from its fingerprints. They were taken and given to the *Los Angeles Examiner* to be enlarged and sent to the FBI in Washington, D.C., where they were matched to Short's on a database. She had been

HANDLING FALSE CONFESSIONS

Police investigations are often slowed or sidetracked by people wrongly confessing to the crime. At least 200 people confessed to killing the son of Charles Lindbergh in 1932, and 60 false confessions were recorded for the unsolved 1947 murder of Elizabeth Short, the "Black Dahlia." A variety of reasons are thought to cause people to do this: mental problems, intoxication, coercion by the police, the need for attention, or the desire to protect a loved one who committed the crime.

An extreme example in England was that of Sean Hodgson, who spent 27 years behind bars after falsely confessing to a murder. This created an unsolved murder, and the victim's sorrowful mother noted, "He should not have confessed at the time."

A sheriff removes the prisoner ID bracelet from Eddie Joe Lloyd after DNA proved his innocence.

In the United States, Eddie Joe Lloyd served 17 years in prison for the 1984 rape and murder of a 16-year-old girl in Detroit, Michigan. He confessed to police while he was in a hospital being treated for mental illness. Telling him that his confession would help "smoke out" the real murderer, the police gave him details that only the killer could have known. Lloyd was convicted and sentenced to life although in court he said, "I never killed anybody in my life and I wouldn't." In 1995 he contacted the Innocence Project, a nonprofit group that takes on such cases, and it arranged the DNA test that proved his innocence.

fingerprinted in the past for a crime at a California army base and when she was arrested for underage drinking. Ten days after her body was discovered, Short's black patent leather purse and one of her black shoes were found in a Dumpster several miles away.

A Sensational Story. The brutal murder of a pretty young woman made a sensational story for the media. This put even more pressure on the Los Angeles Police Department, which had brought in hundreds of officers from other agencies to work on the case.

No Fixed Abode. Detectives discovered that Short had no permanent address, since she recently lived in several apartments, rooming houses, and hotels in the Los Angeles area. She had been living in Los Angeles for three years, trying to get into acting and working odd jobs to survive. A week before her death, Short told a friend she was moving to Chicago to become a fashion model. She was last seen on January 9 entering the lobby of the Biltmore Hotel in downtown Los Angeles, after saying she was meeting her sister to go to her home in Berkeley.

Taunting Letters. This case was extraordinary because of its long list of suspects, numbering in the hundreds. The Los Angeles district attorney originally believed 22 people to be serious suspects, with seven of these being doctors—who were suspects because the body was cut with skill. Police also interviewed thousands of people who they thought might have information about her. On top of this, 60 people falsely confessed to the crime. The large number of suspects proved to be too much of a drain on resources, and wild speculations in newspapers turned the case into a three ring circus. Although taunting letters, supposedly from the killer, were sent to the police and Short's address book was sent to the *Los Angeles Examiner,* the district attorney's office finally closed its investigation in 1950.

to Los Angeles Herald-Express

I Will GiVE UP IN Dahlia KILLing if I Get 10 Years

DON'T TRY TO Find Me

A letter supposedly written by Short's killer was sent to the *Los Angeles Herald-Express,* but some believed reporters wrote it to keep the story alive.

Elizabeth Short's body, covered with a blanket, as it was discovered in Leimert Park, Los Angeles.

The Suspects

- **Mark Hansen, 55.** Nightclub owner and known to be a jealous former boyfriend of Short's, Hansen's name was embossed on her address book when it was mailed to the *Los Angeles Examiner*. Short had lived with Hansen and several other girls from his burlesque act in 1946, when he had unsuccessfully tried to seduce her. One of her last telephone calls was to Hansen, and he made contradictory statements to the police about the reason she called him. He also knew three doctors who were among the suspects.

- **Walter Bayley, 66.** A surgeon, whose home was just one block away from where the body was discovered. His daughter was a close friend of Short's sister. An autopsy after Bayley's death in 1948 showed he was suffering from a degenerative brain disease. After he died, his estranged wife claimed that Bayley's mistress had known a terrible secret about him.

- **Robert Manley, 25.** The last person seen with the victim alive, he helped her to check-in her suitcases at a bus station. Suffering from

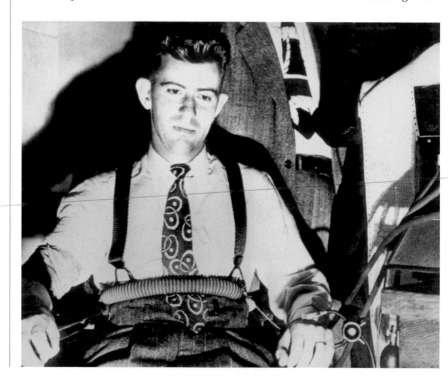

Robert Manley, a suspect in the Short murder, takes a polygraph test in Los Angeles. He passed and was released but later suffered nervous breakdowns.

mental problems, he had once been committed to a psychiatric hospital after hearing voices. He was the person who identified Short's possessions found in the Dumpster. Police were unable to press charges after Manley took a polygraph test and took sodium pentothal, the truth serum, and passed both.

- **Dr. George Hodel, 46.** He ran a venereal disease center, but had studied surgery in medical school. His son, Los Angeles homicide detective Steve Hodel, is certain his father, who died in 1991, was the murderer. In a 2003 book accusing his father, Hodel said he found two snapshots in his father's photo album of a young woman that looked like Short. He also examined letters sent by the killer to the police and confirmed that the handwriting closely resembled that of his father. Dr. Hodel's daughter also accused him of incest, but he was cleared.

- **Orson Welles, 31.** The famous actor, director, and producer was named in a book by a former neighbor of the Short family. He came under suspicion because of his temper, the fact he ate in the same restaurant as Short, had "sawed" a woman in half in a magic act, and went to Europe 10 months after the murder.

- **Woody Guthrie, 34.** Police also questioned the famous folk singer as a suspect because he had sent sexually explicit letters to a woman in California.

Lingering Doubts

- Was this tragic murder simply the result of a young woman being in the wrong place at the wrong time and encountering a homicidal predator? Would someone she knew send taunting letters to the police?

- Does such a frenzied attack suggest a person with mental problems, like Walter Bayley and Robert Manley? Since Bayley was a surgeon living close by, why didn't detectives seriously investigate him?

- Should Dr. George Hodel now be considered the chief suspect, since his own detective son believes he murdered Short, and even says his father probably killed 30 other women?

- Does the jealousy of Short's boyfriend, Mark Hansen, provide the clearest motive? What did they talk about during their last telephone call, and why did Hansen give police conflicting accounts of the conversation?

Loretta Grimes reads letters from well-wishers after her two daughters disappeared. When a ransom letter arrived, she followed its instructions, but it was a hoax.

THE GRIMES SISTERS

On the evening of December 28, 1956, Loretta Grimes, a divorcée, gave reluctant permission for two of her daughters, Barbara, 15, and, Patricia, 12, to go out in the worsening Chicago weather. They were going to the neighborhood Brighton Theater, a mile away, to see the Elvis Presley movie *Love Me Tender* (which they had already seen 10 times). It was a two-block walk to the bus stop and a short bus ride away. They planned to watch the movie twice, with the second showing ending at about 11:00 P.M. The girls should have been home by 11:45 P.M., but at midnight they had still not appeared so Loretta sent two of her other children to the bus stop to wait for them. Three buses arrived, but Patricia and Barbara were not on any of them. When a police officer happened to walk past, the siblings told him the girls were missing. Then, at 2:15 A.M., their frantic mother telephoned the police.

Although the police first assumed the girls had run away from home, the next day, a special task force conducted door-to-door inquiries, and even the railroad yards and the Chicago River were searched. The hunt was the largest in Chicago's history, lasting 25 days. Even Elvis Presley issued an appeal to the girls to return home. On January 12, 1957, their mother traveled to Milwaukee with FBI agents after receiving ransom letters instructing her to leave money in a downtown church to secure the girls' release. Barbara was to meet her there to take the money to the kidnapper, but no one came. The "kidnapper" later turned out to be a mental patient.

It was not until January 22, 1957, that the girls' naked, frozen bodies were found by a construction worker off the secluded German Church Road on the banks of Devil Creek near Willow Springs, southwest of the city of Chicago. They had been dumped next to the road, over a guardrail beside a ravine.

The Investigation

Immediately after the corpses were discovered, more than 160 police, along with news reporters, began searching through the woods, and destroyed any evidence that might have been there. The girls' clothing was never found, and the killer had been careful not to leave any fingerprints or other evidence at the scene. Locals also conducted their own search for evidence and distributed flyers asking the community for help.

Autopsy Results. The autopsies concluded that the girls had died of shock and exposure to the cold on the day that they had disappeared. However, the bodies bore bruises and puncture wounds that looked as if they had been caused by an instrument like an ice pick. The left side of Patricia's face had also been battered. The autopsy report drew sharp criticism, because it did not highlight the physical attacks that contributed to the girls' deaths. Harry Glos, a chief investigator, believed Barbara had been sexually molested before she was murdered. The bodies had a thin layer of ice on them, which led Glos to suggest they had been alive until January 7, 1957, when there was the last heavy snowfall of the winter.

Rumors. Friends of the girls testified to seeing the girls at around 9:30 P.M. in the popcorn line at the theater. In total, investigators questioned 300,000 people about the killings, narrowing their inquiries down to about 2,000 who faced tougher interrogations.

Chicago police meet to coordinate their search for the sisters. More than 160 police joined the search, but the girls' bodies were found by a construction worker.

Unfounded rumors suggested the sisters led an active sex life, often hanging around a favorite bar and becoming drunk. One theory was that they were abducted for a prostitution ring and murdered when they refused. Their close friends denied the rumors, saying that the girls were normal, decent teenagers. However, the autopsy did prove that both sisters were sexually active, but the coroner did not release this publicly to spare the family.

Ghost Stories. Although a $100,000 reward for information was posted, nothing new was uncovered and nobody stood trial for the murder of the Grimes sisters. The only remaining trace of them is a Chicago superstition that the road where their bodies were found is haunted. Locals have reported hearing an invisible car arrive, something being dumped, and the door slamming shut before the car screeches away.

The Suspects

- **Walter Kranz, 53.** Kranz called the police on January 15, 1957, to report a dream he'd had in which the girls were in a park. The location of his dream later turned out to be less than a mile from where the bodies were found. Nothing else linked Kranz to the crime, and he was released.

- **Max Fleig, 17.** Fleig took a polygraph test and, while failing it, confessed to the murders. Since the law stated that juveniles could not be given a polygraph test, the police had to release him. No other evidence connected him to the sisters, but Fleig was later imprisoned after being convicted of a brutal killing of a young woman a few years later.

- **Edward L. "Benny" Bedwell, 21.** A drifter from Tennessee with an Elvis-style haircut, he was seen in a restaurant getting drunk with the sisters. Bedwell also confessed to the murders three times, saying he had wild drinking and sex sessions with the girls. He even showed police how he had killed them. Once he had been booked on murder

Even though they had seen Elvis Presley's movie 10 times and the weather was bad, Barbara and Patricia headed into the night to see two consecutive showings at the Brighton.

- Even if the police had beaten Edward Bedwell, would the suspect have gone to such extremes as to reenact the murder for detectives?

- Should the teenager Max Fleig, who confessed to the crime, have been released because detectives illegally gave him a polygraph test? After a jury later convicted Fleig of a similar killing, why didn't police review his earlier confession?

- Was this an impulse murder or one that was carefully planned? Was the motive sexual? Does the absence of any trace evidence at the crime scene indicate a professional killing?

- Was there a cover-up to protect the girls' reputation and the feelings of their family?

charges, he recanted his confession, claiming the police had beaten it out of him. The state attorney agreed and all the charges were dropped. The man who arrested him, Cook County Sheriff Joseph Lohman, believed until his death in 1969 that Bedwell had murdered the girls. Police later arrested Bedwell in Florida for the rape of a 13-year-old girl, but failed to convict him.

- **Kenneth Hansen, 23.** Arrested in 1994 for the murders of three Chicago boys in 1955, police hoped to be able to link him to the murder of the Grimes sisters, but failed.

A model of Marilyn Sheppard's head was used by forensic experts to guess which blunt weapon was used. A flashlight replicated the wounds.

MARILYN SHEPPARD

Dr. Sam Sheppard, 30, claimed to be dozing on the early morning of July 4, 1954, on a daybed downstairs in his home in Bay Village, a suburb of Cleveland, Ohio, when his wife's screams from the upstairs bedroom woke him. Rushing to her, Sheppard encountered "a form in a light garment" and was knocked unconscious. When he came around he found his 31-year-old pregnant wife, Marilyn, lying murdered on her twin bed. He checked on his 7-year-old son, who was still sleeping in the next room, and ran downstairs to pursue a "bushy-haired intruder" in a white shirt, overtaking him on a nearby beach at Lake Erie. They struggled and the man once more knocked Sheppard unconscious.

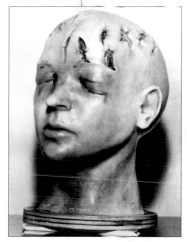

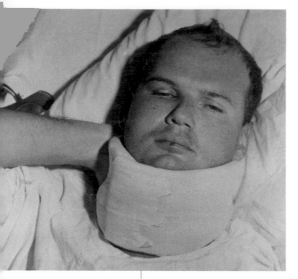

Dr. Sheppard rests in a Cleveland hospital after his wife's murder. The medical collar protects his neck that he said was injured in a struggle with the killer.

The Investigation

Before the coroner arrived at 8:00 A.M., the crime scene had already been badly compromised by police, relatives, neighbors, and press wandering through the house. After examining the body, he found that Marilyn Sheppard had been beaten severely with 35 wounds to her head.

Domestic Violence. The police immediately viewed Sam Sheppard with suspicion, considering the killing to be a case of domestic violence. They could find no evidence of a break-in and no fingerprints. His dog, known to bark at strangers, had remained silent that morning, and his son had slept soundly through the reported struggle in the next room. The T-shirt that Sam Sheppard had been wearing when the neighbors arrived soon after the murder had also disappeared, and he told police he didn't know where it was.

Sam Sheppard had sustained neck injuries and chipped teeth, and was taken to the local hospital. After intense questioning there, one police officer informed him, "I think you killed your wife."

Secrets and Lies. Sam Sheppard worked as an osteopath, and the high-profile investigation that followed his wife's murder soon uncovered his three-year affair with a nurse at his hospital. Although Sam Sheppard admitted his marriage was in trouble, at an inquest he denied sexual relations with the nurse even though she disputed it. He refused to take a lie-detector test on the advice of his lawyer and was arrested on July 30, 1954. The same day a *Cleveland Press* editorial ran the headline: "Why Isn't Sam Sheppard in Jail? Quit Stalling—Bring Him In!"

Other Suspects

- **The mysterious intruder.** The man Sam Sheppard said he wrestled with was never found, despite witnesses saying they saw a "bushy-haired man" near the house that day.

- **Richard Eberling, 25.** He cleaned the windows at the Sheppard home and was found in possession of one of Marilyn's rings, although he had stolen it from her sister-in-law. Eberling stated that

WHEN UNSOLVED CRIMES BECOME COLD CASES

Cold cases are all unsolved crimes that have all hit a dead end before being labeled cold. Some police departments set a time limit. In Winston-Salem, North Carolina, a detective originally assigned to a homicide works on a case for up to three years. Then, if all known leads have come to nothing, the case goes to the cold case homicide unit. Some departments use more general guidelines. In Henrico County, Virginia, a case becomes cold "when the original investigator has eliminated any and all potential leads and evidence, or needed witnesses do not exist."

In Canada the Criminal Investigation Bureau, which handles provincial murder investigations, can reopen any unsolved case if new information or investigative technology becomes available. Definitions of cold cases are kept general. The Historical Case Unit of the Saskatoon Police Service will look at files if "all avenues have been exhausted by the initially assigned investigators." The Cold Case Unit of the Halifax Regional Police does this when all leads have been exhausted or no new ones have been developed for "an extended period of time."

Britain also does not limit the definition of cold cases. In 2004 "Operation Advance," a joint project by the Home Office and Forensic Science Services, reanalyzed serious unsolved crimes as old as 1989 using modern DNA techniques. Cold cases were examined by 34 police forces and resulted in 30 convictions.

Homicide investigations that find no significant leads or witnesses in the first 72 hours will probably become cold cases, according to the National Criminal Justice Reference Service (NCJRS) of the U.S. Department of Justice. Many crimes stay unsolved and cold because of staff shortages. This means cold cases often take more time and work than the original investigation. New detectives must look for what is missing and then go out and find it.

The NCJRS adds that cold cases are among the most difficult and frustrating investigations that detectives face. Often evidence is old or misplaced, witnesses have died, and new detectives are unfamiliar with the original details.

On the positive side, fresh eyes are valuable in reassessing crimes that have exhausted investigators. Worried witnesses may become less fearful and more open with the passage of time. Cold cases are also reactivated when a criminal strikes again using the same methods.

A vault containing the coffin of Roger Vaillancourt is raised in November 2005, in Foley, Minnesota. Fifty years after Vaillancourt died in what was thought to be an accident, police have reopened the case.

while washing the Sheppards' windows, he had cut his finger and bled in the house. His blood DNA was tested to compare with blood in the bedroom, but the results were inconclusive. Eberling was jailed in 1984 for the murder of a rich, elderly woman, and he died in prison in 1998. Both a home nurse for the elderly woman he killed and a fellow convict said Eberling had confessed to the Sheppard crime.

July 17, 1954, Cleveland, Ohio: Dr. Lester Adelson, deputy county coroner of Cuyahoga County, examines X-rays of the hands, feet, and head of Marilyn Sheppard who was found bludgeoned to death in Bay Village early July 4.

The Trials

Sam Sheppard's trial began on October 28, 1954, under the glare of national coverage, with many reporters convinced of his guilt. He testified, retelling his struggle with an intruder, and the defense produced two witnesses who said they had seen a bushy-haired man near the house that day. They also argued that the bedroom had been extremely bloody, but Sam Sheppard had only one small spot of blood on his pants.

Found Guilty. The prosecution pointed to Sam Sheppard's affair as the motive for murder, with his lover, Susan Hayes, testifying that they had made love. Also damaging was the coroner's testimony that a bloodstain on the pillowcase could have been made only by a surgical knife. The jury agreed with the evidence and Sam Sheppard was convicted of second-degree murder and sentenced to life in prison.

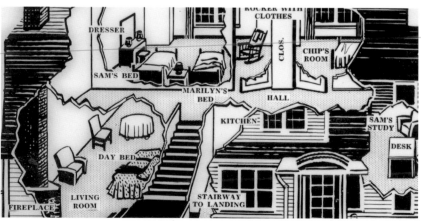

An artist's cutaway drawing of Dr. Sheppard's summer house in Bay Village, Ohio. The drawing was a main exhibit during his 1954 murder trial.

The Fugitive. Appeals for a new trial were turned down, and in 1961 the famous defense lawyer F. Lee Bailey took over when Sam Sheppard's lawyer died. Sheppard received more sympathy in 1963 when the popular television series *The Fugitive* was released based on the Sheppard murder, although the drama featured a one-armed intruder and had the innocent husband on the run. A movie with the same title was released in 1993.

Dr. Sheppard (center) enters the Ohio penitentiary to begin his life term. He is shackled to a parole violator (left) and led by Deputy Sheriff David Yettra.

Release and Retrial. In 1964 Sheppard was released from prison after nearly 10 years, when a judge ruled that his trial had been unfair due to excessive press coverage and the original judge's failure to control the courtroom. One newspaper columnist said during that trial, the judge had told her, "Well, he is guilty as hell. There is no question about it."

Sam Sheppard's second trial began on October 24, 1966. Heading the defense, Bailey argued that the crime scene indicated a woman could have been the murderer. A prosecution expert testified that blood found on Sam Sheppard's wristwatch came from splattered blood, but a defense expert said it came from contact. Bailey even suggested, though no proof existed, that the mayor had carried on an affair with Marilyn Sheppard, and that his wife had killed her. Bailey's convincing argument that the evidence was weak against Sam Sheppard resulted in his being found not guilty.

"Not Innocent." Sam Sheppard became a heavy drinker and died of liver disease in 1970 at the age of 46. His son, Samuel Reese Sheppard (nicknamed "Chip"), conducted a campaign to clear his father's name, bringing a civil case in 1996 to have his father found innocent, and to sue for wrongful imprisonment. His father's body was exhumed for DNA testing, and the son's lawyer contended this showed the blood in the bedroom was not Sam Shepherd's. The jury, however, decided that Sam Sheppard was "not innocent" and not wrongfully imprisoned.

- Why didn't Sheppard call for help as he chased and fought with the "bushy-haired intruder"?

- What happened to the missing T-shirt Sheppard had been wearing on the morning of the murder, and how could he not recall taking it off? Why did he have only one small spot of blood on his clothes after examining his wife's body in the blood-covered bedroom?

- Since he had a doctor's knowledge of drugs and poisons, why would Sheppard resort to bludgeoning his wife to death?

- Why did police handle the suspect Richard Eberling so lightly after he said his blood was in the Sheppards' house, was later found guilty of murdering another woman, and had confessed to two witnesses that he had killed Marilyn Sheppard?

THE ZODIAC KILLER

During the late 1960s and early 1970s, a serial killer terrorized northern California around the San Francisco area, slaying at least five known people. During his killing spree, the murderer taunted the police and press with coded letters, signed with a zodiac symbol. He also claimed to have killed 37 or more victims.

Part of a letter sent by Zodiac on November 9, 1969, to the *San Francisco Chronicle*. He listed facts to prove he was the murderer.

The Victims

- **Betty Lou Jensen, 16, and David Faraday, 17.** The first deaths officially attributed to the Zodiac Killer occurred on December 20, 1968, in the town of Benicia, about 20 miles (32 km) northeast of San Francisco. At around 10:20 P.M., Jensen and Faraday were parked on a lovers' lane, when another car arrived and the driver ordered them to get out. Faraday was shot in the head and Jensen was shot five times in the back.

- **Darlene Ferrin, 22, and Michael Mageau, 19.** Six and a half months later, on July 4, 1969, the victims were parked at midnight in Vallejo, 4 miles (6.4 km) from

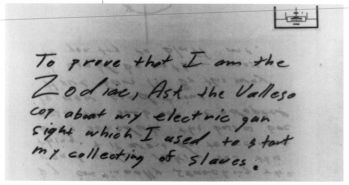

To prove that I am the Zodiac, Ask the Valleso cop about my electric gan sight which I used to start my collecting of slaves.

Three of Zodiac's victims were (left to right) taxi driver Paul Stine who was shot dead, coed Cecelia Shopard, stabbed to death, and her boyfriend Bryan Hartnell, who survived.

the first murder site. Another car parked behind theirs, and a man approached with a flashlight and revolver. Using the light to blind them, he shot them both several times. Ferrin died and Mageau survived. He described the assailant as about 5 feet 8 inches (1 m 73 cm) tall and heavyset. Within a half hour, a man telephoned the Vallejo police department claiming responsibility for this and the earlier killings.

- **Bryan Hartnell, 20, and Cecelia Shepard, 22.** On September 27, 1969, these college students were having a picnic on a small island in Lake Berryessa, 60 miles (97 km) northeast of San Francisco. A man approached them wearing a black hood with a bib that bore a cross-circle symbol. After making Shepard tie up her boyfriend, he tied her up and stabbed both the students multiple times. Using a felt-tip pen, the assailant then drew the cross-circle on their car door and added the words:

    Vallejo
    12-20-68
    7-4-69
    Sept 27-69-6:30
    by knife.

A man called the Napa county sheriff's office at 7:40 P.M. to confirm his attack. The pay phone he used was just a few blocks away and a palm print was taken, but never matched. Shepard died later and Hartnell survived; both managed to give descriptions of the man.

- **Paul Stine, 29.** Taxi driver Stine picked up a man in San Francisco on October 11, 1969. He had driven only one block before his passenger shot him once in the head. The killer took Stine's wallet and car keys, and ripped off his shirt-tail dipping it in the murdered man's blood. Three teenagers saw the crime and called police as the man walked away. They later helped a police artist to draw two composites of the killer, whom they estimated to be between 35 and 40 years of age.

The Letters

Detectives' hopes were raised when the killer began sending letters. On August 1, 1969, three local newspapers received the first ones in which the killer took credit for the first two attacks. He also added a cryptogram with 408 symbols, divided so that each newspaper received a third of the puzzle. This cryptogram represented his identity, the killer said, and he threatened to kill more people if it was not published on the front pages of each of the newspapers, which they were.

Signed, "Zodiac." Six days later one of the newspapers, the *San Francisco Examiner*, received another letter, using the name Zodiac for the first time. In the letter the writer said that he could be caught if the police managed to crack the code.

On October 14, 1969, the *San Francisco Chronicle* received a Zodiac letter containing a swatch of the shirt tail of taxi driver Paul Stine. Other letters followed, and on December 20, 1969, exactly a year after the first murders, the Zodiac wrote to Melvin Belli, a well-known lawyer, asking for his help to stop the killings. Letters in 1970 to the press and police claimed other killings. The last letter arrived nearly four years later, postmarked January 29, 1974, in which the killer merely said how much he enjoyed *The Exorcist* movie.

WHEN MURDERS BECOME MOVIES

A wide variety of movies have recounted famous murders. *Chapter 27*, an independent film released in 2007 at the Sundance Film Festival, was about the murder of John Lennon by Mark David Chapman in 1980 in New York. Unsolved killings have also sometimes been turned into movies, such as *The Black Dahlia* released in 2006 about the 1947 murder of Elizabeth Short in Los Angeles.

On the other hand, some television movies have been rushed out before the suspect's trial has even ended. *The Perfect Husband: The Laci Peterson Story* recounted the murder of pregnant Laci and ended with her husband, Scott, being charged with the crime. The film outraged Laci's parents because the story centered on Scott, and it also angered Scott's parents because he had not yet been convicted (but he was later).

At least one movie has resulted in the release of a wrongfully jailed man. *The Thin Blue Line* (1988) was an award-winning documentary about Randall Adams, who was then in jail for the 1976 killing of a police officer in Dallas, Texas. Adams had been within three days of execution before the U.S. Supreme Court had the sentence commuted to life. The movie's portrayal of the case revealed that five witnesses had committed perjury during the trial, and the publicity surrounding the movie led to Adams's conviction being overturned and him being released in 1989 after 12 years in prison.

The Black Dahlia movie in 2006 dramatized the story of Elizabeth Short's murder.

Movies have also been released about real-life murders that never happened. Although both the French and British governments conducted lengthy investigations into the car accident that killed Princess Diana and Dodi Al Fayed, a 2007 television movie opted to portray the conspiracy theory touted by Dodi's father, Mohamed Al Fayed. *The Murder of Princess Diana* claimed she was killed by British intelligence officers.

The San Francisco police released sketches of the Zodiac killer in 1969 based on descriptions by witnesses to the slaying of the taxi driver in San Francisco.

The Suspects

- **Arthur Leigh Allen, 39.** The only person to be arrested out of the 2,500 people that the police reviewed, Allen was a convicted child molester and had also been arrested for having a firearm in his car. He was suspected by his friend Don Cheney who said Allen had asked him how to disguise handwriting and had told him that someone could elude detection by committing motiveless murders. Allen had the same model of typewriter that had been used for the letters, wore a watch with a Zodiac sign, and had bloody knives in his car on the day of the Lake Berryessa murder—he said he had killed a chicken. However, he passed a polygraph test and his fingerprints, handwriting, and DNA did not match the Zodiac's. Allen was never charged and died in 1992 from natural causes.

- **Richard Marshall, 40.** A former Navy man trained in codes.

- **Theodore Kaczynski, 26.** Later convicted as the Unabomber; cleared of any involvement by the police and FBI.

- **Jack Tarrance.** In 2000 the FBI was alerted to Tarrance by his stepson Dennis Kaufman, who had noticed that Tarrance's handwriting matched that of the killer and the police sketch resembled him in his younger years. After Tarrance died in 2006, Kaufman found a black hood like the one worn in the 1968 murder, a knife possibly covered in blood, and rolls of film containing gruesome images.

- **Guy Ward Hendrickson.** In 2009 a California real-estate agent, Deborah Perez, claimed her stepfather was the Zodiac Killer, who even took her with him to two of the killings when she was seven. Perez claims to have the taxi driver's horn-rimmed glasses. Hendrickson, a carpenter, died in 1983.

RICHARD "DICKIE" HOVEY

Richard Hovey, 17, also known as "Dickie" in his hometown of Fredericton, New Brunswick, Canada, dreamed of becoming a rock star. He was a talented musician who played lead guitar in a local band called Teddy and the Royals, but Hovey knew if he was to make the big time he needed to be in a big city. In the late spring of 1967 he hitchhiked to Toronto with his guitar case slung over his shoulder to work as a musician in the city's hippie haven at the time, Yorkville Village. After two weeks of filling in occasionally with a band in the Mynah Bird Club, and a week after his seventeenth birthday, Hovey disappeared forever. Within months, the decomposed remains of two unidentified young men were found in separate areas north of Toronto. Both were naked and had their hands tied behind their backs. One was discovered on December 17, 1967, in a wooded area in Balsam Lake Provincial Park near Coboconk, and the other corpse was found on May 15, 1968, against a hedgerow on a farm near Schomberg. Police linked the two deaths and fear began that a serial killer was on the loose.

Richard Hovey poses with his guitar, which has never been found.

The Investigation

The Ontario Provincial Police (OPP) kept the skeletal remains secure in plastic containers at the Toronto morgue. Police were stumped by the lack of clues and had no way to identify the bones. They issued a news release asking the public for information, but this produced little interest so the cases were filed away. In 2006 nearly 40 years after the deaths, they reopened the cold cases to take advantage of new DNA techniques.

New Forensic Techniques. The OPP offered a $50,000 reward for information that would help solve the murders. They called in forensic anthropologist Kathy Gruspier, who confirmed that the victims were teenagers and added details about their physical features, such as their height and bone structures. They conducted autopsies and had forensic artist Pete Thompson reconstruct the victims' faces from the skulls. The images were then broadcast on national television and a website. When officers held a press conference regarding the case, relatives of Hovey and, separately, a friend called within 24 hours from Fredericton identifying one of the faces as the missing musician.

Mystery Victims Are Identified. Police went to New Brunswick to interview Hovey's brother, Kevin, and his two sisters, Marcia and Carolyn, and to obtain blood samples. When their DNA matched a sample from the skeletal remains they knew the young musician had been found. His body was flown home to be buried at long last by the family and detectives began a new hunt for the murderer. On March 9, 2009, the OPP announced that family members viewing the reconstructed image had identified the second victim as Eric Jones, 18. His brother, Oscar, said the victim had left home in Noelville, Ontario, to start a new life—moving to Toronto to live with an aunt. Jones had moved out of her house a month later, in April 1967, which was around the last time he had been seen alive.

Sexual Abductions. Detectives believe someone in the gay community attacked Hovey and Jones. The victims were probably picked up in downtown Toronto and driven to rural areas. OPP Detective Inspector Dave Quigley, the lead investigator in the case, also thinks they may have gone willingly at first. And it was not the first time this had

Ontario Provincial Police on November 14, 2006, released the reconstructed faces of the two murder victims.

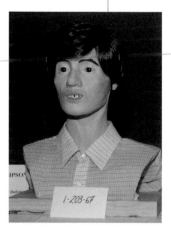
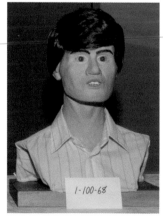

THE BONE DETECTIVE

Kathy Gruspier helped police to identify Richard Hovey and Eric Jones by describing their physical features from the skeletal remains. A world-renown forensic anthropologist, she even keeps two body bags in her SUV so that she's ready for the next call to a crime scene. "I'm on call 24–7," she explains. Besides identifying bones, she also specializes in how they were placed and moved, as well as the tools that may have been involved in particular murders.

Gruspier, a busy single mother, is Ontario province's first forensic anthropology consultant to the Office of the Chief Coroner, and took up the post in 1992. She regularly testifies in criminal proceedings, and her international work identifying bones has taken her to Cambodia, Jordan, Kosovo (in 1999 she was a member of the Canadian Forensic Investigation Team probing crimes against humanity), and East Timor in 2000 for the United Nations. In 2003 she received the NATO medal for her work in Kosovo, and the Canadian Peacekeeping Service Medal.

Gruspier also has a law degree and teaches law and forensic science courses at the University of Toronto at Mississauga, where she is an adjunct professor of Forensic Science.

As well as aiding police in tracking down criminals, Gruspier sometimes discovers that suspicious bones involve no crime. In 2003 she examined bones from a construction site in Peterborough, Ontario. They were thought to be suspicious human remains, but soon discovered to be animal bones. In 2004 laborers unearthed a skull near Swansea Town Hall in Toronto that was believed to be from a murder victim. Gruspier measured the skull and examined the teeth before disclosing that it was in fact an aboriginal man in his 20s who probably died of tubercular meningitis. She noted that the good condition of his teeth showed that he had died before Europeans arrived with their cavity-causing foods.

happened; in the summer of 1967 two other young men were abducted and then sexually attacked.

Hovey's Final Steps. Police sent out a request for friends of Hovey to contact them. "We want to retrace Richard Hovey's final steps," said Quigley. They talked with members of the band that he sometimes played with, Bobbi Lee Justice and the Scepters, who had recorded a CD, *Still Searching For Your Soul,* as a tribute to him. The police also began to think about what had happened to Hovey's beloved, painted Sears guitar, because the only evidence left on the body by the killer was the white shoelace that was used to bind Hovey's hands.

The police hold a press conference about the two youths' murders. Hovey's body was identified nearly 40 years after it was discovered.

They also interviewed eyewitnesses who were the last people to see him alive. Some of them recalled watching him get into a light-colored Corvair driven by a "muscular black man" whom detectives believe was the murderer. As the car had driven away it had turned onto a street that eventually leads out of the city.

The Suspect

The Corvair sighting was the first definite link to the man that police considered a suspect—the convicted sex offender and killer James Greenidge. He was first jailed in 1955 for raping a 14-year-old girl and served 5 years of a 10-year sentence.

Convicted Sex Killer. Greenidge fitted the witness's description of the man seen driving Hovey away; his car also matched the Corvair that was seen. In the summer of 1967 he murdered a 17-year-old boy and dumped his body north of Toronto. He then stabbed a 21-year-old man in the throat and chest and left him in a field to die, but the victim survived to identify both Greenidge and his car.

Greenidge was convicted of manslaughter and attempted murder and was imprisoned from 1968 to 1977, he then spent time in a minimum-security facility before being paroled in 1978. About that time, another youth was murdered in the Toronto area, and police again suspected Greenidge, who was known to have gay affairs. However, police suspicions were based on circumstantial evidence and it remains a cold case. Meanwhile, Greenidge changed his name to James Gordon Henry and moved to Manitoba, but was soon back in prison serving a life sentence for the 1981 rape and murder of a 24-year-old woman in Vancouver.

Lack of Evidence. Without a confession or any strong evidence, the Ontario police are left with the unsolved murders of Richard Hovey and Eric Jones. However, detectives are still pursuing the break that will convict the murderer. Greenidge was denied parole at his hearing in 2007, when the parole board reviewed his lifelong pattern of crime and noted, "Your violence has escalated with every offense."

Jimmy Hoffa was a powerful union leader but served a prison term for criminal activities. When released, he attempted unsuccessfully to head his union again.

JIMMY HOFFA

One of America's most notorious trade union leaders, Jimmy Hoffa, 62, disappeared on July 30, 1975, in a suburb of Detroit and was never seen again. He had gone to the Machus Red Fox Restaurant for a 2:00 P.M., meeting with two men from the Mafia. After arriving on time, Hoffa waited in the parking lot for almost a half hour before going to a pay phone outside a hardware store to call his wife and say he was leaving if the others failed to arrive soon. He then disappeared. He was almost certainly murdered, and the police continue to keep the case open.

By 2008 the FBI had compiled more than 16,000 pages of documents on the Hoffa case.

The Investigation

Police identified the men that Hoffa was waiting for as a Detroit crime boss, Anthony "Tony Jack" Giacalone, and Anthony "Tony Pro" Provenzano, a head of the Teamsters Union in New Jersey, who was also a mob member. The FBI determined that the meeting was to be a peace conference between Hoffa and Provenzano, after years of hostility between the two.

Lack of Evidence. Witnesses saw Hoffa and several other men get into a car in the parking lot at 2:45 P.M. Detectives traced the car to Joe Biacalone, the son of Tony Jack. He claimed he had loaned the vehicle to Charles "Chuckie" O'Brien, a close Teamster associate of Hoffa's. Police believe Hoffa was killed soon after entering the car. O'Brien, whose fingerprints were in the vehicle, vowed Hoffa had not gotten in. Although traces of blood were found in the car, O'Brien claimed it was fish blood from frozen salmon. Police dogs also picked up Hoffa's scent in the backseat and trunk, but authorities still felt the evidence was too weak to indict O'Brien.

A Shady Past. The FBI is convinced the Mafia killed Hoffa because of his past history. In 1957 he became president of the Teamsters, the union that mainly represented the trucking industry. The Mafia helped him to get elected to this position, and he freely acknowledged his friendships with gangsters. U.S. Attorney General Robert Kennedy encouraged investigations into charges that Hoffa had engaged in fraud, misuse of union money, violence, and jury tampering. He was convicted in 1964 and three years later began a 13-year sentence, but after relinquishing the union presidency in 1971, President Richard Nixon commuted his sentence.

A forensic team use a metal detector in a residential area of Hampton Township, Michigan, to search for clues about Hoffa's disappearance.

THE COLDEST COLD CASES

Why do detectives continue to work on homicide cases that seem to lack real evidence? The answer is that unknown or unrecognized evidence does exist, so investigators keep fishing tirelessly for the big break. This is why detectives have been looking for the body of union leader Jimmy Hoffa since 1975.

In Britain the 1986 disappearance of 25-year-old Suzy Lamplugh (see page 164), a real estate agent, who has not been seen after leaving her London office to show a "Mr. Kipper" around a house. Police scaled down their search 15 months after she became missing, but kept the file open. In 1994 Lamplugh was officially declared dead though her body had not been found. The case was reopened in 2000 after a tip-off said her body was buried at an old airfield, but this proved wrong. Despite the passage of time, Detective Superintendent Jim Dickie who was leading the investigation said, "I have not given up hope that a piece of vital information will come in to us."

Neither have police in Perth, Australia, who are still hoping to solve murders that took place more than a decade ago in the wealthy suburb of

Police search for Suzy Lamplugh's body through woods in Somerset, Britain.

Claremont. Sarah Spiers, 18, disappeared in 1996, and her fate is still unknown. A year later, the bodies of Jane Rimmer, 23, and Ciara Glennon, 27, were found. Up to 90 investigators have worked in a special task force for the Western Australian Police. They have tried different tactics, even sending questionnaires to suspects asking, "Are you the killer?"

In 2008 they used a television program to show surveillance camera images of Rimmer talking to a man, and more than 150 viewers telephoned with information. Despite years of frustration, Detective Superintendent Jeff Byleveld noted, "We still have a very live investigation."

Officers look for evidence near the gravesite of Ciara Glennon in Claremont, Australia.

Reporters stop Tony Provenzano on August 6, 1975, outside his expensive Florida home to ask about his involvement in Jimmy Hoffa's disappearance.

As soon as he was released, Hoffa began a campaign to regain control of the Teamsters. This irritated union officials and mobsters who did not want to reinstate an ex-convict who was at odds with the FBI. Mafia bosses warned Hoffa several times to retire, but in the end his persistence to regain power most probably cost him his life.

The Missing Body. Hoffa was declared legally dead in 1982, and in 2001 the DNA from a hair taken from Hoffa's hairbrush was successfully matched to a hair found in the car. The search for his body, however, has never ended. Various rumors suggest it was dumped near the Verrazano-Narrows Bridge in New York, buried at a toxic waste site in New Jersey, ground up at a meat processing plant, buried under the helipad in Savannah, Georgia, and even mixed into concrete used to construct the New York Giants' stadium in New Jersey.

In 2004 detectives pulled up the floorboards of the Detroit house where Hoffa supposedly died, and two years later, after receiving a tip-off, the FBI searched a farm in Milford Township, Michigan. Neither searches uncovered anything. During the FBI's investigation of the Hoffa suspects, however, they turned up numerous other unrelated crimes, and more than 30 mobsters were prosecuted and given prison sentences.

The Suspects

- **Anthony Provenzano, 57.** The prime suspect, he was in jail for racketeering when he first met Hoffa, who was an inmate in the same prison. Hoffa was concerned that Provenzano's illegal activities had caused federal investigations of the Teamsters. Although Provenzano had an airtight alibi on the day of the murder, being in New Jersey with union officials, police assumed he still had something to do with the murder. He was convicted in 1978 of the 1961 murder of a man whose body was supposedly put through a tree shredder. After a decade in prison, he died there at the age of 81.

- **Anthony Giacalone, 56.** Detectives think Giacalone set up Hoffa's fatal meeting, but he was at his gym at the actual time of the murder. He later spent 10 years in prison for tax evasion and died in 2001, while awaiting trial for racketeering.

- **Russell Bufalino, 71.** A Mob boss who was named by an informer as the person who ordered Hoffa's death. Bufalino had traveled from Pennsylvania to Detroit, but his whereabouts the day Hoffa disappeared are unknown.

- **Frank "The Irishman" Sheerhan, 55.** A Mafia hit man who confessed to his lawyer that he shot Hoffa twice in the head at a house near the restaurant. He said Hoffa's body was taken to a funeral parlor two minutes away and cremated. The FBI had listed Sheerhan as a prime suspect before he received a 32-year sentence for racketeering. He died of cancer in prison.

Lingering Doubts

- The Mafia works behind a veil of silence, but who ordered the killing and who carried it out? How many people know where the body is buried?

- Why did police say they lacked evidence against Charles O'Brien after he said that Hoffa was not in the car he drove, even though bystanders saw Hoffa in it and his blood and scent were found in the vehicle?

- If Tony Provenzano was in charge, as police believed, why did he openly set up the meeting with Hoffa instead of killing him secretly?

- Frank Sheerhan's deathbed confession contained many plausible details, but was he protecting the real killer or trying to inflate his own Mafia reputation? What prompted the two other Mafia members to confess?

Bob Crane smiles for the camera in 1975 when *The Bob Crane Show* was aired. He became a well-known actor in the 1960s.

BOB CRANE

The American actor Bob Crane was best known as the star of *Hogan's Heroes,* a World War II comedy, which ran from 1965 to 1971, set in a Nazi prisoner-of-war camp. On June 29, 1978 (two weeks before his fiftieth birthday), Crane was found battered to death in an apartment in Scottsdale, Arizona, where he was appearing in a play. His body was discovered after 2:00 P.M. by an actress who was in the same play and had an appointment with Crane to record a voice track for the performance. Finding the door unlocked, she entered and walked through to the bedroom where she found Crane's body, curled up in a fetal position on the bed with a cord around his neck that was tied into a bow. The bed and nearby wall were covered with blood.

The cast of *Hogan's Heroes* included (left to right) John Banner, Werner Klemperer, Crane, and Cynthia Lynn.

The Investigation

A medical examiner determined that Crane had probably been asleep when someone used a blunt instrument to deliver two fatal blows to the left side of his head. The assailant, most likely a strong man because of the depth of the wounds, then cut an electrical cable from the VCR and tied it with a tight knot around the dead man's neck. Investigators suspected the weapon was a camera's tripod, because Crane was a photography enthusiast, but the murder weapon was never found.

Invited in to Kill. There was no sign of forced entry and the police concluded that Crane had most likely let his killer into the apartment. A half-empty bottle of scotch was found on a countertop, which was strange because Crane disliked scotch. On the bed next to him was a large black almost empty bag with its two zippers open,

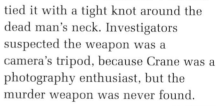

Among the pallbearers at Bob Crane's funeral in California were two cast members of *Hogan's Heroes*, Robert Clary (center) and Larry Hovis (right).

suggesting that the killer had taken away whatever was inside. Crane's lifestyle was thoroughly investigated. It was discovered that he was a collector of pornography, and he had filmed sex sessions with some of the many women he had taken to bed. Police considered the possibility that the killer could be a jealous husband or rejected lover.

The Suspects

- **Patricia Crane, 42.** Bob Crane's wife was also an actress, who used the stage name Sigrid Valdis and married Crane after they appeared together in *Hogan's Heroes*. She was known to be jealous, but was at home in Los Angeles at the time of the murder, so she was never considered a likely suspect.

- **John Carpenter, 50.** Crane's close friend had left Scottsdale the morning before the actor's body was found. He raised suspicions when he called Crane's apartment twice while police were there and did not ask for Crane or show surprise at their presence. Detectives impounded the car that Carpenter had rented the previous day and found several spots of blood that matched the actor's blood type, but this was not considered strong enough evidence. In 1989, after DNA came into use, police again tested the spots in Carpenter's rental car, but they proved inconclusive.

Detectives then began the slow process of investigating Carpenter that stretched on for 14 years before they arrested him for the murder in 1992.

The Trial

Jurors were told that Crane and Carpenter had a close, but sleazy, relationship. Carpenter was an electronics expert, who supplied the actor with videotape to record his sex acts, while Crane found women for his friend.

Brain Tissue. The main evidence against Carpenter, and the reason he was charged, involved a speck of tissue seen on the door panel of the

Police gather outside the apartment where actor Bob Crane was beaten to death.

car he had rented the night of the murder. It was only noticed in a photograph that had been taken of the car, the actual material itself was long gone. When experts working for the police looked at this tiny, ¹⁄₁₆-inch (3-mm) mark, they said they believed it to be human brain tissue. The defense countered this with their own experts who said it was impossible to make this claim.

Carpenter's Behavior. Evidence was also presented about Carpenter's unusual behavior both before and after the killing. A waitress testified that the day before, she had noticed tension between the two men as they dined together. A motel manager said Carpenter seemed anxious to leave the city quickly the next day, and the police were suspicious of his unexplained calls to the apartment. These inferences, the defense pointed out, added up to nothing but circumstantial evidence.

Crane's wife testified as a prosecution witness against Carpenter, but some have suggested this was to deflect suspicion from herself. The Cranes themselves had regular arguments about money and Bob Crane's philandering.

Blackened Reputations. The most sensational drama was the prosecution's attempt to blacken Carpenter's reputation by showing the jury a 10-minute tape of him and Crane having sex with a woman. The judge instructed jurors to regard the tape as proof the two men had a relationship, but not as evidence that Carpenter was a bad person. The prosecution hoped to convince the jury that Crane had tired of Carpenter's hanging around and asked him to leave. But there was no evidence that the two men had a traumatic falling out. "I never even had a fight with Bob," Carpenter stated. "And he was the goose who laid the golden egg for me, in terms of meeting ladies." The defense said no proof of a rift existed, and turned the jury's attention to an unidentified blond hair found in Crane's bedroom, suggesting the revenge was related to a sexual liaison.

Tho jury brought back a verdict of not guilty—one of its members later said they had not been convinced that the photographed speck was incriminating. "Nobody knows what it was," ho said, "not even the doctors."

Dana Bradley's family described her as a bright and very social child. Her decision to accept a ride proved fatal.

DANA BRADLEY

December 14, 1981, was an exciting day for 14-year-old Dana Bradley, who was looking forward to her mother's birthday celebration in the evening. She left her school, in St. Johns, Newfoundland, in the afternoon and met three of her friends at a convenience store. At 4:30 P.M., she called her grandmother to say she would be home in an hour. Although she told her friends she would take the bus home, since a bus stop was only minutes away, Harry Smeaton and his brother, who were selling Christmas trees at a roadside stand, saw her hitchhiking at 5:15 P.M. After a couple of minutes a car

pulled up near the bus stop, and the male driver offered Dana a ride. A passing truck driver also saw her run up to the car and lean in to talk with the driver. Dana tried without success to open the passenger door, so the driver leaned over and opened it. She got in and was never again seen alive.

Four days later, at about 3:00 P.M., a man was in some woods near Maddox Cove, just outside St. Johns, looking for a Christmas tree when he discovered the young girl's body. When police arrived, they saw that she had died from blows to the head with a blunt object. Strangely, the murderer had laid the victim out neatly in her school clothes, with her schoolbooks tucked under her arm.

The Investigation

The investigation became the largest murder hunt in Newfoundland's history, and one of the biggest ever seen in Canada. Police interviewed thousands of people and pursued countless leads. They also used the media to appeal to the murderer, believing he had left the girl's body in a peaceful pose because he was in some way remorseful. Other than the witnesses who saw Dana get into a stranger's car, the police had virtually no clues, since heavy rain had washed away any available evidence.

Witness Reports. Help came from several eyewitnesses. The Smeaton brothers, who had seen the abduction, were able to give descriptions of the man for a police sketch and also recalled the type of vehicle he was

Police created and distributed images of the suspect after several witnesses recalled details about the man involved in Dana's abduction.

THE MOUNTIES IN FACT AND FICTION

Known worldwide for their integrity, dedication, and smart red uniforms, the Royal Canadian Mounted Police (RCMP) have been pursuing criminals for more than 130 years. They do not "always get their man," as their slogan declares, but they do keep on their trails and capture an impressive number.

The Mounties' colorful uniforms have added to their dashing, heroic image.

The organization began in 1873 as the North-West Mounted Police, dedicated to securing Canada's claim to its western regions. The following year, 275 Mounties traveled around 930 miles (1,500 km) west to build Fort Macleod in southern Alberta. By 1885 the force had increased to about 1,000. In 1904 King Edward VII signed a document that made the organization the Royal North West Mounted Police, and in 1920 it took its present name.

Today, the RCMP is a federal force covering 75 percent of Canada's geography, and providing policing services to all provinces and territories except Ontario and Quebec. Its National Police Services offers resources to more than 500 law enforcement and criminal justice agencies in Canada. This includes a repository of 3.5 million criminal records. Among other duties, the force also protects the prime minister and foreign dignitaries.

Admiration for the RCMP has led to Hollywood movies and other fictionalized accounts of their bravery. The 1936 Broadway operetta *Rose Marie* was turned into at least four movies—best known is the 1939 film *Susannah of the Mounties,* starring Shirley Temple. Television added *Due South*, a popular drama about a Mountie helping the Chicago police, which was produced by Canada's CTV and ran from 1994 to 1999. The Mounties even became a cartoon when *The Dudley Do-Right Show* appeared on television screens in 1969, followed three years later by a movie with real actors.

driving. The suspect was in his late 20s with a slim build and unkempt collar-length hair. He was around 5 feet 8 inches (1.7 m) tall. His car was a four-door, 1970s Plymouth Valiant with rust spots along the doors and fenders; witnesses could not agree on the color and suggested it might have been either green, yellow, or beige.

More witnesses had seen a man near the clearing where Dana's body was discovered. At 11:30 P.M., over eight hours after she was found, a couple noticed the same type of car parked on a nearby road with the

> WE WERE ACTUALLY ONLY 25-30 FEET AWAY FROM WHERE SHE GOT ABOARD. SHE GOT IN AND THEY DROVE OFF. WE DID COMMENT ON A LITTLE GIRL LIKE THIS, HITCHHIKING, GETTING ABOARD WITH A STRANGER AND NEVER THOUGHT NO MORE OF IT THAN THAT.
>
> —HARRY SMEATON

passenger door open and its interior light on, showing a beige interior. A man, who fitted the suspect's description, was standing a few feet from the vehicle.

Not Forgotten. In 1991 NTV News in St. Johns broadcast a reenactment of the crime. This drew numerous tips, but still no answers. Members of the public continue to give the police approximately 50 tips on the case each year, and the murder remains seared into the minds of many Newfoundlanders, but the case remains unsolved. A local songwriter and singer, Ron Hynes, penned "The Ghost of Dana Bradley" in 2002, and in 2003 Darrin McGrath authored the book *Hitching a Ride: The Unsolved Murder of Dana Bradley*.

The Suspects

As the investigation grew, police identified around 250 prime suspects.

• **David Somerton, 36.** In 1986 an anonymous note was sent to Jack Lavers, chief investigator for the Royal Canadian Mounted Police (RCMP), which pointed the finger at Somerton. He had previously been convicted and served time in New Brunswick for armed robbery and quickly confessed to the Bradley crime, giving details that were consistent with how the crime occurred. Somerton claimed he buried the murder weapon near the body and left his car at the local dump. Police searched both sites without success, clearing trees and digging at the crime scene. Somerton then recanted, saying the pressure of 18 hours of interrogation and being on heavy medication led to his confession. "I was doing anything to get them off my back to make it out of that room," he said. Because the RCMP had no physical evidence to link Somerton to Dana he was not charged with murder, but he was charged with public mischief and sentenced to two years in prison for misleading the RCMP.

Police continue to suspect his involvement, and Somerton accuses them of harassment, telling them to bring charges or leave him alone. His criminal record was extended in 1996 when he was convicted of an indecent assault on a teenage girl and three years later pled guilty to sexually assaulting a minor.

- Why did Dana change her mind about taking the bus? Did she know the car driver who offered her a ride?

- Since witnesses gave a good description of the murderer's car, why has it never been found? Does this indicate that the driver did not live in the area?

- For what reason did the killer place the body in a formal pose? Does this reflect his regret or a sick attempt at humor?

- Was the killer the man sighted near the crime scene more than eight hours after Dana's body was found? Why was he there?

- Who sent the police the letter that named David Somerton as the killer? Why did he confess, giving details about the case?

- Although real evidence against Shannon Murrin seems to be thin, should police investigate him in regard to this case?

- **Shannon Murrin, 29.** Police considered Murrin as another possible suspect, but this was based on weak circumstantial evidence. Murrin was later tried unsuccessfully for the 1994 murder of Mindy Tran in Kelowna, British Columbia. He fitted the description of Dana's suspected killer and was originally from Newfoundland, visiting for Christmas in 1980. Murrin left Kelowna suddenly in the fall of 1981, which added to the circumstantial evidence.

Peggy Hettrick was born in Lovell, Wyoming. Her schoolmates recalled her beautiful blue eyes and gorgeous red hair.

PEGGY HETTRICK

Peggy Hettrick, 37, was a petite, redheaded woman who managed a clothing store in Fort Collin Colorado. On February 11, 1987, she left a local restaurant at 1:00 A.M., to walk to her nearby apartment. Along the way, someone came from behind, stabbed her once in the back, and dragged her more than 100 yards (91 meters) into a field. The following morning, a bicyclist discovered her partially clad body.

The Investigation and Suspects

Officers at the scene soon discovered that Hettrick's body had been sexually mutilated with almost surgical skill.

A lab technician carries out a DNA analysis during an investigation.

HOW DNA TESTS WORK

When DNA results are presented in court, the verdict is usually assured. The testing and analyzing of DNA is so complex, jurors would not question the findings (although some lawyers do). Collecting enough samples, reading the profiles, and coming up with matches can be painstaking work, but new systems are speeding up the process.

To make a match between two samples, such as a person's known DNA and traces found at a crime scene, a forensic scientist needs to separate the double-stranded DNA into single strands to look at the repeated base sequences. Chemicals and an electrical current are used to make the separation, and a fluorescent dye is applied to each fragment. A laser beam fluoresces the fragments, and a band of the suspect's DNA is displayed on a graph next to a band of the DNA found at the crime scene. If the colored peaks on the graph are the same, a match is indicated.

The early use of DNA in criminal cases often faltered because the samples were not large enough or were degraded. The development of the polymerase chain reaction (PCR) technique allows laboratories to make millions of copies from an extremely small sample, such as a few skin cells. This used to take about three hours, since the sample had to be heated and cooled up to 40 times, but recent advances in technique have cut the time to only 40 minutes by using convection to keep the DNA mixture moving in a circular flow.

The introduction of mitochondrial DNA analysis (mtDNA) overcomes the problem of extremely degraded samples. While the other tests are done on DNA extracted from the nucleus of a cell, mtDNA tests analyze a different part of the cell when the nucleus is not present.

This seemed to indicate that a doctor, or a person experienced with knives, had committed the crime. The victim's purse was found next to her body and had not been disturbed.

Hettrick's Lifestyle. Detectives carefully built up a picture of Hettrick's lifestyle. In addition to working at the Fashion Bar in a Fort Collins shopping center, she was writing a novel and had another manuscript that she hoped to have published. Known as a regular customer at local bars, she was in the Prime Minister Pub and Grill on the night of her murder, along with her former boyfriend Matt Zoellner. Witnesses noticed that during the evening she became upset and declined his offer of a ride home.

Schoolboy Killer. Investigators immediately suspected Timothy Masters, a 15-year-old high-school student. He told police he had seen the body the morning after Hettrick was killed on his way to catch the school bus, but failed to report it because he thought it might be a mannequin. Masters lived with his father in a mobile home that overlooked the murder scene. Although Masters claimed not to have walked through the trail that had been made by the body's being dragged, his footprints were found there. Two days after the murder, detectives searched the boy's room and school locker. They found a knife collection, pornography, writings about violence, and pictures he had drawn that resembled the crime—one was of a sexual mutilation and another showed a man dragging a woman who was pierced with arrows.

Other Suspects. These facts soon ruled Matthew Zoellner, Hettrick's former boyfriend, out of the investigation. But another possible killer was Dr. Richard Hammond, an eye surgeon whose bedroom window overlooked the murder scene. He was arrested in 1995 after he hid cameras in his home to secretly film women in his bathroom. Several days after being arrested, he committed suicide without ever being named as a suspect in Hettrick's murder. Yet the day after the murder, he had stayed at home, breaking appointments.

Arrested at Last. Although Masters was their only true suspect, the police had no physical evidence that directly linked him to the crime,

Peggy Hettrick's body was discovered in the middle of a field, having been dragged there by her killer from the road some 100 yards (91 m) away

Tim Masters speaks at a press conference after being released from prison. He had served nearly a decade before DNA proved his innocence.

such as blood, hair, or fibers. While Masters served eight years in the U.S. Navy, the police spent over a decade building the case against him. Investigators came close to an arrest in 1992, when they learned that the suspect had told high school classmates details about Hettrick's mutilations. Masters claimed that details had been passed on to him by a friend who had helped police at the crime scene, and detectives were able to verify this.

Finally, after a forensic psychologist, Dr. Reid Meloy, concluded that Masters's drawings and writings indicated he was the killer, police arrested him on August 10, 1998, in California where he worked as an aircraft mechanic.

The Trial

Prosecutors argued that Masters's gruesome writings and drawings, his love of knives, and his knowledge of the crime area all added up to his guilt. They also presented evidence that the defendant's footprints were discovered in the bloody trail that had been made by dragging the victim, although Masters told police he never had walked that way. His defense was that just being in the area did not imply murder and no other physical evidence existed.

Circumstantial Evidence. The jury, however, decided the many pieces of circumstantial evidence were enough to prove that Masters was guilty. He was convicted on March 26, 1999, and sentenced to life. Some jurors said the many small details linking him to the murder were too overwhelming to ignore. Among the most damning was his failure to report seeing a body, his footprints on the trail, and his violent drawings. One juror stated: "He admitted his guilt through pictures to us."

An Innocent Man. His lawyers appealed the decision, but it was upheld in 2001 and a second appeal to the Colorado Supreme Court was denied in 2002. By this time an advanced DNA test had been developed, and tests were done on the clothes that Hettrick had been wearing when she was murdered. They showed skin-cell DNA belonging to her former boyfriend and no other DNA. In addition, Masters's lawyers uncovered four documents that police had withheld from the defense during the trial. They asked for a new trial, naming the late Dr. Richard Hammond as the key suspect. On January 22, 2008, a judge threw out Masters's conviction and released him after he had served almost a decade in jail. In 2009 Masters brought a lawsuit accusing the police and the prosecutors of withholding evidence that would have pointed to other suspects. The lead detective in the case admitted that fingerprints and hair belonging to someone else had been found in Hettrick's purse. Nobody else has been charged with the murder.

JULIE WARD

On September 7, 1988, the British photographer Julie Ward, 28, disappeared in Kenya while on a safari. She was nearing the end of her seven-month visit in the Masai Mara game reserve. Taking one last excursion to photograph wildebeests, she and an Australian, Glen Burns, became stranded when their jeep broke down. He returned to the Kenyan capital, Nairobi, for help but Julie repaired the jeep, picked up their tents at the campsite, and ignored advice by driving back toward Nairobi alone. Six days later, her mutilated and charred body parts were found.

Kenyan investigators quickly decided that she had either been torn apart and eaten by wild animals or had committed suicide. When the police refused to conduct a murder inquiry, her father, John Ward, began an

Julie Ward was an avid wildlife photographer and animal lover. The Julie Ward Center for rescued big cats was opened in 1999 in South Africa.

The scene where Julie Ward was killed shows the ashes of a fire used to burn her remains. Her father, John Ward, discovered the ashes and parts of her body.

investigation in January 1989 that led to a Kenyan court ruling in October that she had been murdered.

The Investigation

As soon as Julie was reported missing, John Ward traveled to Kenya from Bury St. Edmonds in Suffolk, England, to examine the scene. He hired spotter planes to hunt for his daughter's remains. Her jeep was found abandoned with "SOS" written on the roof in dust. Within days of her murder, it was her father who discovered her severed leg and half of her jaw in the grass, and also ashes where her remains had been burned, over five miles from the jeep. Six weeks later her skull was found. By 2009 the 75-year-old, retired businessman had visited the crime scene more than 100 times and had spent almost $4 million of his own money looking for evidence. Julie's camera was missing, so he circulated its serial number worldwide. His wife, Jan, also made investigative trips to Kenya.

Cover-up. Ward believed the official investigation was obstructed by Kenyan authorities, who were worried about its effect on tourism, and by British officials, who wanted to maintain friendly relations with an old Cold War ally. When he pointed out that wild animals or a person committing suicide would not have been set fire to the body, a British official suggested that Julie had been struck by lightning.

Local Kenyan rumors also suggested that smugglers, connected to public figures, had killed her after she had witnessed their activity, and that a prominent Kenyan politician had had her killed for having an affair with his son.

In 2004 an independent police report for Scotland Yard said British officials in London and Nairobi had engaged in "inconsistency and contradictions, falsehoods, and downright lies," and concluded that this "not surprisingly led to John Ward believing that there was an active conspiracy to prevent him from identifying his daughter's killers."

Suspects and Trials

John Ward's persistence forced a murder inquiry in 1990 in which Scotland Yard detectives assisted the Kenyan police. Despite Ward's protests, the British detectives quickly concluded that two rangers stationed a mile away from the jeep had murdered Julie after a sexual assault. The suspects, Peter Kipeen and Jonah Magiroi, were put on trial in 1992. They were acquitted six months later due to lack of evidence, but the trial judge stated a cover-up had occurred to protect the lucrative tourist industry.

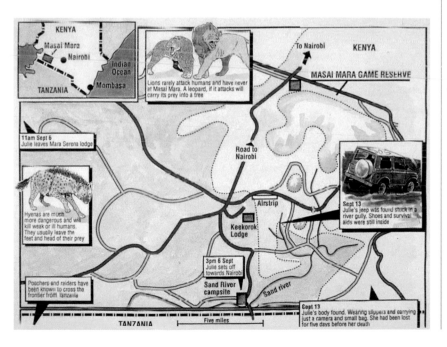

A map of the area where Julie Ward lost her life, showing where her body and her jeep were found. She had spent seven months in the Masai Mara game reserve in Kenya.

A year later, Valentine Kopido, who said he was a former government chauffeur, claimed Julie was killed after she stumbled onto smuggling linked to Israelis and an important Kenyan politician. Scotland Yard investigated his story in 1996 and exposed it as a fabrication.

Cooperation and Arrest. Ward campaigned tirelessly, keeping the pressure on Kenyan authorities until they finally began to cooperate fully in 1997. A special police team was put on the case and that year

MURDER OR SUICIDE?

A favorite ruse of many killers is to make a death seem like a suicide. The body of a battered victim can be thrown from a building, a strangled person hung from a noose, and a gun placed in the corpse's hand.

Such a case occurred in 1982 when the Vatican banker Roberto Calvi (see page 226) was found hanging from a scaffold under London's Blackfriars Bridge with his pockets full of bricks and $15,000 in cash. He had been convicted of illegally exporting currency. The coroner recorded suicide, but a

second inquest said the reason for his death was unknown. A theory arose that Calvi was strangled by the Mafia, before being hanged. The case was reopened in 2003 as a murder inquiry. Three Italian mobsters, a financier, and two others were charged with murder, but in 2007 they were acquitted.

Another high-profile death was the murder of lawyer Vincent Foster, a Deputy White House counsel for

Roberto Calvi's body lies near London's Blackfriars Bridge minutes after being discovered.

President Bill Clinton. A worker found his body in Fort Marcy Park in Washington, D.C. Police arrived at what appeared to be a suicide, and found a pistol in Foster's right hand.

The death was a mystery. No one had heard a gunshot in the park, and the man who found the body had not seen a gun. Police found a blonde hair on his clothing that revived an old rumor that he was conducting an affair with Hillary Clinton. He had come with the Clintons from Little Rock, Arkansas. Carpet fibers were also found, and some believed this indicated the body had been wrapped in a carpet. Detectives found that someone had entered Foster's office the day he died to remove his work on the Whitewater property scandal, in which the Clintons were partners in a property development company that failed and led to fraud convictions of the other partners. However, three official investigations all decided he committed suicide.

charged Simon Ole Makallah, the chief gamekeeper of the Masai Mara, with Julie's murder. He had aroused Ward's suspicion by quickly leading the search party to Julie's abandoned jeep and then going directly to her body. Ward said Makallah had been his main suspect "from the first day I saw him." Scotland Yard, however, had even used the man as their guide during their initial investigation.

Another Innocent Suspect. Makallah's trial began in Nairobi on March 1, 1999, and on September 17, the judge declared him innocent, saying, "Nothing added to nothing makes nothing. The case was based on purely circumstantial evidence." After his acquittal, Ward asked for a retrial due to violations of court procedures, but this was denied. For her part, Julie Ward's mother, Jan, declared, "Maybe this really is the time to draw a line under it and call it a day."

By 2009 John Ward had visited Africa 100 times in the 21 years since Julie's murder and had spent $4 million (£2.7 million) seeking her killer.

British Inquest. Scotland Yard continued to work on the cold case, and on April 26, 2004, a formal British inquest was held in Ipswich. The Kenyan pathologist who conducted the autopsy stated that he had described Julie's bone injuries as "clean cut" but this was changed to "torn" by Kenya's director of public health to indicate an animal attack. The pathologist also recalled the Kenyan police commissioner saying Julie had been a "loose girl who had been with different men on different nights" and said she could have cut herself up. Rumors were also presented, with a former British consular official testifying that the son of the Kenyan president at the time, Daniel arap Moi, was implicated. The inquest concluded that Julie Ward was unlawfully killed, but they were unable to say by whom.

Hope for a Conclusion. Kenyan authorities regard John Ward as a grieving father who will only accept that Julie's death was a homicide. They believe no evidence points to this, since Scotland Yard and their own detectives have made extensive investigations for more than 20 years and only arrested three men on circumstantial evidence too thin to convict them.

Julie's parents continue to hope that DNA can be found and matched. They also hope someone will come forth with new information, perhaps a local person who had passed through the game reserve and happened to see their stranded daughter. *The Observer* newspaper reported on October 11, 2009, that a new inquiry has been agreed to by Scotland Yard, which wants to look closer at the DNA evidence.

Lingering Doubts

- If the chief gamekeeper was innocent, how did he find Julie's jeep so quickly and then discover her body as if by chance?

- Was it incompetence or desperation that made Scotland Yard accept the suspicious gamekeeper as their guide, while the clues grew old?

- Why wasn't a thorough inquiry conducted about the rumors of smuggling that might involve high Kenyan officials? Would British authorities obstruct the investigation to keep the Kenyan authorities happy?

Mindy Tran was abducted in her own neighborhood, but it took two months before her body was discovered.

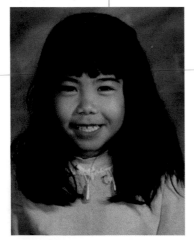

MINDY TRAN

Eight-year-old Mindy Tran was riding her bicycle just after supper near her home in Kelowna, British Columbia, Canada, on the warm evening of August 17, 1994. At 6:45 P.M. two of her friends were watching her as she rode up and down quiet Taylor Road and stopped to talk with two women. They also saw a white van driving slowly through their Rutland neighborhood. Mindy was last seen putting her bike down between two rocks and walking along the road toward her home before she vanished.

The search was one of the largest in Canadian history, with hundreds involved. It was officially called off on August 22, but on October 11 that year a 68-year-old man with a divining rod helped police discovered Mindy's body. Police had lent the searcher a strand of the girl's hair from her headband, and he held it against the divining rod until it pointed to the body. Mindy's remains lay in a shallow grave, covered with leaves and twigs in Mission Creek Regional Park about 1 mile (1.6 km) from her home.

The Investigation

An autopsy found that the attacker had beaten the girl, breaking her nose twice, and then strangled her with her own shorts. She had been sexually assaulted.

Mode of Abduction The police file on the case was huge, filling 44 file boxes, and the Royal Canadian Mounted Police (RCMP) in Vancouver sent a team to help the local police with the investigation. Witnesses provided three sightings of the white van in the neighborhood, close to the time Mindy vanished, and many more white van sightings after she disappeared and before her body was found. Witnesses also reported seeing a girl resembling Mindy on August 19 as she struggled with a man in a brown pickup truck. Police followed this lead for several weeks before discounting it.

Detectives came to the conclusion that a vehicle had not been used in the abduction, because Mindy's remains were found so close to where she disappeared. Instead, they asked the locals if they had seen a man carrying a suitcase, since it might have contained her body.

The Suspect

Police interviewed all of the neighbors and immediately, based on circumstantial evidence; one person fell under suspicion—Shannon

Mindy Tran's parents look on while police and neighbors discuss search procedures. Witnesses said they had seen a girl struggling with a man in a truck.

Murrin, 43. Murrin, a neighbor of Mindy's, was an auto-body worker who had lived in many places in Canada and had a criminal record of burglaries and bank robberies. The media described him as a transient and an alcoholic, and one officer on the case reported that he was a bad character. Mindy's bike was found in front of Murrin's duplex; one witness said they had seen Mindy walking toward Murrin's front door, while other witnesses had seen a man resembling Murrin carrying a suitcase.

On January 5, 1995, Murrin was hospitalized for 11 days after being nearly beaten to death by three men who claimed a RCMP officer asked them to get a confession. He received a two-year sentence for pulling a firearm on his attackers, and during his time in jail, from 1995 to 1997, seven prisoners claimed he confessed to Mindy's murder. On January 14, 1997, police charged Murrin with the murder.

The Trial
Murrin's trial began on August 4, 1999, and lasted almost seven months. More than 80 witnesses gave evidence and the prosecution presented DNA results from a British laboratory that matched Murrin to three hairs found in Mindy's underwear at the burial site. This was the first presentation to a Canadian jury of mitochondrial DNA (mtDNA), after a Canadian DNA test had proved inconclusive. The prosecution also had two witnesses who said they saw Murrin with a suitcase. But their chief witness was Douglas Martin, 43, a criminal whose many convictions

The suspect Shannon Murrin is driven off in a police vehicle. A jury acquitted him but the police continued to believe that he was guilty.

THE CANINE UNIT

Police investigating missing persons, unidentified remains, and unknown suspects, often call upon a canine team to put them on the right scent. One of the best is the canine unit of the Ontario Provincial Police (OPP). Established in 1965 the unit now has 27 teams; each team is made up of a dog and a handler and is on call 24 hours a day. Besides searching for criminals, bodies, and evidence, some dogs are trained to detect explosives and drugs.

Canine units have an important part to play in searching for missing children, like Mindy Tran, and adults. Robberies also require their special skills. In August 2009 an OPP team went to Lambton Shores, near Lake Huron, to help track down some house burglars. The dog began tracking from the house and soon located discarded stolen property. It then followed the suspect's scent for more than three hours, before locating him in hiding.

OPP's breed of choice for general work is the German shepherd, because of its keen sense of smell and hearing as well as its dependability and good temperament. Labrador retrievers are preferred for finding human remains that are buried or underwater. The dogs are chosen between the ages of 18 to 24 months and undergo an intensive 16-week training at the OPP Academy Canine Training Center. Tracking is emphasized, which includes the ability to follow a scent over heights, tunnels, stairways, and water, in all types of weather. The dogs are also trained on command to protect their handlers. The officers also have to be in excellent physical condition to keep up with their dogs. The animals live at the handlers' homes and have a special bond with them. When an OPP officer retires, so does the dog, usually returning to live permanently with its handler.

A constable from the Canine Unit of the Ontario Provincial Police pets police dog Ki, an 8-year-old German Shepherd, after the dog was inducted into the Purina Hall of Fame Monday, May 7, 2007.

included perjury. He testified that Murrin had confessed to him in prison when he was in the next cell.

A Strong Defense. The defense claimed that Murrin had been at a friend's house when the girl was taken, and they argued that the police had the witness supporting this main alibi change his account by saying Murrin was there an hour later. One of the three men who had beaten Murrin also testified that RCMP Sergeant Gary Tidsbury had asked them to take the suspect to Mission Creek Park to get a confession. When he pulled a loaded gun at his home, they beat him unconscious, drove him in the back of a pickup truck to the park, and almost beat him to death. Murrin brought a civil lawsuit against Tidsbury and the three others, and on December 31, 2009, it was settled out of court and the details were not released.

Internal Investigations. After almost a week of deliberations, the jury acquitted Murrin, who jumped from his chair in the courtroom and clapped his hands. The RCMP, however, said they had no plans to investigate the case further, since they believed the appropriate person had been charged.

In July 2001 the RCMP released the results of an internal investigation of the case, exonerating Tidsbury, but saying he should have been replaced as the lead investigator, because the court case was damaged by a public perception that he may have been involved in Murrin's beating. The review also said too many officers had searched for Mindy when she was missing and that not enough had investigated the possible murder.

Capable of Murder? In May 2009 Joey Oliver, 39, was sentenced to 11 years for a double manslaughter committed in August 1993 near St. John's, Newfoundland, although he claimed Murrin was responsible for the double murder. Oliver claimed he had confessed to the crime because Murrin had threatened him and his family if he talked. Murrin denied Oliver's claim and has never been charged for the crime.

Lingering Doubts

- Did the divining rod actually locate the body? Why would police use such an unusual method of detection?

- Why was so much time spent on finding the two vans if the body was located close to Mindy's home?

- Did Tidsbury ask the three men to physically force Murrin into a confession? Why were the men not charged, but Murrin sent to jail for pulling a gun on them? Was this a police cover-up?

- Was Joey Oliver telling the truth when he claimed Murrin committed the killings instead of him? Why has Murrin not been investigated for this crime?

- Why would the prosecution rely on a criminal as their key witness? If seven convicts had claimed that Murrin confessed to them, why was Martin the only one giving evidence in court, especially since he once committed perjury?

JONBENÉT RAMSEY

Six-year-old American child beauty-pageant queen JonBenét Ramsey was murdered in 1996 at her family's large home in the college town of Boulder, Colorado. Her parents, John and Patsy Ramsey, realized she was missing at 5:45 A.M. on December 26, 1996. Patsy found a two-page, handwritten ransom note on the stairs in the house that demanded $118,000 to keep the girl from being executed by a "small foreign faction." Patsy immediately called 911 to report JonBenét's kidnapping. When the police arrived, they suggested that John and a friend search the large rambling house. They found the little girl's body in the basement wine cellar. The Ramseys had put JonBenét to bed at 9:30 P.M. Her father found her body at 1:05 P.M. the next day.

JonBenét's image became familiar to Americans after her murder. Many video images showed her dressed in beauty pageant costumes.

The Investigation

The crime scene was badly compromised. The police had allowed John Ramsey, who was Boulder's "Businessman of the Year," to carry his daughter's body from the basement and had also permitted friends of the couple to move freely through the house.

Evidence of an Intruder.

The Ramseys claimed that their daughter had been killed by an intruder, but the police found no footprints in the snow on the lawn and no evidence of a forced entry. However, a window near the body was open with a suitcase below it which may have been used as a step. The footprint of a hiking boot

A forensic scientist examines evidence collected around the Ramsey house. The crime scene had been compromised by friends who visited.

was also discovered in the basement dust and did not match those belonging to the family or their friends.

Officers spent a week searching the house, as reporters began to criticize the confused investigation. Police took eight days to send DNA from the girl's clothing for an official analysis. Bloodstains on her pajamas and underpants were mixed with DNA from a white male. This DNA was not her father's, and hairs and fibers found at the scene did not come from her parents.

Autopsy Results. The murderer had placed tape over her mouth, bound her wrists above her head with white nylon cord, and used the same cord to strangle her by tightening it around her neck with a broken paintbrush handle. The killer then covered her body with a blanket. Investigators said the broken paintbrush and the paper used for the ransom note had not come from the house.

The autopsy revealed JonBenét's skull was fractured and she had possibly been sexually assaulted. Her head bore two small, burnlike injuries that some investigators believed resembled the marks made by a stun gun.

The Suspects

JonBenét's parents, John and Patsy, were immediate suspects. The leading investigator, Steve Thomas, believed the parents had made up the intruder story after Patsy accidentally killed her daughter by striking her after she wet the bed. However, another investigator working on the case was convinced that someone had broken into the house and attacked the girl. The only other person at home that night was JonBenét's half-brother, 10-year-old Burke Ramsey, who was never a suspect.

Focus on the Parents. Besides taking samples of the parents' hair and blood, police also looked at their handwriting. The Colorado Bureau of Investigation said that indications pointed to Patsy's writing the ransom note, but they could not be definite.

John Ramsey holds up a photo of his slain daughter as he and his wife, Patsy, hold a news conference in Atlanta, Georgia, on May 24, 2000.

Police also took handwriting samples from employees at John Ramsey's computer company, and from the man who had played Santa Claus at a family party.

Two days after the murder, the parents flew to their former home city of Atlanta, Georgia, to bury their daughter. Boulder police followed them, but the Ramseys denied their request to take polygraph tests. Media coverage often seemed negative toward Patsy, a former beauty queen, who many felt had pushed her daughter into child beauty competitions.

John Mark Karr's false confession raised hopes in 2006, but these were dashed by DNA tests that proved he was not involved in the murder.

An Umbrella of Suspicion. In March 1997 police searched the Ramseys' summer home in Charlevoix, Michigan. The next month, Boulder District Attorney Alex Hunter confirmed that the police were focusing on the Ramseys. A grand jury convened on September 15, 1997, to hear evidence, but the district attorney decided that no indictments would be issued since the evidence was insufficient. On December 5, 1997, the new leading investigator, Mark Beckner, said the Ramseys "remain under an umbrella of suspicion."

The couple turned down a Boulder police request for another interview in January 1998, because investigators refused to show them the evidence. The following month, the police lost some of the evidence, including palm prints from family friends.

In May 2000 the Ramseys passed a polygraph test given by an independent examiner, but police rejected the results because they would not take one given by the FBI. In 2003 Boulder County District Attorney Mary Keenan said the evidence pointed more to an intruder than Mrs. Ramsey.

Exoneration for the Ramseys. Patsy, suffering from cancer, died in June 2006, two months before John Mark Karr, who was living in Thailand, confessed to killing the girl. He was arrested on August 17, 2006, and returned to Colorado, but was released after forensic tests did not match his DNA to that found on the girl's clothing.

In July 2006 the police exonerated John and Patsy of having a role in their daughter's death. John had once said that some people would always believe he and his wife had killed JonBenét, even if police charged someone else with the murder. In 2008 the Boulder County District Attorney Mary Lacy gave John Ramsey a note saying no member

Billie-Jo Jenkins was fostered by Lois and Sion Jenkins from the age of nine. Her real father had been imprisoned and her mother could not cope alone.

of the family was under suspicion, and she also offered a public apology to them. The following year, the Boulder County police announced they were reopening the cold case and would form a special task force, including FBI agents, to review all the past evidence.

BILLIE-JO JENKINS

The body of Billie-Jo Jenkins, a 13-year-old British schoolgirl, was discovered on February 15, 1997, in a thick pool of blood on the patio of her foster family's large Victorian home in Hastings, East Sussex. She had been painting the patio doors at the time. Her foster mother, Lois Jenkins, 35, was taking a seafront walk with two of her four daughters. Her foster father, Sion, 39, was shopping with their two other daughters, Annie, 12, and Lottie, 10. When they returned from the store, the girls' screams brought their father rushing to the horrific scene. He found Billie-Jo lying full length with the left side of her face against the concrete. Her skull had been crushed and, strangely, the corner of a garbage bag had been pushed into her left nostril.

The Investigation

Police quickly determined that Billie-Jo had been hit on the head five times with an 8-inch (20-cm) iron tent peg

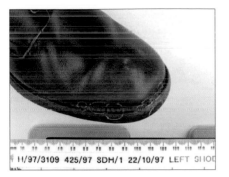

that was found near her body. One of the Jenkinses' daughters had left it on the patio earlier that day while she was cleaning out a utility room. Forensic scientists said the girl had been beaten unconscious and died within minutes. She had not been sexually assaulted.

Sion Jenkins made a television appeal asking if anyone could help the police find the killer, but within days he was arrested himself after tiny blood spots were discovered on his jacket, trousers, and shoes. Jenkins later claimed the police had decided he was guilty 24 hours after the murder.

Evidence in the case included Sion Jenkins' shoe which allegedly had Billie-Jo's blood on it. He said he had found her in a pool of blood.

The Suspects

- **Sion Jenkins.** Billie-Jo's foster father was a respected deputy head teacher (assistant principal) at a local boys' school. He and his wife, Lois, had fostered Billie-Jo since 1992. The pattern of 150 microscopic specks of blood on Jenkins's clothes seemed to be overwhelming evidence, although he claimed they came from the girl's dying breath as he cradled her in his arms. Investigators were convinced by Jenkins's statement that he had only returned to the house for only about three minutes, while his daughters waited in the car for their trip to a hardware store. He said he had gone into the dining room to turn down Billie-Jo's music without being aware of her through the patio doors.

- **An unknown stalker or prowler.** Weeks before her death, Billie-Jo had told friends that a stalker had been following her. Her foster parents were also worried about a prowler who had been seen in the empty property next door. They had even considered moving for their own security.

- **A psychiatric patient.** On the same day Billie-Jo died, a psychiatric patient was seen acting suspiciously in the park next

Sion Jenkins' fleece jacket was covered with tiny specks of blood, but his defense said the dying girl had "breathed blood" onto it when he held her.

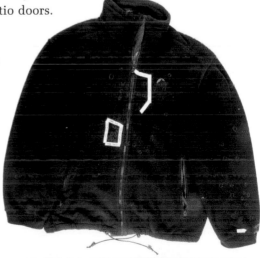

to the Jenkinses' house. Police arrested the man but released him a few days later.

- **A dark-haired intruder**. Jenkins suddenly recalled another possible suspect while he was researching his book, *The Murder of Billie-Jo Jenkins*. He had met a dark-haired man in his own hallway just after the murder. The stranger said he was a plain-clothes policeman and reassured him, "She is going to be okay," then walked away. The man has never been traced, although Jenkins asked the police to put together an image to help identify him.

The Trials

Sion Jenkins endured a nine-year ordeal, during which time he had three trials and his wife left him and moved to Tasmania in Australia with their four daughters.

The First Trial. In his first trial, in 1998, Jenkins told the court how he had panicked and become confused after discovering Billie-Jo's body. He failed to call an ambulance immediately, he said, because he did not want to leave his crying daughters in case the intruder was still in the house. The prosecution's case hinged on the fine mist of blood found on

A horse-drawn hearse with Billie-Jo's coffin nears the City of London Cemetery on April 24, 1997. The cemetery's chapel was filled with mourners for her funeral.

Jenkins's clothes. Experts said the droplets could only have come from blood sprayed during the attack. Although Jenkins claimed the spots came from blood in the girl's nostril, he had initially said in his emergency call that she was not breathing when he held her.

Jenkins's defense received no help from his wife, who was convinced of his guilt and also influenced their two daughters who did not testify on his behalf. The jury's verdict was guilty and he was jailed for life. The following year, he appealed but the conviction was upheld.

Retrial. After Jenkins spent six years in jail, new forensic evidence about the blood became available and a retrial was held in July 2005. The defense, relying on a pathologist's examination of the girl's lungs, argued that Billie-Jo's airway had been blocked after the attack, and pressure in her lungs could have caused a sudden spray of blood. Presented with this new evidence, the jury was unable to reach a decision. Some evidence against him was not allowed in court—his wife claimed that Jenkins had hit her, but a judge ruled that this information would prejudice the jury.

The Second Retrial. Jenkins's second retrial was held three months later, in October 2005, and again resulted in a hung jury. His now-divorced wife told the court that Billie-Jo was beginning to "use her femininity" to get her way with Jenkins and other men. The two daughters, however, testified in support of their father. Evidence that the girl's blood on his clothes contained fragments of her bone was refused by the judge because it was presented too late. The Crown Prosecution Service decided against more retrials, and he was formally acquitted. Jenkins has since remarried and will never be prosecuted again for Billie-Jo's murder. The indecisive verdicts set him free.

BILLY-JO'S MURDERER HAS ESCAPED DETECTION BECAUSE OF THE DREADFUL ERRORS IN THE POLICE INVESTIGATION AND THEIR SINGLE-MINDED AND DESPERATE DETERMINATION TO CONVICT ME AT ALL COSTS.

—SION JENKINS

The Notorious B.I.G. was born in Brooklyn, New York, and became important in East Coast hip-hop music with the Junior M.A.F.I.A. group.

THE NOTORIOUS B.I.G.

Christopher Wallace, known professionally as the Notorious B.I.G. or Biggie Smalls, was one of America's most influential rappers when he was killed in a drive-by shooting on March 9, 1997, in Los Angeles. B.I.G., 24, had just left a music industry party at the Petersen Automotive Museum and was being driven to his hotel. As his Chevrolet sport utility vehicle pulled up to a red stoplight, someone yelled to the singer, asking him to lower his window. As he did this, a black Impala car pulled up on the right side of B.I.G.'s vehicle and the driver, an African-American man who was alone in the car, looked B.I.G. in the eye for a moment, pointed a blue steel pistol, fired four shots into his chest, and sped away. B.I.G.'s driver rushed him to a hospital less than five minutes away, but he was pronounced dead at 1:15 A.M.

The Investigation

Although detectives from the homicide division of the Los Angeles Police Department (LAPD) were on the scene that night, they left the following morning and did not work on the case again until a month later. A former LAPD officer said this was unexplained.

Nation of Islam. Dozens of people were on Wilshire Boulevard when the shooting occurred, and several witnesses helped the police create a composite sketch of the killer. Some thought he looked like a member of the Nation of Islam (a black religious group) because he was wearing a blue suit and bow tie. Four spent shell casings from a 9 mm automatic pistol were found at the scene.

Vehicle Entourage. There were three vehicles in B.I.G.'s entourage. Sitting in the back of B.I.G.'s Chevy were two of his friends, the Junior M.A.F.I.A. rapper James "Lil' Caesar" Lloyd and B.I.G.'s best friend Damien "D-Rock" Butler, and traveling in the car in front was Sean "Puffy" Combs, his driver, and three bodyguards in the back. Combs headed Bad Boy Entertainment, B.I.G.'s record label. The director of security for Bad Boy Entertainment was in the car behind.

Notorious B.I.G. poses with his close associate, Sean "Puffy" Combs. Combs was traveling in the car in front when B.I.G. was shot

Witnesses told the police that two cars appeared to be involved in the attack. When B.I.G.'s driver stopped for the red light, a Toyota made a U-turn and tried to push in between his car and the one carrying the director of security. After the shooting, the Toyota made another U-turn and accelerated away.

Gang Battles. Investigators were most interested in the continuous feud between the top East Coast and West Coast rap companies. This had degenerated into gang battles in Los Angeles and elsewhere between the Bloods, who supported B.I.G., and the Crips, who backed rapper Tupac Shakur, 25. In June 1996 Shakur released a song in which the lyrics bragged that he'd had sex with B.I.G.'s estranged wife. Three months later, on September 7, Shakur was murdered in a drive-by shooting in Las Vegas, dying six days later. Although B.I.G. was recording in a New York studio at the time, police believed he was involved in the shooting that was carried out by a gang member.

The only witness willing to tell police who may have shot Shakur was one of his backup singers, Yafeu "Kadafi" Fula, 19, but Las Vegas police only managed to speak with him briefly before he was shot two months later in Orange, New Jersey, in another unsolved murder.

Suspects

The simplest explanation is that an unknown member of the Crips gang murdered B.I.G. to avenge Shakur's death, which is also currently unsolved. But Russell Poole, a detective with the Los Angeles Robbery-

Homicide Division, took another view. "Biggie's murder was much more sophisticated than anything I've ever seen any gangbanger pull off," he noted. "This was professionally executed." He and others, including the *Los Angeles Times*, believed the Crips might have murdered B.I.G. because Bad Boy Entertainment's Puffy Combs had used off-duty police instead of Crips as bodyguards for a Los Angeles event.

Some, however, say the Crips carried out the killing for another reason. B.I.G. had promised to pay them for murdering Shakur, but then reneged on the deal, so the Crips made him pay the ultimate price.

The Record Label Conspiracy. A conspiracy was claimed in a 2002 book, *LAbyrinth*, by Randall Sullivan, which was based on Detective Russell Poole's work. The conspiracy suggests that Marion "Suge" Knight, the cofounder of Death Row Records (Shakur's label), joined up with a former Los Angeles police officer and gang member, David Mack, to have B.I.G. murdered. Shakur had been Death Row Record's best-selling rapper, so killing B.I.G. would in turn remove Bad Boy Entertainment's best money maker. The book also named Amir Muhammad (also known as Harry Billups), a member of the Nation of Islam, as B.I.G.'s killer because he was fingered by an informer and closely fit the composite sketch. Amir disappeared and was never located by police.

The funeral procession of B.I.G. passes fans and onlookers at St. James Place in Brooklyn, New York. The rap artist lived there before his success.

Record Sales. Another conspiracy theory suggests that Shakur and B.I.G. were both murdered by record executives in order to avoid paying them large fees and to increase sales of their records—rappers are more popular when they are dead. Death Row records had more than 200 of Shakur's unreleased songs. Some people believe the company murdered their own star for financial reasons and then killed B.I.G. to make Shakur's death seem gang-related.

Other Suspects. In 2005 the Los Angeles television channel KTTV and a hip-hop magazine, *XXL*, implicated Tyruss Himes, a former friend of Shakur's, in the murder. Himes sued for defamation, but the case was thrown out of court. Also that year, B.I.G.'s relatives filed a wrongful death lawsuit against the city of Los Angeles, naming Mack and Amir Muhammad as defendants, but the case was dropped. In 2007 the relatives again sued the city, this time claiming Rafael Perez, supposedly associated with Death Row Records, admitted to police that he and Mack had participated in B.I.G.'s death.

Renée Sweeney was a music student who had a bright future ahead of her. She was not supposed to work on that fatal day.

RENÉE SWEENEY

Renée Sweeney, 23, was a fourth-year student at Laurentian University in her hometown of Sudbury in northern Ontario, Canada. She worked part-time as a clerk in the Adults Only Video store in the city's south end to help pay for her education. In early January 1998 she told friends that she believed a stalker had been following her, so she began parking directly in front of the store for security.

On a cold and snowy January 27 at about 11:00 A.M., a man entered the store when she was alone. Sweeney walked over to meet him as was the store's custom, and he launched a vicious knife attack on her. She received multiple stab wounds as she struggled with him, knocking over shelves

THE LADY IN THE WELL

In June 2006 construction workers found more than they had bargained for while digging up old gasoline tanks at a convenience store in Saskatoon, Saskatchewan, Canada. The location was previously an abandoned wooden well, and they unearthed the blackened skull of a woman who may have been murdered sometime between 1920 and 1924. The area was cordoned off and forensic specialists took three days to unearth other body parts and clothing that included a long skirt, high-collared blouse, and fitted jacket.

Forensic investigators determined that the woman was injured and probably dead when thrown into the well. They determined that she was a healthy Caucasian about 25 to 35 years old and standing 5 feet 1 inch (1.5 m) tall. Since she wore an 18-carat gold chain, police believe she was middle class or wealthier. At the time of her death, she lived in Sutherland, the small railroad town that is now a Saskatoon suburb.

The body was well preserved by the gasoline-and-water mixture in the well. Forensic experts were able to secure a surprisingly good DNA profile from the victim's preserved hair. Police have so far been unable to identify the woman. Several people, including one from France, telephoned believing they were her relatives. Mitochondrial DNA samples were taken from the most likely female family members, but none matched, include the three most likely candidates.

A forensic art specialist from the Royal Canadian Mounted Police has reconstructed the woman's face using the skull's shape to model her features. It is hoped someone's old family photograph will resemble the facial reconstruction.

If this was murder, police realize the killer is most likely dead, but they continue to search for the identity of the petite lady in the well.

and scattering videos over the floor. Her attacker left her on the bloodstained carpet and went into the bathroom to clean her blood off his hands and clothes. By the time he returned, Sweeney had dragged herself behind the counter. He walked over and stabbed her until she died. Sweeney's death was the first homicide of the year in Sudbury, known as "the mining capital of Canada" for its nickel and copper mines. When her mother had asked how she could work in such a store, Sweeney had replied, "Mom, I can defend myself."

The Investigation

Forensic scientists found that Sweeney had been stabbed more than 30 times. Knife wounds to her hands showed the intense fight she had put up. The attacker had taken less than $200 from the cash register, but detectives did not consider this a normal robbery. They reasoned that someone intent on stealing cash would not choose that store located in a strip mall and certainly not at 11:00 A.M. And the murderer had come from the back of the building in waist-deep snow, leaping over two fences, which would have been an unusual route for a planned robbery.

IT WAS A VICIOUS ATTACK . . . AND WITH THAT NUMBER OF STAB WOUNDS, TRADITIONALLY THAT WOULD MAKE IT PERSONAL.

—STAFF SERGEANT SHEILAH WEBER

DNA Sweep. The forensic experts recovered many fingerprints and samples of DNA at the crime scene, some from beneath Sweeney's fingernails. They compared the DNA with samples from the community and have eliminated more than 1,350 people as suspects. This was the third major DNA sweep by the Royal Canadian Mounted Police (RCMP), and officials had to coerce four men into giving samples by issuing DNA warrants. No matches were found, although the police had entered the DNA on the FBI's national database.

They also noted that the cash register had recorded an $80 cash purchase at 10:43 A.M., and their request for the shopper to contact them failed. This could mean either he was the killer or just a customer embarrassed to be in the sex shop.

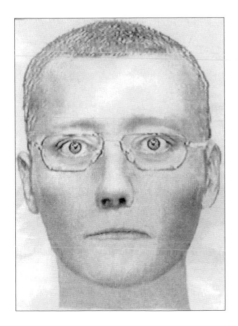

Slim Young Man. Witnesses provided a description of the killer, saying he was a slim white male in his early twenties with short dark hair, about 140 pounds (52 kg), and from 5 feet 10 inches (1.77 m) to 6 feet (1.8 m) tall. He wore glasses and was dressed in jeans and a gray hooded top underneath a dark green-blue jacket. Two composite drawings of the suspect were distributed by the RCMP and the Greater Sudbury Police Service. Its similarity to Chris Myoro, 25, charged with an Ottawa homicide of a 27-year-old woman in 2003, led to the Sudbury

A police composite sketch of the suspect was drawn from details provided by witnesses who saw the slim man in the store and then running outside.

A blood-soaked jacket was abandoned by the suspect along with a pair of gardening gloves. Police were able to obtain a DNA profile from both items.

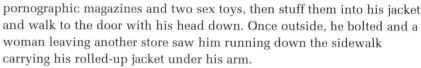

police considering him a suspect. They sent DNA taken from Sweeney's body to Ottawa for comparison but there was no match. (In 2008 Myers pleaded guilty to the murder of Ardeth Wood and received a sentence of 25 years in prison.)

Witnesses and Evidence

The first witnesses were a young university couple who entered the store and spotted a man standing alone behind a magazine rack. They saw him take three pornographic magazines and two sex toys, then stuff them into his jacket and walk to the door with his head down. Once outside, he bolted and a woman leaving another store saw him running down the sidewalk carrying his rolled-up jacket under his arm.

Dozens of officers and a canine tracker followed the path the murderer had taken. He had run through bushes into vacant land in knee-deep snow, and the dog led police to his blood-soaked jacket and pair of white cotton gardening gloves hidden under large rocks. The jacket was a large-sized High Sierra brand made in Korea, and detectives said it was lightweight with no lining which suggested he was a local man who had come from a warm house or car on this day when the temperature was -17°F (-27°C). In an inside breast pocket they found a large diaper pin.

From footprints left in the store and outside in the snow, police identified his shoes as being black-and-white Brooks running shoes. They never recovered the murder weapon or the items the killer took from the store.

Tip-Off. In 2007 police still received more than 1,150 tips, which they investigated, and in October 2007 they took part in a national television program, *Crime Files Cold Case,* that reenacted the murder on

Carole Strachen (left), Renée Sweeney's mother, is comforted by her daughter, Kim Sweeney, following a memorial service on the first anniversary of Renée's death.

- Who was the stalker that frightened Renée? Had she passed along his description to her friends?

- How could such a brutal attack occur in the store, knocking over shelves, without attracting attention at 11 A.M.?

- Did the killer and victim know each other? If the police believe this was not a robbery, why did the killer take around $200 from the cash register?

- Was the murderer a local man? The police seemed to think so because he wore light clothing, but did the failed DNA sweep prove otherwise?

the Court TV Canada network. "There's no new evidence," Sergeant Weber said, "but there are new investigative avenues we're pursuing." A $25,000 reward is offered for information leading to the identification or conviction of the murderer who in 2009 was still on the RCMP's "Most Wanted for Murder" list. In 2008 on the tenth anniversary of her murder, the Sudbury police established a task force to concentrate on the case. Laurentian University now offers a $500 Renée Sweeney Scholarship in music or history.

JILL DANDO

One of Britain's most shocking murders occurred in broad daylight on April 26, 1999, when Jill Dando, 37, a popular news anchor and co-host of a BBC crime program, was shot dead on her doorstep in London. She was walking to her door at around 11:30 A.M. when the assailant calmly approached her from the sidewalk. He grabbed her arm from behind, forced her to crouch as she screamed, and pressed the gun's muzzle against her head to silence the

Jill Dando relaxes with Nick Ross, her co-host of the BBC's crime reenactment program, *Crimewatch*, from 1995 to 1999. Her death was later reviewed by the show.

Police officers and forensic scientists scour the murder scene, hunting for evidence on Gowan Avenue, where Dando lived in London's affluent Fulham neighborhood.

shot. The killer then fled on foot and was seen only fleetingly by two neighbors.

The Investigation

The police arrived quickly on the scene, but had no success as they searched the busy streets for the gunman. Despite the long row of houses on both sides of Dando's street, nobody had witnessed the actual shooting. A next-door neighbor was able to give a general description of a man he had seen walking quickly from the scene with what appeared to be a cell phone. Others reported seeing a man, covered in sweat, waiting for a bus on the next street.

Although the weapon was never located, the 9 mm bullet casing found at the scene indicated that it was shot from a blank-firing pistol that had been modified for live ammunition.

A Massive Investigation. Within hours, the police were seeking a motive. Who would want to end the life of this popular television star known for her sunny personality? Robbery was quickly ruled out since nothing was taken, including her jewelry and watch. A massive investigation began that lasted for more than a year. The police collected almost 14,000 e-mails, which had been sent to the BBC, and 486 names found in Dando's Filofax. They compiled a list of some 2,000 possible suspects, among whom were 140 with "an unhealthy interest" in the victim. Detectives took more than 2,500 statements and recovered more than 3,700 exhibits.

The Suspects

- **A convicted criminal.** The investigation centered on Dando's television work. Her program, *Crimewatch,* gave details of criminal cases and sought help from the public to solve them. Criminals, and even gangs, had been convicted as a result of the show, so the police initially wondered if she was killed in revenge. A professional killer seemed likely because the fatal bullet had been crimped to prevent blood spraying onto the shooter.

- **Serbian supporters.** Dando had also received hate mail from Bosnian-Serb supporters three weeks before her murder, after she had broadcast an appeal for money to aid Kosovan orphans during the war in former Yugoslavia. Related to this was a National Criminal Intelligence Service report suggesting that a Bosnian-Serb warlord might have paid a hit man to kill the BBC personality in revenge for NATO's bombing of a Belgrade television station days earlier.

- **An obsessed stalker.** Police also looked briefly at Dando's personal life. She had recently become engaged, so a jealous former lover might have been involved, but this proved to be a false theory. Through the process of elimination, investigators became certain that Dando was the victim of a stalker, probably a loner, who was morbidly fascinated by her television image. Her brother told the police she had been harassed by an obsessed fan just days before, and a man in a baggy suit and a hat was seen loitering close to her house on the day of the murder. Investigators determined that her car had not been followed.

- **Barry George.** A sufferer of mental illness, George was known for his obsession with famous people. He lived just half a mile (800 m) away from Dando's

Cartridge cases at the murder scene were presented during Barry George's trial. They contained six distinctive hammer marks never known in Britain or elsewhere.

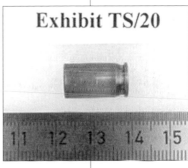

Exhibit TS/20

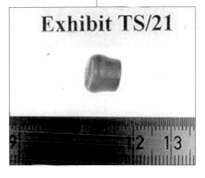

Exhibit TS/21

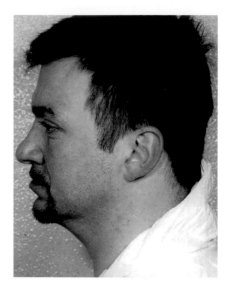

home. When police searched his house, they found 2,248 photographs he had secretly taken of women, along with a gun holster and a photo of him wearing a gas mask and holding a starting pistol, like the one thought to have been used in the murder. George was obsessed with Princess Diana. He had once been arrested outside Kensington Palace with a hunting knife and rope as he tried to break in to see Diana, Princess of Wales. In 1983 he had been convicted for attempted rape and served 23 months in jail. On May 15, 2000, a little more than a year after Dando's murder, police arrested and charged him with the crime.

The Trials

The main evidence in the prosecution's case was a trace of firearm discharge found in the pocket of George's overcoat—he maintained it was planted by the police. In addition to this forensic evidence, a witness stated that she had seen George in the street nearby when the shooting took place, and detectives said the suspect had offered contradictory alibis. George was convicted by the jury, and on July 2, 2001, he received a life sentence.

Appeals and Retrial. Two appeals in 2002 and 2007 failed, with judges maintaining that the discharge residue was consistent with that found on Dando's hair and clothing. However, a retrial was granted in 2008 after George had served eight years in a high-security prison. Fresh evidence about the residue was presented, and the court was told it was "just as likely the particle came from some extraneous source." Many had already wondered how a person with such a disorderly life could have planned and committed the murder without leaving forensic evidence.

The judge now ruled that the residue could no longer be considered, and on August 1, 2008, the jury cleared George of the crime.

- The first jury found George guilty mainly because of a trace of gunpowder found in his pocket matched the gunpowder residue on Dando. Could this be a coincidence unrelated to her death? Did police plant this evidence, as he claimed?

- Who was the man in a baggy suit seen loitering near Dando's house on the day of the murder? Is he the "sweaty man" seen later at the bus stop?

- Since she had been stalked before, is it likely that an unknown, deranged fan had decided to become famous by killing Dando, as what happened to John Lennon?

- Does the execution style of the murder point to a hit man? Who is the most likely to have hired him, a local criminal gang or Serbian nationalists?

NATALEE HOLLOWAY

In 2005 more than 120 Alabama high school seniors were on a trip to the Dutch Caribbean island of Aruba when 18-year-old Natalee Holloway disappeared and was possibly murdered. The group first realized she was missing on May 30, 2005, when the group was flying back to Mountain Brook, an affluent suburb of Birmingham, Alabama. Her passport, cell phone, and packed suitcases were found in her hotel room at the Holiday Inn.

Natalee had been last seen the previous night by classmates outside Carlos'n Charlie's, a popular nightspot in Oranjestad, leaving in a car with three local youths. The U.S. media covered the story intensely for a year and still continues to update information on the suspects and searches for her body.

The Investigation

The Aruban police had never encountered such a high-profile international case, and the invasion of aggressive journalists seemed to rattle their confidence. Many normal procedures for collecting evidence were overlooked. The police had a prominent suspect in 17-year-old Joran Van der Sloot, the son of a local lawyer who was training to be a judge. The youth admitted driving Natalee from the

Benvinda de Sous, the lawyer for the family of missing Natalee Holloway, announces the reward for her safe return had been increased from $200,000 to $1 million.

nightspot with his two friends to a deserted beach. Police, however, did not examine his car or search the grounds of his family's home.

The students admitted they drank heavily on their last night, despite having seven adult chaperones. The Aruban Deputy Police Chief, Gerold Dompig, suggested Natalee may have drunk too much alcohol or taken too many drugs and died on the beach, where someone buried her.

A Missing Body. Understandably, the first mission was to locate Natalee's body. An intense search began on the island and surrounding waters, involving Aruban authorities and hundreds of volunteers, and eventually aided by FBI agents, Dutch soldiers, and a team of divers from Texas. Aruba was combed thoroughly for two years and some searches still continue, but Natalee's body has never been found.

Slow Progress. The investigators were criticized for their slow progress by Natalee's parents, Beth Twitty, her former husband, David Holloway, and her new husband, George "Jug" Twitty. The Aruban police, on the other hand, complained that the family's pressure had pushed them into early arrests before adequate evidence could be collected. Beth Twitty eventually called for a boycott of Aruba and received the support of Alabama Governor Bob Riley.

U.S. volunteers probe Aruban waters searching for the teenager's body. Hundreds of people joined the hunt, alongside FBI agents and Dutch soldiers.

MURDER OR NATURAL CAUSE?

Coroners can come to an incorrect conclusion if a death resembles a natural cause, such as a wasting disease or a heart attack. Even an autopsy might fail to trace the original act that caused a physical trauma leading to death.

This was especially a difficult problem before the advent of modern forensic sciences. When the French emperor Napoleon Bonaparte died on the island of St. Helena in 1821, while being held as a prisoner of the British, the cause was ruled to be stomach cancer. However, recent DNA tests on Napoleon's hair by the FBI and other laboratories discovered he had been ingesting arsenic for over four months until his body contained hundreds of times more than normal amount. The new findings presented in 2000 declared that he was murdered.

Napoleon's coffin was opened on St. Helena on October 16, 1840, when his remains were removed to France.

Medical witnesses often disagree over the cause of death. When Martha "Sunny" von Bülow went into an irreversible coma in 1980 at her Rhode Island estate, her husband Claus, was convicted of murdering her with insulin injections. Although she did not require insulin, a vial of it and syringe were found in one of her husband's bags. Von Bülow's stepchildren and his wife's maid testified against him. He received a 30-year sentence, but this was reversed in 1984 due to improper court procedures. At his second trial in 1985, he was declared innocent after experts testified that his wife died from taking drugs and alcohol. She remained in the coma until her death in 2008 at the age of 76.

The Suspects

Joran Van der Sloot and his friends, the brothers Deepak and Satish Kalpoe, have remained the only real suspects throughout, although the first to be arrested were two former hotel security guards. They were implicated when Van der Sloot falsely declared that he had returned Natalee to her hotel and had seen the guards approach her. This was soon disproved, however, and the guards were released after a week.

Arrests Are Made. The three youths were arrested on June 9, 2005, on suspicion of kidnapping and murdering the girl. Within a few days,

Joran Van der Sloot, the prime suspect in Natalee's disappearance, appears on a Dutch television show on February 1, 2008. It drew a record of more than seven million viewers.

Joran van der Sloot

How are you gonna prove this story is a lie?

based on their statements, police also arrested Van der Sloot's father, Paulus Van der Sloot, and a disc jockey who had backed the youths' story—both were soon freed.

Joran Van der Sloot kept changing the facts. He said he had left Natalee on the beach near the Marriott Hotel. Then he claimed the Kalpoe brothers had dropped him off at home and had driven away with the girl, which they denied. Despite this confusion, the brothers were released for a month and then rearrested. All three men were given their freedom on September 1, 2005, since the police had found no body or substantial evidence against them.

Changing Stories. After being freed, Van der Sloot seemed eager to tell another version. He said Natalee wanted to have sex but he had no condom. She then asked him to stay, but he had school the next morning. Finally she asked to be left alone on the beach, so when Van der Sloot was picked up by Satish Kalpoe, Van der Sloot left her there. Satish Kalpoe, however, said he did not go back to drive Van der Sloot home. During the investigation, a few other local youths were arrested for their connection to Van der Sloot, but all were released.

Dutch police took over the case in September 2006, and 20 investigators descended on the Van der Sloot home on April 27, 2007, digging into the soil but finding nothing. A month later, the Kalpoe family home was finally searched. On November 21, 2007, the three suspects were rearrested again, but soon released. The prosecutor declared the case closed on December 18, 2007.

Confessions. In February 2008 Van der Sloot began to confess to being involved in her death. Riding in the vehicle of a Dutch businessman who had befriended him, Van der Sloot was unaware that he was being recorded by hidden microphones and cameras. He said that Natalee had become convulsive on the beach and stopped breathing, then a friend advised him to return home while he disposed of the body. Confronted with the tapes, however, Van der Sloot said he been smoking marijuana and had lied to tell the man what he wanted to hear.

White Slavery. Then, on November 24, 2008, Van der Sloot recorded a televised interview with Fox News in which he said he had sold Natalee into white slavery, and that she had been taken to Venezuela. He added that he had used some of the money to pay off the Kalpoe brothers, and his father had paid off two police officers that knew about the crime. The interview was broadcast, but Joran again retracted the statements.

> WE WERE PLANNING ON GOING TO MY HOUSE, BECAUSE SHE SAID SHE WANTED TO GO TO MY HOUSE. MY INTENTION WAS TO TAKE HER TO THE HOUSE TO HAVE SEX WITH HER.
>
> —JORAN VAN DER SLOOT

Lingering Doubts

- Van der Sloot's bizarre confessions and retractions have raised his profile as the prime suspect. Was his motive to confuse the police or just to bask in the media spotlight?

- Did the local police go easy on Van der Sloot because he is the son of an Aruban lawyer?

- How could Natalee completely disappear on the small island? Since Van der Sloot and his friends had access to boats, was one used to dump her body far out at sea?

- Why did Natalee go willingly with three strangers without notifying her classmates or one of the seven adult chaperones? Was she a victim of a date rape drug? Did her murder result from a sexual attack that went awry?

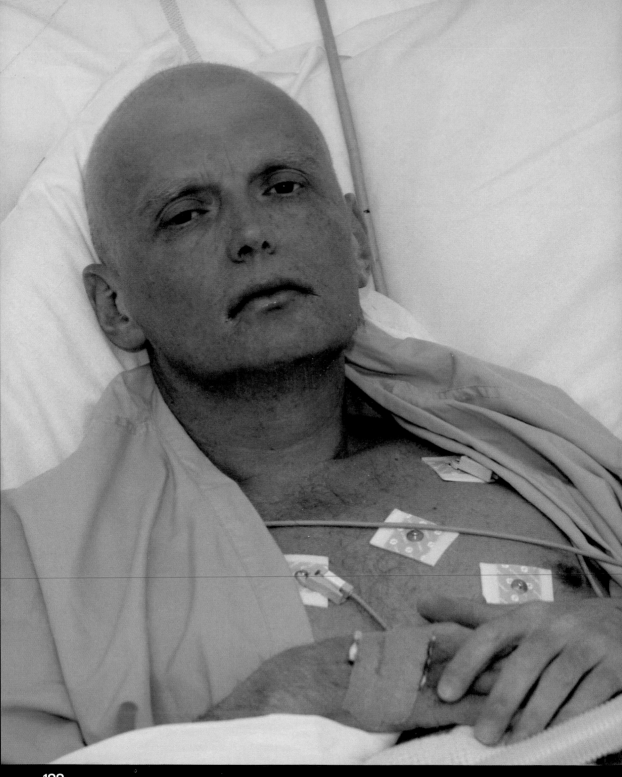

POLITICAL ASSASSINATIONS

History has been altered many times by political murders. Most assailants have been obvious. We know who stabbed Julius Caesar and shot Abraham Lincoln and, despite some doubters, we know who killed John F. Kennedy and Martin Luther King Jr. But other assassins use anonymous bombs, hide within protective regimes, or just disappear with luck.

FRANCISCO "PANCHO" VILLA

GEORGI MARKOV

BENIGNO AQUINO JR.

OLOF PALME

TOM WALES

RAFIK HARIRI

ANNA POLITKOVSKAYA

ALEXANDER LITVINENKO

BENAZIR BHUTTO

IMAD MUGHNIYEH

FRANCISCO "PANCHO" VILLA

After first living as a bandit, the Mexican revolutionary general, Francisco "Pancho" Villa (1878–1923), became a national hero, helping Venustiano Carranza's army defeat Victoriano Huerta. Villa then fought Carranza and was defeated in 1915 by General Álvaro Obregón. When the United States sided with Carranza, Villa took a force of about 500 men into New Mexico in 1916 and killed 18 American citizens. A U.S. Army expedition pursued him in Mexico for 11 months without success. When Carranza was assassinated in 1920 and Obregón became president, Villa retired to an armed ranch at Canutillo in the state of Chihuahua, Mexico.

On July 20, 1923, Villa was driving home after becoming the godfather to a friend's child. As his car passed through the town of Parral, a man raised his hand and shouted "Viva Villa." This was the signal for assassins in a nearby apartment to open fire as the car slowed to make a turn. Villa died instantly; he was hit nine times by hollow-point bullets that expand on contact. Forty bullets hit the car, also killing three passengers, while another died later. The gunmen escaped on horseback.

The Suspects

Soon after the ambush, reports were sent to President Obregón saying Villa's own men had killed him. Obregón informed his staff and generals that he doubted these accounts. Although telegraph lines out of Parral

Pancho Villa (third from right) poses proudly with members of his staff. His gang numbered about 500 when 56 U.S. cavalrymen pursued them from New Mexico in 1916.

had been cut before the attack, Colonel Felix Lara wired the president within hours to say seven to nine men "apparently all of them rancheros" had committed the murder.

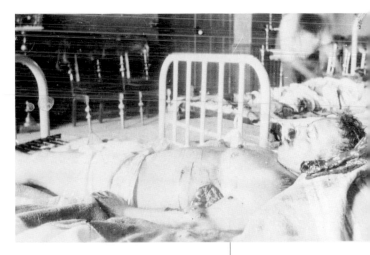

- **Colonel Felix Lara.** Much suspicion has fallen on Lara, although he was Villa's friend. Lara commanded the garrison at Parral and was supposed to provide Villa with a security escort when he needed it. Villa usually traveled with 50 armed guards, but on the day he was shot, he had requested only three armed escorts to meet him just before he drove into Parral. Lara, however, had taken his men to a nearby town, supposedly to rehearse for a national holiday although it was two months away. Rumors suggested that Obregón sent 50,000 pesos to Lara to encourage him to march his troops away on maneuvers. Lara may have left marksmen behind to act as assassins. His suspicious behavior continued after he informed the president about the murders and was instructed to pursue the killers. Lara claimed that he did not have enough horses, although there were plenty in the town that he could have requisitioned.

The corpse of Pancho Villa was taken to his ranch, and he was buried a day later. On February 6, 1926, grave robbers broke into his tomb. His skull was taken and never recovered.

- **Jesus Herrera.** The last surviving male member of the Herrera family, two of whom had been officers under Villa, but they betrayed him and switched sides. In revenge, Villa had captured and executed another Herrera family member and his two sons. Herrera, who called Villa "a savage beast," had tried to assassinate Villa several times between 1919 and 1923, and in turn Villa also hired hit men to kill Herrera. Both men were well protected, but Villa feared his persistent enemy. He wrote to Obregón for help, but the president took three weeks to reply, promising to find a discreet way to end the "painful incidents." Three months later, Villa was murdered.

- **Álvaro Obregón, 43.** Villa and Obregón had held an uneasy truce for years, but the president still feared the possibility of Villa meddling in the 1924 elections when he might have become a

General Alvaro Obregón in 1917, two years after defeating Villa at the battle of Celaya and three years before he became president of Mexico.

candidate, or even called for another uprising. Since the country feared the ruthless Obregón, many assumed that he either ordered the assassination or knew of the plot and chose to ignore it.

- **Jesus Salas Barraza, 35.** This powerful figure, who nursed old grievances against Villa, admitted to the assassination. They had fought together against Victoriano Huerta, but Barraza then joined Obregón against Villa. Voters made him a congressman in 1922. A few days after the assassination, after Obregón had said the congressman was immune from prosecution, Barraza claimed responsibility, an act that let other officials off the hook. He was arrested trying to escape to the United States and sentenced to 20 years in prison. Three months later, the governor of Chihuahua commuted Barraza's sentence. He was made a colonel in the Mexican Army in what seemed to be a perfect cover-up.

- **Plutarco Elías Calles, 45.** The Mexican minister of the interior at the time, he had retained a hatred for Villa after fighting him in the revolution.

- **Jesús Agustín Castro, 35.** The governor of Durango was a former enemy of Villa. He supported Venustiano Carranza, who tried in vain to hunt down Villa in 1918 and 1919.

- **Unknown Enemies.** Villa's rampages as a bandit and revolutionary had killed thousands, and his conquests of many girls and women would have provoked the revenge of husbands, fathers, and brothers. He had also seized the haciendas of wealthy families in Chihuahua for his own use.

- **José Sáenz Pardo.** In 2008 María Fernanda Carrillo Sáenz Pardo, 28, came forward, claiming to be the granddaughter of one of Villa's assassins. She wanted the United States to pay her the $50,000 reward that was reportedly offered for his capture or death. She claimed Villa had killed members of her grandfather's family, so he had joined with six other men to assassinate him. He later received a military commission and military escort for many years, which suggested he had made an agreement with President Obregón. Regarding the granddaughter's request, the U.S. Embassy in Mexico City said a resolution authorizing a $50,000 bounty was once introduced in Congress, but never passed.

Georgi Markov was a novelist who became a communist defector. He settled in London in 1970 and the next year joined the Bulgarian section of the BBC's World Service.

GEORGI MARKOV

The Bulgarian dissident Georgi Markov, 49, a journalist with the BBC in London, was attacked on September 7, 1978, on his way to the organization's World Service headquarters. As he waited in line with other commuters at a bus stop near Waterloo Bridge, Markov felt a stinging pain in his right thigh. He looked back to see a heavy-set man picking up an umbrella. "Sorry," the man mumbled in an accent and then hurried across the road to take a taxi. Despite the pain, the journalist gave it little thought and continued to his office.

By the evening, Markov had a high fever. He visited a hospital and was treated for blood poisoning. As his health worsened, he told his wife, Annabel, he was sure a Communist agent had stabbed him with a poison-tipped umbrella. By September 11, 1978, he was dead.

The Investigation

An autopsy found no poison in Markov's body, but the doctors did discover a tiny, platinum-iridium pellet in his thigh. It was the size of a pinhead, with two holes drilled into it at right angles. Investigators were certain the holes had held the toxic substance that killed Markov. In January 1979 a coroner's inquest concluded that he had been "unlawfully killed" by a poison called ricin, which has no antidote. Its symptoms mimic other diseases, so doctors could have easily missed poisoning as the cause of Markov's illness and death. Ricin deaths are often attributed to natural causes.

The "Nonperson." Scotland Yard began an investigation into Markov's background. He was a prizewinning writer and a radio and television political commentator in Bulgaria with contacts in the Politburo. In 1969 he defected to the West, embarrassing Bulgarian authorities when he joined the BBC as a freelance scriptwriter for Radio Free Europe in Munich, turning out more than 130 programs. The Bulgarian authorities classified him as a "nonperson."

More Victims. British detectives were aware that Vladimir Kostov, one of Markov's friends and also a Bulgarian defector who commentated for Radio Free Europe, had suffered a similar attack three weeks earlier as he left the Etoile Metro station in Paris. He experienced a sharp pain in his back and fell ill for several days, but survived. Doctors found the same type of pellet in Kostov's back. And a month after Markov's death, another of his friends, Vladimir Simeonov, a Bulgarian defector working for the BBC in London, was found dead at the bottom of his stairs.

James Bond Gadgets. Scotland Yard reasoned that only a national intelligence service, such as the KGB or Bulgaria's Darzhavna Sigurnost

A replica of the umbrella that was used as a weapon to kill Georgi Markov was displayed at the International Spy Museum in Washington, D.C., in July 2002.

(DS), could develop and use a James Bond-type gadget, such as an umbrella that fired or injected poisoned pellets. They suspected that the device had been developed at a top secret KGB laboratory known as the Chamber.

Bulgarian Secrets. Technical staff of the KGB had probably put together the assassination that would have involved senior members of Bulgaria's DS secret police. General Vladimir Todorov, the former head of Bulgarian intelligence, was convicted and sentenced in 1992 to 16 months in jail for destroying 10 official volumes about Markov's death. A second person accused of destroying the documents committed suicide. Although crucial evidence was disposed in 1998, on the twentieth anniversary of the assassination, Bulgaria's President Petar Stoyanov said the authorities would continue to investigate the case.

The Police Forensic Science Services Laboratory in London analyzed the platinum sphere that contained the small amount of ricin poison used to kill Markov.

An Open-and-Shut Case. British authorities began a new review of the case in 2006. In May 2008 British counter terrorism detectives spent two months in Sofia interviewing approximately 40 witnesses, including General Todorov. They also viewed archival documents on the case. On September 11, 2008, the Bulgarian government officially closed the book on the crime, invoking its 30-year statute of limitations. Their own investigation, they said, had produced inconclusive results. The British inquiry into Markov's death remains open.

The Suspects

The month after Markov's death, Bulgaria's President Todor Zhivkov claimed that Western intelligence services had killed Markov to slander his country. Markov's scripts for Radio Free Europe were critical of Zhivkov's autocratic rule, and one theory suggests that the president had asked the KGB to silence him. The assassination could have been a gift from the secret service, since it occurred on Zhivkov's birthday.

A Danish-Italian Hit Man. The name of a suspected hit man surfaced in 2005 in *Kill the Wanderer*, a book by Hristo Hristov, a Bulgarian investigative journalist who analyzed 97 volumes of intelligence

Annabel Mary Markov, the widow of Georgi Markov, was driven away on January 2, 1979, after an inquest in London determined that he had died from ricin poisoning.

documents from the Bulgarian State Security Service that he had managed to gain access to after a six-year legal struggle. It named Francesco Gullino, a Danish man of Italian origin, who was known as "Agent Piccadilly" in the DS. He had been recruited as a spy after Bulgarian police arrested him for smuggling drugs in 1971.

According to the files, Gullino made three trips to London in 1977 and 1978, to "neutralize" and "liquidate" Markov. It stated that $81,000 (£50,000) was spent on the operation, with Gullino receiving less than half of the money.

The Missing Suspect. British and Danish detectives did not interview Gullino until 1993, because he was a Bulgarian spy and had been formerly protected by the Communist regime. He admitted to espionage, but denied killing Markov. They also questioned Lyuben Gotsev, a top-ranking state security officer, who in 1990 became the nation's deputy foreign minister. Gullino was not arrested and has not been seen since. As recently as 2008, Scotland Yard hoped to press charges against him, but Bulgaria's full cooperation is no longer forthcoming.

Lingering Doubts

- If the Bulgarian files are correct, it seems likely that Gullino was the hit man. But how much can Communist documents naming a foreigner as an assassin be trusted?

- The papers state that Gullino was the only agent in London at the time of Markov's death, but Danish investigators claimed they had no real evidence allowing them to detain him. Why was he released when he admitted to espionage? And where has he been hiding since 1993?

- Was the assassination order actually given by Vladimir Todorov, the secret service chief who disposed of the files? Why doesn't the U.K. government seek his extradition, or inquests and trials for those who allegedly directed the assassination?

- Since there was an attempted assassination on another Bulgarian dissident in Paris weeks before in the same manner, did British agents have advance warning that Markov's life was in danger?

BENIGNO AQUINO JR.

In the late 1960s, the Filipino senator, Benigno "Ninoy" Aquino, became a prominent opposition leader against the repressive regime of President Ferdinand Marcos and his notorious wife, Imelda. Soon after Marcos declared a state of martial law on September 21, 1972, Aquino was arrested and imprisoned on false charges of murder, illegal possession of firearms, and subversion.

While he was in jail, in April 1975, Aquino went on a 40-day hunger strike to protest against his military trial. Regardless of his physical condition, he was dragged to the tribunals and only gave up his fast on the fortieth day. In 1977 he was convicted and sentenced to death by firing squad. The execution was not carried out right away, and when Aquino suffered two heart attacks in 1980 he was allowed to travel to the United States for heart surgery in Dallas, Texas.

While Aquino was recovering, he and his family became exiles for three years in Newton, Massachusetts, a suburb of Boston, where he lectured at Harvard University and the Massachusetts Institute of Technology. He also traveled around the country, giving critical speeches against Marcos.

When Marcos's health declined in 1983, after a kidney transplant, Aquino decided to return to his homeland and appeal for the president to resign. He flew alone, leaving his family to follow in two weeks. The danger was apparent, and he stated, "If it's my fate to die by an assassin's bullet, so be it."

Aquino descended from the plane at Manila airport on August 21, 1983, wearing a bulletproof vest. Three armed bodyguards accompanied him. Marcos had deployed a security ring of approximately 1,200 military and police personnel around the tarmac. Despite the heavy security, a gunman shot 51-year-old Aquino in the head, killing him instantly. The suspected assassin, Rolando Galman, was dressed as a maintenance mechanic and was hidden under one of the jetliner's engines. He was immediately shot and killed by police.

The Investigation

The autopsy revealed that Aquino had been shot at close range in the back of his head. The fatal bullet had traveled in a downward path from

Benigno Aquino has a discussion in San Francisco, California, shortly before he made the dangerous journey back to the Philippines after years in exile with his family in Massachusetts.

behind his left ear and exited his jaw. This suggests that it was fired from an elevated position.

Marcos's Investigations. For his part, Marcos immediately appointed a fact-finding commission. This was criticized, however, because it was headed by the Supreme Court chief justice. Marcos countered the criticism by creating an independent board of inquiry that convened on November 3, 1983. It held 125 days of hearings, summoned 196 witnesses, and compiled approximately 20,300 pages of testimony. Although no one could identify the assassin, one passenger testified that she saw a man in a military uniform rush up behind Aquino and point a pistol at the back of his head before the gunshot was heard.

The independent board took a year to reach its opinion, which was split. The majority report, issued on October 23, 1984, indicted several members of the military, while the minority report agreed that the assassination had been a military conspiracy. However, it declined to indict anyone.

The Suspects and Trials

Nine hours after Aquino's death, Marcos announced that the assassin was Rolando Galman. He also claimed that the Philippine Communist

A soldier drags Benigno Aquino to a military van moments after he was fatally wounded at the Manila airport as he descended from the aircraft.

JFK'S ASSASSINATION: PROOF OR PUZZLE?

If doubts remain about senior officials who might have planned Aquino's death, these suspicions pale in comparison to the conspiracy theories that still surround the 1963 assassination of American President John F. Kennedy in Dallas. A Gallup poll has consistently shown that 75 percent of Americans believe the gunman, Lee Harvey Oswald, was not the only person involved.

These suspicions persist despite the findings of the U.S. government's 888-page Warren Commission report that was based on 552 witnesses and 3,100 exhibits. The report concluded that Oswald acted alone. The government published 26 volumes of supporting documents in the same year, and three years later U.S. government investigations agreed with the commission's conclusions.

American President John F. Kennedy, First Lady Jacqueline Kennedy, and Texas Governor John Connally ride through Dallas, Texas, moments before the assassin struck.

Regardless of these reports, conspiracy theorists point to the murder of Oswald by Jack Ruby, two days after Oswald's arrest. Ruby had connections with organized crime, which has led many to believe that the organization was behind JFK's death and the elimination of the assassin. The Mafia had suffered at the hands of Kennedy and his brother, Attorney General Robert Kennedy, who led investigations into its activities. Ruby died in jail in 1967, just before a new trial date was set.

Suspicions have also been directed at the U.S. government, particularly the CIA. This theory formed the basis of Oliver Stone's 1991 movie, *JFK*, which also suggested that Vice President Lyndon Johnson had been involved. It is believed this fictional account is responsible for persuading 85 percent of Americans that some conspiracy existed.

Suspects in other theories include both the Cubans, since Kennedy approved the failed 1961 Bay of Pigs invasion by Cuban exiles, and Cuban exiles living in the United States, who were displeased by JFK's decision against a big invasion of Cuba following the failure. The idea that the CIA had killed the president was related to his criticism of the agency and the high-profile firings that occurred after the Bay of Pigs.

Former Filipino soldiers convicted of killing Aquino cheer when released from prison on March 4, 2009. Those who plotted the assassination have never been identified.

Mourners view the dead body of Aquino in his home in suburban Quezon City near Manila. Millions were estimated to have joined his funeral procession through Manila's streets.

Party was behind the murder and that the decision had been made by its general secretary, Rodolfo Salas. Marcos suggested the motive was revenge, claiming Aquino had made links with the organization, but then betrayed it.

Cover-up. Among the 26 men indicted in the board's majority report were General Fabian Ver, Marcos's chief of staff, and two other high-ranking officers, General Prospero Olivas and General Luther Custodio. They were among 25 military personnel and one civilian charged with the assassination. After a brief trial, all the suspects were acquitted on December 2, 1985, which provoked cries of a cover-up.

New Government, New Trial. When Marcos was deposed in 1986 Aquino's widow, Corazon "Cory" Aquino, was elected president. Her new government initiated another investigation that found 16 members of the military guilty. In 1990 they were sentenced to life, but the blame for pulling the trigger rested on Rolando Galman, the civilian dressed as an aircraft-maintenance man. Military officers had supposedly recruited Galman for the job.

Private Army. The convicted men claimed the shooting was ordered by Marcos's wealthy business partner, Eduardo "Dandling" Cojuangco Jr., who ran the largest private army in the Philippines. In 2003 a former sergeant, Pablo Martinez, who later became a Christian minister, said he had gone to the airport with three men on an illegal order by "the invisible group," who plotted the assassination. He claimed that two of the men were associated with Cojuangco, but the Aquino family later proclaimed Cojuangco's innocence.

The Plotters Remain Unfound. Although the justice system identified members of the military who were involved on the day of the assassination, those who actually plotted Aquino's death have never been named. Many have always suspected Marcos, since the act eliminated a charismatic politician who was a threat to his presidency and regime.

Others believe it was someone who planned to succeed the dying president. The Philippines' Deputy Speaker, Raul Gonzalez, said the possibility of finding the person or group who plotted the assassination has become remote. "I think the country is still looking for the mastermind," he said, adding that even if Galman was the real killer, nobody knew his motive.

The convicted men had their life sentences reduced, and the remaining 10 suspects were released from jail in March 2009.

Lingering Doubts

- The masterminds behind the assassination are still unknown, even after the investigations, trials, and the six-year term of President Corazon Aquino. If the case is this complicated, why did Marcos name Galman as the killer so quickly?

- Is it possible Galman acted alone because he had a political or personal grudge?

- Because a witness said the shot came from a man in uniform and the autopsy found that the bullet was fired from an elevated position, why is Galman still considered the killer?

- The theory that Aquino's escorts assassinated him is a convenient reason to implicate Marcos. But would the military want to eliminate an opposing politician if the order had not come from the president or his officials?

- Because Marcos's agents were considered capable of using concealed methods to kill Aquino, such as poison, why would they carry out the assassination so openly, in front of television cameras and possible witnesses?

OLOF PALME

The Prime Minister of Sweden, Olof Palme, 59, and his wife, Lisbet, went to the Grand Theater in downtown Stockholm to watch a movie on the evening of February 28, 1986. Afterward, they walked toward the subway station for the trip back to their apartment about 1 mile (1.6 km) away. Palme had dismissed his bodyguards earlier, which he often did because he was a popular leader who enjoyed doing ordinary things and mingling with the public. At 11:21 P.M., as the couple turned into Tunnelgatan Street and were passing an artists' supply shop, a man suddenly came up behind them and fired two shots at close range. One bullet entered Palme's back, the other grazed his wife. The assassin quickly ran off down the street, and disappeared into the dark. Palme died almost instantly.

The Investigation

Since the Palmes only made the decision to see the movie at 8:00 P.M., detectives searched the Palme's apartment and offices for bugging devices, but found none. No one had witnessed the shooting, and police found no weapon or bullets. Two days later, passersby came across two .357-millimeter copper-tipped bullets in the snow near the murder scene. The bullets came from a Magnum revolver that was capable of piercing armor. Hundreds of investigators were put on the case, and in the first 10 years they received 18,000 leads. They failed in their search for the gunman, however, and no extra evidence was discovered. Despite many conspiracy theories, detectives never produced a motive for the killing.

Swedish Prime Minister Olof Palme makes a speech in 1986, the year he was assassinated. Palme was a popular leader who enjoyed personal contacts with the public.

The Suspects

With the many leads offered to the police, the main sucpects were narrowed down to the following:

- **Victor Gunnarsson, 32.** A right-wing schoolteacher who was known to be an extremist, Gunnarsson was a member of the European Workers Party. Detectives searching his house found party pamphlets that contained propaganda about the liberal prime minister. Gunnarsson was arrested after the shooting, but he was soon released when police could not link him to the assassination. He moved to the United States and was murdered in 1993 in North Carolina by a former policeman who became jealous over a woman.

- **The Kurds.** Police arrested 20 Kurds who were living in Sweden in 1987. They acted on a tip-off that their Kurdish Worker's Party (PKK) terrorist organization was responsible for the assassination because Palme had turned down their leader's application for asylum. Three of them were charged with "suspicion of being accessories" to the murder, but they were later released. However, several of their homes were bugged, and these actions led to the removal of Hans Holmer as the police officer in charge of the investigation.

- **Craig Williamson, 36.** In 1996, a former South African police officer, Colonel Eugene de Kock, claimed that Williamson, a former South African policeman, had assassinated Palme because he had strongly opposed South Africa's apartheid regime. Williamson's boss disputed these claims, alleging that Anthony White, a Zimbabwean working with the South African security services, was the killer. Swedish detectives went to South Africa, but could not find any evidence to back up these claims.

- **Christer Pettersson, 42.** This Swedish drifter was a drug addict and alcoholic with a long criminal record. He was a prime suspect, and was arrested for the murder in 1988. Lisbet Palme picked him out of a videotaped police line-up, saying she had looked up from her dying husband an instant after the shooting and seen Pettersson just a few feet away. He had already served three prison sentences, including one for the manslaughter of a young man. More recently he had committed petty crimes, and was arrested two weeks before the assassination for trying to steal a jar of spaghetti sauce.

- **The CIA.** The American agency was suspected because of Palme's criticism of the Vietnam War.

- **Mossad.** The Israeli intelligence agency came under suspicion because of Palme's support of Palestinian causes.

- **A Marxist Terrorist.** Palme had tried to cut off Swedish arms sales to Iran and Iraq.

Christer Pettersson arrives at his apartment in a Stockholm suburb in October 1998 after the Supreme Court turned down the prosecution's request for a new trial

The Trial

Christer Pettersson's trial opened in December 1988, nearly three years after the assassination. The only damaging evidence against him was Lisbet Palme's identification of him as the killer "without any doubt." Pettersson claimed he had spent the night gambling in a club, but no

LEADERS WHO SHUN PROTECTION

Olof Palme was reluctant to be surrounded by bodyguards during his leisure time, confident that Stockholm was a safe place. His desire for the occasional freedom of an ordinary citizen has been shared by other heads of state, but few have been tempted to make public appearances without protection. An early exception was Julius Caesar who dismissed his security force just before his assassination in 44 B.C.

American President Harry Truman particularly disliked security agents. He enjoyed his "daily constitutional," a morning walk along the sidewalks of Washington, D.C., and took delight in sneaking out of the White House before the Secret Service could react. He often spoke of "having trouble with the boys in the Secret Service," and once ordered them off as he walked down the street to a meeting, carrying three briefcases full of papers. In 1950, however, two Puerto Rican nationalists tried unsuccessfully to assassinate him, resulting in the death of a White House policeman and one of the attackers. Truman ended his solitary walks along the city's streets, but was driven to more secure, outlying areas by the Secret Service to continue them there.

A more recent American politician who has decided to forego security is Alaska's Governor Sarah Palin. One of her first decisions after being elected to the state's highest office in 2006 was to dismiss her security guards, vowing she could take care of herself. However, this changed when she became the Republican vice presidential nominee in 2008.

Besides going without security for the sake of freedom, many politicians have a fatalistic view about being attacked. President Truman noted that "if you're in an office like that and someone wants to shoot you, they'll probably do it, and nothing much can help you out." Pakistani politician Imran Khan put it in simple terms: "My enemies could have bumped me off, with or without security agents."

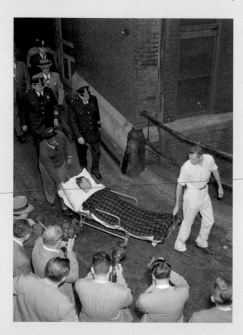

Oscar Collazo, the surviving Puerto Rican who tried to kill President Truman, is taken to a hospital.

witnesses were found to back up this fact. The court judgment said that Mrs. Palme's testimony had been corroborated, proving the defendant "fired both shots beyond any reasonable shadow of doubt."

A panel of two judges and six jurors reached a guilty verdict, although two judges dissented because of the two years it took for Lisbet Palme to identify the suspect.

Four months later, however, the verdict was overturned on appeal. This was due to a continuing doubt about Lisbet Palme's identification, and also because the murder weapon was never found and Pettersson had no motive.

A woman lays a flower on the grave of Olof Palme on February 28, 2006, the twentieth anniversary of his death. He was buried in a church cemetery only a block from where he was assassinated.

A New Trial Is Denied. In 1997 prosecutors asked for a new trial, saying four new witnesses had seen Pettersson at the murder scene. The Supreme Court turned down the appeal since there was still no weapon. Even the chief prosecutor acknowledged that a confession by Pettersson would not be enough to convict him. The suspect gave a television interview in 1999, in which he declared he could not recall what happened that night, adding "I don't believe I did it, but I could have done it." A Swedish psychiatrist diagnosed Pettersson with a brain injury that impaired his memory.

Lingering Doubts

- Why was Pettersson released on appeal when the prime minister's wife and four other witnesses put him at the scene of the murder? Officials cited lack of motive, since he had no grievance against Palme. However, Pettersson had already killed someone and had a history of drug and alcohol abuse. Why didn't officials accept that it was possible to have a motiveless murder?

- How could the assassin carry out his plan on a public street and then run away without being captured? Was he assisted by others?

- The killer seemed to have information on Palme's whereabouts that night, and the use of armor-piercing bullets does not seem like part of a small-time plot. Did a politically motivated organization or a government arrange the assassination?

TOM WALES

On October 11, 2001, Tom Wales put in a full day at his office in Seattle, Washington, where he was an assistant United States Attorney. Wales, 49, had held this position for more than 18 years and was known as an excellent prosecutor of white-collar crimes. At about 10:40 P.M., he was sending e-mails at his computer in the basement of his home when a gunman in the small backyard fired several times through the picture window. A neighbor immediately called 911 to report the gunshots. Hit in the neck and torso, Wales died the next day in the hospital. He was survived by his former wife, Elizabeth, and two adult children, Tom and Amy.

The Investigation

Although the FBI was devoting great manpower to New York's Twin Tower disaster that had occurred a month before Wales's murder, they moved quickly to investigate his death under the code name of SEPROM (Seattle prosecutor murder). No federal prosecutor in U.S. history had ever been slain because of his work. Agents believed the motive could have been tied to Wales's role as a prosecutor or to his advocacy of gun control.

A "Perfect Murder." The Seattle police responded immediately after the shooting and made a thorough search of the crime scene. They found several bullets and spent shells but no murder weapon. Ballistics experts identified the .380-caliber handgun as a Makarov, a semiautomatic type made in Soviet bloc countries until the late 1960s. The bullet grooves revealed that a special hardwearing silver replacement barrel had been fitted. About 3,600 were bought in the United States before Wales died, and agents are still tracing them. No other evidence existed at the crime scene, and one investigator said, "This may be as close as you come to a perfect murder."

Lone Man Seen. Residents in Wales's quiet Queen Anne neighborhood said they saw a lone man fleeing the scene after the shooting but could not give a better description. In 2004 FBI agents reviewing police records found reports of a stranger spotted near Wales's

Tom and Amy Wales speak at a ceremony in a federal courthouse in Seattle on October 11, 2006, the fifth anniversary of their father's murder. More than 150 people attended, including Wales's former wife.

GUN CONTROL?

Tom Wales was president of the statewide Washington CeaseFire, a group that promotes gun control. He spent more than a decade building it into an organization that, as he proudly noted, "takes on the NRA at every turn." The National Rifle Association (NRA) opposes any serious restrictions on Americans' right to bear arms, as stated in the Second Amendment to the U.S. Constitution. Gun-control advocates fight a battle in the United States, where guns are freely available and can be carried openly in some states. In 2008 firearms were used in 67 percent of all murders; guns caused 29,625 deaths that year, with 11,672 being homicides. Among young people aged 15 to 24, guns are yearly among the top three causes of death.

Firearms have thus become a key source of evidence in criminal cases. A weapon left at the crime scene will normally reveal fingerprints and DNA and may be traced back to the owner through the serial number. If the firearm is not found, police will conduct lengthy searches of the surrounding area or suspects' homes. It is unlikely that an assassin could recover spent cartridge cases that remain on the scene, as in the Wales' assassination, and these can also provide valuable evidence. Firearm residue can often lead to a conviction when it clings to an assailant's clothes, hand, hair, or face.

The growth of firearms has led to the expansion of forensic lab work Ballistics experts use microscopic methods to examine spent bullets for marks that can match them with the weapon used and perhaps make comparisons with bullets used in other shootings. A test firing of a gun will produce a bullet whose markings may be compared to those from the crime scene.

Hollywood actor Charlton Heston served as president of the National Rifle Assocation from 1998 to 2003.

house two weeks before he was killed. Witnesses described him as a white male who wore his hair in a ponytail and had tobacco-stained teeth with the left front one chipped. Strangely enough, he was pulling a wheeled black nylon suitcase behind him. The FBI released a composite drawing in 2006 but it has failed to help.

The "Gidget" Letter. Five years after the assassination, when some 4,000 people had been questioned and more than 10,000 leads pursued, the FBI office in Seattle received a typed letter from someone claiming to be

the murderer. It was unsigned, and the return address said "Gidget" with the address of a Las Vegas business thought to be unconnected to the crime. No DNA was found on the letter and envelope. The writer said a "nice talking lady" had contacted him for a hit while he was living unemployed and broke in Las Vegas. He never knew her name but drove to Seattle and crouched in Wales's backyard waiting for him to sit at the computer. "I took careful aim," he wrote. "I shot two, or possibly more, times and watched him collapse. I absurdly waited a few minutes and then left. I was sure he was dead."

FBI Agent Robert Geeslin displays a Makarov handgun like the one investigators say was used to slay Tom Wales.

Despite these details, agents are not sure the writer committed the crime. Shawn Van Slyke, a behavioral analyst for the FBI, believes no hit man would take a job from an anonymous stranger, demand no advance payment, and then send a confessional letter to the bureau.

The FBI released this composite sketch of the man seen pulling a suitcase behind him near Wales's house. The sketch, released on the fifth anniversary of Wales's death, did not resemble the prime suspect, James Anderson.

U.S. Attorney Fired. By 2002 the U.S. Attorney in Seattle, John McKay, complained that too little effort and too few resources were being devoted to the case. Soon afterward, he was fired, but the FBI then began to expand its work in the area. Ten investigators from the FBI and Seattle police still work on the cold case, while the U.S. Department of Justice offers a reward of up to $1 million for information leading to an arrest and conviction.

The Main Suspect

The FBI investigation focused on a commercial airline pilot, James Anderson, whom Wales had prosecuted in a fraud case. He also had a company that was converting a military helicopter for civilian use, but was accused of violating Federal Aviation Administration rules. Although most of the charges against him were dismissed, the 40-year-old man filed a lawsuit against Wales and the U.S. Attorney's office claiming malicious prosecution.

In 2004 agents searched Anderson's home, which was 20 minutes from Wales's, and removed 27 boxes of possible evidence. In 2006 they searched the house again and had him provide handwriting samples. Circumstantial evidence collected by the FBI showed that the pilot had flown to Las Vegas at approximately the same time the "Gidget" letter was postmarked. He was also a gun enthusiast opposed to Wales's stance against pilots carrying guns into the cockpit.

Lack of Evidence. The investigation found that Anderson had seen a movie at a theater 10 minutes from Wales's home. A call was made from Anderson's house slightly after Wales was shot. The suspect refused to be interviewed by agents, and the FBI said it lacked enough real evidence for an indictment. Anderson was badly affected by the investigation, leaving U.S. Airways to train for other flying jobs.

> MY FATHER WAS A FEDERAL PROSECUTOR. HE BELIEVED IN JUSTICE AND DUE PROCESS. AND I BELIEVE IN JUSTICE AND DUE PROCESS. I AM MY FATHER'S DAUGHTER. TO MY BROTHER AND ME, US KIDS, HE WAS THE HEART OF HEARTS, OUR CENTER, EVERYTHING.
>
> —AMY WALES

Lingering Doubts

- Why did it take the FBI three years to learn that neighbors had described a suspicious person in the neighborhood. Why was there no match for such a detailed description? What was in the man's suitcase?

- Was the "Gidget" letter a hoax? Was it written to put the police off the trail? Why did the writer choose a real Las Vegas business for the return address?

- Was U.S. Attorney John McKay fired because he complained that he needed more agents on the case? Why were they belatedly supplied after he was replaced?

- Was there enough circumstantial evidence against James Anderson for an indictment? Could he have committed the murder just before the call was made at his home 20 minutes away?

RAFIK HARIRI

Rafik Hariri, 60, former prime minister of Lebanon, was assassinated in Beirut on February 14, 2005, when a massive car bomb was detonated as his convoy traveled along an exclusive seafront area by the St. George Hotel. His bodyguards were among the 22 others killed. About 24 cars were set on fire, and the blast created a deep crater.

Hariri, a billionaire who was mainly responsible for rebuilding war-damaged central Beirut, was returning from a session of parliament. Two former ministers traveling in his motorcade were also injured.

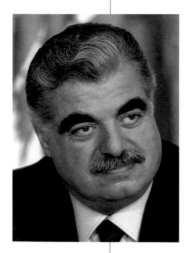

The Investigation

Forensic scientists recovered 33 body parts of a suicide bomber that was killed in the blast. DNA tests on the remains indicate that he was not Lebanese. Detectives are still trying to determine the bomber's native country by analyzing the unusually high levels of lead found in his remains. They have taken geographical samples from Syria and other regions of the Middle East to try and find an area with matching lead levels.

Rafik Hariri grew up in poverty to become a main figure in Lebanon's politics for two decades and serve as his country's prime minister for 10 years.

The Suspects

Immediately after Hariri's death, an unknown Islamist organization claimed it was responsible for the bombing and vowed to launch more attacks on "infidels." This group, An-Nosra wal Jihad fi Bilad al-Sham (Victory and Jihad in Greater Syria), made the claim on a videotape that was shown on Al Jazeera television, saying that they had assassinated Hariri because he had supported the Saudi Arabian regime. Lebanese officials, however, discounted the claim as a bid for notoriety.

Syrian Involvement. Soon after the blast, United Nations (UN) investigators said they had found links to Syrian and Lebanese officials. Many people in Lebanon blamed the Syrians, because Hariri backed the opposition to Syrian occupation. He resigned as prime minister in 2004 after Syria insulted him with threats to extend the tenure of Lebanon's President Émile Lahoud, who gave absolute allegiance to Syria. Islamist extremists in Lebanon also opposed Syria, because it had repressed the Muslim Brotherhood, a political group, in the 1980s.

United Nations Intervention. Massive demonstrations after Hariri's assassination helped push the Syrians out. The UN also oversaw the

arrest of four Lebanese generals who were pro-Syrian. They were imprisoned for four years without charges and then released in May 2009 because of insufficient evidence—on orders from the UN international tribunal that had been launched two months earlier. It also cleared Syrian President Bashar al-Assad of involvement, but it is still looking for links to his government. If the assassination was traced back to Syria, it would be a huge blow to al-Assad and to Syria's international reputation.

Civilians carry a burned body away from the scene of carnage after the February 14, 2005, bomb blast. Hariri's motorcade was hit in the city that he helped restore.

Sunni vs. Shiite. Hezbollah, a terrorist Shiite group rumored to be supported by Syria and Iran, has an aggressive military unit, and it certainly did not like Hariri. He was the leader of the Sunni Muslims who are against the Shia Muslims of Hezbollah, which is led by Hassan Nasrallah. The two men met weeks before the assassination to attempt to iron out their differences, but Hezbollah was worried that Hariri would try to pressure it to disarm if he regained power.

Hezbollah Special Forces. In May 2009 the German news magazine *Der Spiegel* alleged that the UN tribunal had evidence that Hezbollah's "special forces unit" was responsible. This was based on cell phones that were used by the alleged assassins to communicate with one

Emergency personnel pick through the debris to inspect the scene where a massive car bomb killed Rafik Hariri and 22 others in the seafront district of Beirut.

LONG-RANGE ASSASSINATIONS

For years, assassinations had a more personal nature. Roman senators surrounded Emperor Julius Caesar to slay him with knives, John Wilkes Booth held his gun to President Abraham Lincoln's head, and Gavrilo Princip rushed up to the car of Archduke Franz Ferdinand to fire the fatal shots that eventually led to World War I.

Earl Mountbatten's body is removed from the harbor where he was assassinated by an IRA bomb.

Terrorists, especially suicide bombers, still rely on close contact to kill civilians, but the assassinations of many political leaders have become remote-control deaths. The car bomb that killed Rafik Hariri in Beirut is a typical device used to defeat security efforts. A tragic variation of this was the boat bomb, remotely detonated by the IRA, that killed Britain's Lord Mountbatten and two others in 1979 in Ireland.

Rockets can produce the same result from a longer distance, for example, the Israeli air strikes on January 1, 2009, that killed Nizar Rayyan, a senior Hamas leader in the Gaza Strip by targeting his home. Even more spectacular were the deaths of Rwandan President Juvénal Habyarimana and Burundian President Cyprien Ntaryamira, who were killed with eight others when their plane was apparently shot down by assassins in 1994.

another at the time of Hariri's death. One call was to a girlfriend, who was traced back to one of the Hezbollah operatives.

Hezbollah rejected the magazine's report. Nasrallah called it an American and Israeli conspiracy, designed to hurt Hezbollah in the June parliamentary elections that they were expecting to win. At the polls the voters rejected the terrorist organization and kept the incumbent Sunni-led government in power. This group includes Rafik Hariri's son, Saad, who leads the Sunni Future Movement. The sectarian government is required to have a Christian Maronite president, a Sunni prime minister, and a Shiite speaker of parliament.

The United States in Collusion with Israel. The United States and Israel have also been unofficially accused of the assassination. A journalist and former German criminal investigator, Jürgen Cain Külbel, wrote a book in which he claimed two intelligence agencies, America's CIA and Israel's Mosad, plotted the event. He believes the two countries want to bring down the Syrian government by blaming them for the assassination. He

even claimed that the first UN prosecutor had links with the CIA. Külbel says that an hour before the explosion, someone turned off a device in Hariri's car that would have jammed a remote-control bomb. He added that Israel had invented and manufactured the device and was the only country able to deactivate it.

Many extremists in Lebanon suspect Israel had a hand in the event. They say that Israel is known for "targeted assassinations" in the Middle East and has a mission to destroy Hezbollah, whose guerrillas forced them out of south Lebanon after an occupation that lasted 22 years.

Another Civil War. Another theory is that a Lebanese political group believed the assassination would create another civil war that would help its cause. Lebanon's civil war lasted 15 years from 1975 to 1990 and caused at least 100,000 deaths. During the war, political parties formed alliances and then betrayed them, Syrian and Israeli forces gained footholds in the country, and a suicide bombing in 1983 killed 241 U.S. Marines and 58 French troops serving in a multinational force.

Thousands of Lebanese demonstrate in Beirut a week after Hariri was killed. The banner "Syrial Killer" expressed the opinion of many people that Syria was involved in his death.

Lingering Doubts

- Syria remains a key suspect, but why would President Bashar al-Assad try to destabilize the Lebanon regime when it was under Syrian control? Is it possible that some other Syrian officials or military chiefs sent in the suicide bomber?

- Hezbollah was expected to win the June 2005 election, so why would they kill Hariri and risk a public backlash?

- Could the assassination be a continuation of divisions and remaining hate, left over from Lebanon's civil war? Was Hariri the victim of Lebanese assassins who hoped to bring down the government and destabilize the country?

- Who turned off the bomb-jamming device in Hariri's car?

- Should authorities reject the claim by An-Nosra wal Jihad fi Bilad al-Sham (Victory and Jihad in Greater Syria), a previously unknown terrorist Islamic group, that they were behind the assassination?

- How reliable are the claims of the German author Jürgen Cain Külbel that the CIA and Mosad plotted the bombing?

ANNA POLITKOVSKAYA

The award-winning Russian investigative journalist Anna Politkovskaya, 48, was a fierce critic of President Vladimir Putin's government, especially highlighting the Kremlin's brutal military actions in Chechnya. Writing for the *Novaya Gazeta* newspaper, she continually exposed abuses by Russian troops in that breakaway region, and in 2002 she acted as a negotiator with the Chechen rebels who had taken hostages at a Moscow theater. In 2004 she became ill while traveling to report on the Beslan school siege, and poisoning was suspected.

On October 5, 2006, Politkovskaya was interviewed on Radio Liberty and revealed her investigation into the Kremlin-appointed Chechen President Ramzan Kadyrov, saying she hoped he would be tried for human-rights abuses. Two days later, as she was returning from shopping to her Moscow apartment building at 4:30 P.M., an assailant fired four times as she emerged from the elevator into the hallway, killing her as bullets struck her head and chest.

Politkovskaya's murder seemed to have the hallmarks of a politically motivated contract killing. Three days later, Putin said Politkovskaya was an insignificant journalist who was well-known only in the West.

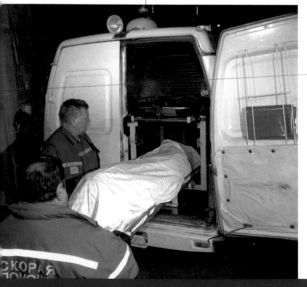

The Investigation

Police found a Makarov pistol equipped with a silencer and four bullets near the body. They took away video footage from the 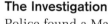 apartment building's surveillance cameras of the assassin entering the apartment building, but this evidence was lost. The image showed the back of a man with narrow shoulders who wore a baseball cap. A lot of evidence was collected, but much of it mysteriously disappeared during the investigation, including computer disks, mobile phone SIM cards, and even a photograph of a main suspect, Rustam Makhmudov, 34, a Chechen man.

Previous Threats. Almost everyone assumed the killing was related to Politkovskaya's brave views expressed in the newspaper. She had received frequent threats and had even fled to Vienna, Austria, in 2001 after e-mails warned that a Russian police officer planned to take revenge for her accusations that he had committed atrocities. The newspaper's deputy editor, Vitaly Yaroshevsky, said: "Anna was killed for her professional activities. We don't see any other motive for this terrible crime."

Arrests and Trials

Investigators said they were unable to identify the person who ordered Politkovskaya's assassination. *Novaya Gazeta*, which conducted its own investigation, hinted that a conspiracy was devised at a high level. The person most widely suspected is Chechnya's President Ramzan Kadyrov. He has denied any involvement, but several of his enemies have suffered violent deaths, including human-rights activist Natalia Estemirova.

Police and Intelligence Involvement? In August 2007 Russian police arrested 10 people they said were a criminal gang involved in the murder. They said the hit man, Rustam Makhmudov, had escaped to Western Europe on a false passport, but they were able to arrest his two brothers, Dzhabrail and Ibragim Makhmudov, along with Sergei Khadzhikurbanov, a Moscow policeman, and Pavel Ryaguzov, a lieutenant colonel in Russia's Federal Security Service (FSB) intelligence agency. Russia's Prosecutor General, Yury Chaika, announced that others in the police and spy agency had provided operational support. The following month, the case was given to a new prosecutor, Alexander Bastrykin.

Flawed Trial. By the time the trial began on November 19, 2008, six of those arrested had been quietly released, leaving the two Makhmudov brothers, the policeman, and the spy to appear in a Moscow military courtroom. They were locked inside a yellow metal cage. The judge announced that the jury wanted the trial to be held in a closed session, but he opened up the proceedings after a juror said this was false. The three-month trial was described by defense lawyers as a fiasco based on shoddy evidence, and others said government officials had deliberately hampered the case. Politkovskaya's son Ilya and daughter Vera attended

Three of the four men tried for Politkovskaya's murder sit inside the defendants' cage at a Moscow court on February 18, 2009. They are (left to right) Pavel Ryaguzov, Ibragim Makhmudov, and Dzhabrail Makhmudov.

Flowers are left at the scene of journalist Anastasiya Baburova's murder in Moscow.

A DANGEROUS PROFESSION

Journalists are constantly in harm's way. Most often they risk their lives covering wars—global and local. The Freedom Forum in Washington, D.C., calculates that World War I claimed two correspondents' lives, World War II saw 68 die, the Korean conflict killed 17, and the Vietnam War claimed 66. The Committee to Protect Journalists (CPJ), based in New York, says 52 reporters have died in Iraq from combat or crossfire from 1992 to 2009, but 89 others died from other causes during this period.

Equally disturbing are the death totals not related to war. The CPJ reports that 792 journalists were killed in the last 17 years and 73 percent of these were murdered. Five were killed in the United States, two in Canada, and one in the United Kingdom. By contrast, 52 reporters have been assassinated in Russia. Of the 17 murdered there since 2000, only one case resulted in the killers being punished. The three killed in 2009 were Natalia Estemirova in Chechnya (see page 185), Anastasiya Baburova in Moscow, and Abdulmalik Akhmedilov in Makhachkala. "Any state that turns a blind eye—or worst—toward the assassination of reporters cannot call itself a democracy," the CPJ stated. "When journalists are threatened, democracy itself is threatened."

A recent shooting in America took the life of Chauncey Bailey, 58, the African-American editor-in-chief of the *Oakland Post* and four other weeklies. A masked gunman shot him in the back and head at close range just before 7:30 A.M. on August 2, 2007, as he walked to work. Bailey was renowned for probing into corruption and gang violence. He was killed by 19-year-old Davaughndre Broussard, an African-American who worked at Your Black Muslim Bakery when Bailey began investigating illegal practices there. Broussard quickly confessed and received a 25-year sentence.

to hear their lawyer say someone higher than the defendants had ordered the assassination. The prosecution stated that the two brothers had kept watch on Politkovskaya's apartment and then gave Rustam a ride to commit the murder. The defense presented unusual evidence, such as an image of Rustam swimming to prove he had broad shoulders unlike the security camera suspect.

On February 19, 2009, after two hours of deliberations, the 12-member jury acquitted the four of organizing the assassination. Ilya and Vera Politkovskaya acknowledged that not enough evidence had been collected to convict the suspects, but said they believed that the four were involved in the assassination.

New Investigation. Journalists said the acquittal cast a shadow over Russia's legal system. On June 25, 2009, Russia's Supreme Court overturned the acquittals of the four defendants and ordered a new trial because there had been procedural violations. However, Politkovskaya's children and colleagues feared that the retrial would hinder finding the assassin and the mastermind, whom they considered to be a very prominent person. On September 3, the Supreme Court agreed, canceled the retrial, and ordered prosecutors to begin a new investigation.

More than 3,000 people gathered in the heart of Moscow for a protest rally over Politkovskaya's death a day after her assassination.

No Progress. *Novaya Gazeta* applauded the decision. "We are pleased there are still some people in Russia who recognize the law," it wrote. "We hope this will lead to a detailed examination of the case." The Politkovskayas' lawyer, Karina Moskalenko, was more cautious, saying "Whether the general prosecutor will use this opportunity, we don't know. So far this hasn't happened. Three years have passed since this tragic event, and the truth still hasn't been uncovered." Others fear that her murder will affect Russian journalism, with fewer writers willing to take the risk of investigative reporting.

Lingering Doubts

- Was the assassination an act of personal revenge, as once threatened by a Moscow policeman, or was it politically ordered? Why was the prosecutor replaced when he said the police and intelligence community were involved? Why did the judge seek a trial behind closed doors? Why was the involvement of Chechen President Ramzan Kadyrov never investigated?

- Why would a hit man leave his gun at the scene? Did police not recover DNA or fingerprints? And why did the other important evidence mysteriously disappear?

- How was the main suspect able to escape from the Russian security force's tight security and never be traced?

- Is the Russian Supreme Court truly independent? Why did it contradict itself, overturning the acquittals, ordering a retrial and then reversing that decision?

ALEXANDER LITVINENKO

A former Russian KGB spy, Alexander Litvinenko, had been granted asylum in England in 2000. On November 1, 2006, he had two meetings in central London, the first in the Pine Bar at the Millennium Hotel to have tea with two Russian men, and then lunch at an Itsu sushi bar with the academic and nuclear-waste expert Mario Scaramella. Within hours of these contacts, Litvinenko began to feel sick and that night vomited several times. This illness, along with stomach pains, continued for three days, and on November 4, he was checked into a north London hospital. A week later he told the BBC Russian Service that his condition was a "serious poisoning."

On November 17 Litvinenko was transferred to University College Hospital in central London, where doctors soon announced that the specific type of poisoning might never be known. After suffering a heart attack, Litvinenko died on November 23. The next day, doctors identified the poison as polonium-210 and said that they believed he was intentionally poisoned.

Hours before he died Litvinenko told a friend, "The bastards got me, but they won't get everybody."

Former KGB bodyguard Andrei Lugovoi speaks at a news conference in Moscow.

Litvinenko's coffin is carried during his funeral in London. He was buried in an airtight coffin because of concerns about radiation.

The Investigation

Detectives examined the years that Litvinenko had spent in Russia. He had led a KGB internal investigations branch, which looked for corruption that sometimes involved the Russian mafia. Former KGB officers often had developed links with criminal elements, which could prove to be a deadly combination.

Justification for the Chechen Invasion. Litvinenko wrote a book alleging that agents of the Federal Security Service (FSB), which replaced the KGB, had coordinated the 1999 bombing of an apartment building that killed more then 300 people. The Russian government, however, blamed the attack on Chechen terrorists in order to gain public support for a Russian invasion of the breakaway republic.

POLONIUM-210, THE MYSTERIOUS POISON

The poison that killed Alexander Litvinenko is one of six metalloids that also includes arsenic and antimony. Polonium, which naturally occurs in the soil, atmosphere, and also everyone's body, was identified in the late 1800s by Marie and Pierre Curie, who received a Nobel Prize for their discovery. The name of the element combines the name of Marie Curie's native country, Poland, and radium.

Polonium-210 is an extremely dangerous synthetic version that is produced by nuclear reactors. Only a minute quantity is needed to kill someone, but it must actually enter the body to be lethal. Since polonium-210 cannot pass through the skin, it is assumed that Litvinenko swallowed it. It can also enter the body if it is inhaled. Once inside, the poison's alpha radiation damages organs and tissues, ionizing electrons, and forcing them out of molecules. It could also corrupt or even cut strands of DNA. The result would be radiation sickness, cancer, or, in Litvinenko's case, rapid death.

The highly skilled British medical team did not quickly identify polonium-210 in the Russian's body because it is difficult to detect when it is absorbed by human tissue. A Geiger counter used next to the body will not record its presence. The first indication of a radioactive substance in Litvinenko's body was found in a urine sample.

Samples of synthetic polonium-210 are kept in sealed disks for research purposes.

Slandering Putin. Once he arrived in London, Litvinenko made allegations against the Russian President Vladimir Putin. The two men had fallen out over FSB corruption in the 1990s, when Putin was head of the security agency. Russia asked the British government to stop Litvinenko and other exiles from making "slanderous statements" and requested their extradition, but this was never granted. A month before his death, Litvinenko was investigating the murder of his journalist friend, Anna Politkovskaya, who was shot dead in Moscow after she investigated Russia's human-rights abuses in Chechnya.

The Meetings. The British investigation discovered that the men Litvinenko had met at the hotel were a former KGB bodyguard, Andrei Lugovoi, and Dmitry Kovtun, who was once with the Russian security services. Detectives also learned that the later meeting at the sushi bar was for Scaramella to give Litvinenko documents about the death of Politkovskaya. The two also discussed e-mail threats that they had both received.

Traces of Polonium-210. Police forensic scientists found traces of radioactive polonium-210 at the hotel bar; on a cup, teapot, and on the clothes of the bar staff. This led investigators to believe that the poison had been put into Litvinenko's tea. They also discovered polonium-210 at the sushi bar, Litvinenko's home, at nine other addresses, and on two British Airways planes. Scaramella and Litvinenko's wife, Marina, both tested positive, but had not fallen ill. In Germany police identified polonium-210 in two houses used by Kovtun, who was also at the hotel meeting.

Britain's Health Protection Agency reported finding 120 people showing traces of the radiation, and estimated that 450 people worldwide may have been affected. This included Boris Berezovsky, a Russian billionaire who was exiled in Britain and was also Litvinenko's friend. He told police he believed Lugovoi was involved in the assassination.

The Suspects

Nine British police officers traveled to Moscow on December 4, 2006, to make inquiries, but Russia refused to extradite the suspects to Britain. The British were, however, allowed to interview Andrei Lugovoi, the former KGB bodyguard who they believed was the main suspect.

A Government Plot. Boris Berezovsky believes officials high in the Russian government devised the assassination, claiming "Everything about Mr. Lugovoi's words and presentation made it obvious that he is acting on Kremlin instruction." Litvinenko's widow agreed, saying that the murder was carried out with the knowledge of Vladimir Putin.

Although there was a strong suspicion that Russian officials were involved in plotting Litvinenko's death, the British believe the only suspect is Lugovoi. He and his family had medical checks after polonium-210 was found in their bodies, but Lugovoi claims the British have made him a scapegoat: "They [Britain] think that they found a Russian James Bond that penetrates the nuclear facilities and, in cold blood, poisons his friend, and at the same time poisons himself, his friends, his wife, and children."

German forensic investigators examine a BMW car in Haselau, Germany, for signs of radiation. It belonged to Dmitri Kovtun, an associate whom Litvinenko had visited.

Lugovoi Accused of Murder.
On May 22, 2007, the British
director of public prosecutions
announced that Lugovoi should
be charged with the murder.
Lugovoi, who is now head of a
private security firm in Russia,
responded by saying the killing
was carried out by Britain's MI6
intelligence agency, Berezovsky,
or the Russian mafia. He added
that the British secret services
had tried to recruit him to find

"compromising information" on President Putin, and he also claimed
that Litvinenko and Berezovsky were British spies.

Marina Litvinenko,
the widow of
Alexander, signs
copies of *Death
of a Dissident* in
2007 in London.

Russia Refuses Calls for Extradition. On July 5, 2007, Russia officially
refused a British extradition request for Lugovoi. Britain therefore
expelled four Russian diplomats from the Russian embassy in London,
and Russia retaliated by expelling four British embassy staff from
Moscow. The chance of an extradition has since faded because Lugovoi
was elected to the Duma, the lower house of the Russian parliament.

State Involvement. Although Britain asked for Lugovoi to be extradited,
it has never named him as an official suspect. In July 2008 a senior U.K.
security official used general terms to say the Russian government was
behind the killing. "We very strongly believe the Litvinenko case to have
had some state involvement," he told the BBC. "There are very strong
indications that it was a state action.

Lingering Doubts

- How could polonium-210 be found in so many places and on people who did not have direct contact with Litvinenko?

- Does this murder represent the Russian mafia's revenge for Litvinenko cracking down on organized crime while at the FSB? Would a criminal organization use a sophisticated poison such as polonium-210 or does this point directly at Russia's secret service?

- Was Vladimir Putin involved? Why did the Russian government refuse to extradite Lugovoi?

BENAZIR BHUTTO

A leader of the Pakistan People's Party (PPP), the largest political party in the country, Benazir Bhutto served as prime minister from 1988 to 1990, and from 1993 to 1996. She was forced out of office both times on corruption charges, but she was never convicted. Despite this, the ruling military government imprisoned her for five years, most of it spent in solitary confinement. In 1999 she left Pakistan to live as an exile in Dubai with her husband and three children.

The country's president, General Pervez Musharraf, granted her amnesty in 2007, and Bhutto returned that year on October 18 with hopes of regaining power. That same day, she narrowly escaped assassination during her homecoming procession in Karachi, when two suicide bombers blew themselves up near her motorcade, killing 140 people and wounding hundreds more. Musharraf declared a state of emergency, suspended the constitution, and placed Bhutto under house arrest to stop her leading a protest march in Islamabad against his state of emergency.

Bhutto, the favorite to become prime minister in the January 8, 2008, elections, urged Musharraf to resign, saying she would never serve alongside him as prime minister. On November 29, 2007, Musharraf was sworn in for his second term as president, and on December 15, he lifted the state of emergency and restored the constitution.

Benazir Bhutto was educated at Harvard and Oxford universities before becoming one of the highest-profile female leaders in the world during her volatile political career.

On December 27, two weeks before parliamentary elections, Bhutto attended a huge political rally of the PPP at a park in the city of Rawalpindi. She was fired upon by someone in the crowd as she was standing in the open sunroof of her car, waving to her supporters, and being driven away from the rally. Seconds later a suicide bomber near her motorcade blew himself up, killing more than 20 people and wounding 50 others. Bhutto, 54, was rushed to a nearby hospital where doctors declared her dead.

With her death, the Bhutto family's tragic political dynasty ended. Her father, Prime Minister Zulfikar Ali Bhutto, was executed in 1979, two years after a military coup; her brother, Murtaza Bhutto, returned from exile to lead a campaign against the military government, but was shot dead in 1996; and her other politically active brother, Shahnawaz Bhutto, was found dead in 1985. Musharraf resigned in 2008 and Bhutto's husband, Asif Ali Zardari, was elected to replace him. He has vowed to defeat terrorists in the tribal regions bordering Afghanistan, who he said were involved in his wife's death.

The Suspects

Witnesses to the assassination said the shot was fired by a sniper, who then detonated himself. Some people believe this indicates that government sympathizers were involved, because tight security seemed lacking in Rawalpindi, which was also the headquarters for the intelligence service and the military. A police cordon surrounded the park, but the assassin was able to breach it.

- **Musharraf's Involvement.** Most analysts do not believe Musharraf ordered the assassination. After the October attempt on her life, Bhutto blamed homegrown militants—the Taliban and al-Qaeda. She also complained about poor security, suggesting that the sympathizers in Musharraf's administration were complicit in the attack. Her requests for cars with tinted windows and four vehicles to surround hers at all times were never implemented. Neither was her plea for devices to jam cell-phone signals that could tip off

SIX MONTHS AFTER BHUTTO'S DEATH THE PAKISTANI AUTHORITIES' INVESTIGATION OF HER KILLING APPEARS TO HAVE GROUND TO A NEAR-HALT, WITH THE TRAIL GROWING COLDER.

—*LOS ANGELES TIMES*

The scene just after Benazir Bhutto was shot shows the devastation caused by a suicide bomber who killed another 20 people following her motorcade.

The Pakistani militant Qari Saifullah Akhtar was one of those arrested in 2008 for involvement in Bhutto's murder. He was soon released for lack of evidence.

assassins about her movements. Government jammers, provided after the October assassination attempt, failed to work. The country's Inter-Services Intelligence agency (ISI) has had radical Islamists in its ranks for many years. Bhutto's election would have also diminished the power of the intelligence service and the army.

- **Angry Islamic Militants.** With the assassin dead, authorities are left with the monumental task of identifying the group that ordered and coordinated Bhutto's murder. Radicals said she was too Westernized and accused her of being an American puppet, advocating secularism and democracy. They also opposed a woman leading the government. Immediate suspicions fell upon Pakistan's Islamic militants who were linked to al-Qaeda. One estimate figured that more than 500 men are training to be suicide bombers in 50 camps run by al-Qaeda in the Pakistan-Afghanistan region. Bhutto had angered them by condemning militants and suicide bombers, and asking the government to redouble its fight against Islamic militancy.

British Scotland Yard detectives photograph the site of Bhutto's death. They arrived in Pakistan to help its government's full inquiry into the assassination.

- **Taliban Warlords.** Weeks before her death, threats to assassinate Bhutto were made by two militant warlords in northwestern Pakistan: Taliban leaders, Baitullah Mehsud and Haji Omar. Khalid Khawaja, a former Pakistani intelligence officer, said Bhutto was a great threat to tribal people on the Afghanistan border. "She was certainly hated to that degree by those elements who are victims

THE U.S. SECRET SERVICE

Although an adequate police force seemed to be in place, the assassination of Benazir Bhutto demonstrates the laxness that can seep into a government's security service.

Most Western countries maintain tight, but discrete, protection for heads of government, as demonstrated by Britain's Special Branch and the Canadian Royal Mounted Police, both of which keep a low profile. This contrasts with the high visibility of the U.S. Secret Service. When the American president leaves the White House, he is accompanied by dozens of Secret Service agents. At public events they are easily recognized in their dark suits bearing lapel pins and presidential seals. Armed agents usually wear sunglasses to survey the crowd and always wear communication earpieces. The U.S. Secret Service covers every minute detail when there is a special event. For example, when President Barack Obama was inaugurated in 2009, agents took charge of airspace restrictions for planes and water security around Washington, D.C. They also secured rooftops, closed downtown roads, conducted security screenings of people along the parade route, and prohibited certain items, such as backpacks.

Even with this high-level efficiency, the agency has suffered a few failures since it began protecting presidents in 1901. The most notable lapses were the assassination of President John F. Kennedy in Dallas in 1963, and the wounding of President Ronald Reagan in Washington, D.C. in 1981.

Wearing their trademark sunglasses, U.S. Secret Service bodyguards accompany President Barack Obama on a public appearance.

of the American terror," said Khawaja, who claims to be friends with Osama bin Laden. Fingers were also pointed at other nations, such as Saudi Arabia, which was opposed to Bhutto because of her Western friends and ideas.

- **Al-Qaeda Claim Responsibility.** Al-Qaeda used websites to claim responsibility for her death, saying the plot was organized by Ayman al-Zawahiri, the second highest al-Qaeda official. He had previously released a video criticizing Bhutto's return and ordering attacks on all candidates.

Arrests Are Made. George W. Bush, the U.S. president at the time, used general terms to condemn "murderous extremists who are trying to undermine Pakistan's democracy," and Musharraf vowed to find the

- Since terrorist groups have often falsely claimed responsibility for attacks, should al-Qaeda's assertion be believed? Is it more likely that an individual or small tribal group carried out the attack with the approval or support of al-Qaeda?

- Did Musharraf know about the plot? If so, why did he not impose a higher security alert? And why did he not respond to Bhutto's request for tinted car windows and a protective convoy?

- What possible role was played by the military or security agencies, where Islamic fundamentalists make up a sizeable number? Was the breakdown in security a sinister plan or just a case of incompetence?

terrorists. In 2009 Pakistan's Joint Investigation Team arrested five suspects who they said were involved in Bhutto's killing through their links with the country's Taliban leader, Baitullah Mehsud. Later that year, the United Nations put together a special fact-finding commission to look into the assassination.

IMAD MUGHNIYEH

One of the world's most-hunted terrorists, Imad Mughniyeh, 46, was assassinated by a car bomb at approximately 11:00 P.M., on February 12, 2008, in Damascus, Syria. It happened when he approached his car as he left a ceremony at an Iranian school. The explosion in the upscale Kafar Soussa district also killed a passerby. Scores of police and intelligence officers rushed to the scene to seal off the area and remove the body.

The Victim

Known by his followers as "the shadowy man," Mughniyeh was the former security chief of Hezbollah, the Lebanese Shiite Muslims terrorist organization. He had been in hiding for 15 years while Western countries, especially the United States and Israel, tried to follow his elusive tracks. The FBI offered $5 million for Mughniyeh's capture or death, and he was wanted by 42 other countries. Some believed he had plastic surgery to escape detection, moving in his later years between Lebanon, Iran, Turkey, and Syria using as many as 47 different false passports.

Terrorist Attacks. Mughniyeh was born into a farming family in the southern Lebanese city of Tyre and spent a year studying at the American

University of Beirut. He had been on the FBI's most-wanted list since the 1980s. It considered him to be behind two 1983 bombings in Beirut, Lebanon. The first, a car bomb at the U.S. Embassy, killed 63 people, including 17 Americans; the second, using trucks, targeted the barracks of peacekeeping forces, killing 241 U.S. Marines and 59 French paratroopers. A year later, he was thought to be behind the kidnapping and assassination of William Buckley, the CIA station chief in Beirut. The United States also indicted him for the 1985 hijacking of a TWA airliner when a U.S. Navy diver was murdered and his body dumped onto the tarmac of Beirut airport. Israeli investigators believed Mughniyeh organized Hezbollah attacks in Buenos Aires, Argentina, when a 1992 bombing of the Israeli embassy killed 29 people, and two years later 85 people died when a Jewish center was bombed. Mughniyeh was also linked to the 1996 bombing of the Khobar Towers in Saudi Arabia, which killed 19 Americans.

9/11? It was also reported that Israel's military intelligence service, Aman, suspected that Mughniyeh was involved in the 9/11 attacks on the World Trade Center and the Pentagon in 2001. "The world is a better place without this man in it," said a U.S. State Department spokesman, describing Mughniyeh as a "cold-blooded killer, a mass murderer, and a terrorist responsible for countless innocent lives lost."

The Funeral. Mughniyeh's funeral was held two days later at a Hezbollah stronghold in Beirut. The city was already tense, waiting for

Hezbollah terrorists meet the media after hijacking a TWA airliner in 1985. They killed a U.S. Navy diver before releasing the other hostages.

a mass rally that day to mark the third anniversary of the assassination of the former Lebanese Prime Minister Rafik Hariri (see page 122). Mughniyeh's brother had also been killed in 1994 in Beirut by a car bomb that may have been intended for Imad.

The Investigation

Three days after the assassination, different news reports said Syrian government officials believed that Western intelligence organizations, such as the CIA, were involved, and other newspapers said Syrian security forces had arrested non-Arab

Schoolchildren visit the war museum opened in July 2008 in Beirut by Hezbollah in tribute to Imad Mughniyeh. It contains his personal belongings, including the clothes he was wearing when assassinated.

foreigners, as well as several Palestinian suspects. Names were never released and no one was charged. The Syrian government announced it was conducting investigations to find the assassins, but it remained silent regarding suspects. Iran said it would assist in a joint investigation team.

Syrian Embarrassment. Syria had been targeted by some Islamic extremists in the recent past, including an attempt in 2006 to storm the U.S. Embassy when three terrorists and a Syrian guard died. Mughniyeh's killing was an embarrassment to the secular regime of President Bashar al-Assad, who was trying to bring his country out of international isolation. His government had not been completely happy with the extremist residing in Syria and was shocked that someone could assassinate Mughniyeh while he was under their protection in the supposedly secure capital. Others have suggested that Syria's security services were complicit in the death.

The Suspects

- **Mossad.** Hezbollah, which battled Israel to a near standstill in the Lebanon war of 2006, was certain the assassination was carried out by Israel's secret service, Mossad. It issued a statement saying Mughniyeh "died a martyr at the hands of the Israeli Zionists." Iran joined in, also praising him as a martyr and describing the death as "yet another brazen example of organized state terrorism by the Zionist regime." Hezbollah's leader Hassan Nasrallah vowed that his group would retaliate against Israeli interests anywhere in the world. For its part, the Israeli government issued a denial, saying it rejected the attempt by terrorist groups to blame it. Israel, however, had reacted with fury a month earlier when Nasrallah boasted that the organization was keeping the body parts of Israeli soldiers.

- **The Lebanese Government.** Another possible suspect was Beirut's pro-Western government, which opposed Hezbollah and its Syrian backers. Mughniyeh first emerged during Lebanon's civil war from 1975 to 1990, and Hezbollah has been in a power struggle with the American-backed government.

- **Syria or Iran**. Taking another view, *Time* magazine has even suggested that Mughniyeh's Syrian or Iranian friends might have decided that he had become an inconvenience. It said they may have wanted to show that they could be relied upon to control terrorists in the Middle East "as long as the U.S. doesn't try to go after the regimes in Damascus or Tehran."

IT'S NOT A MATTER OF JUST PRESSING THE BUTTON. AN OPERATION LIKE THIS WOULD TAKE TREMENDOUS AMOUNTS OF INTELLIGENCE— HUMAN INTELLIGENCE, NOT ELECTRONIC INTELLIGENCE. YOU NEED THE ABILITY TO FIND PEOPLE, TO CHECK THE LOCATION, TO INSTALL THE DEVICE, AND TO ESCAPE.

—ELIEZER TSAFRIR, MOSSAD CHIEF IN BEIRUT

Lingering Doubts

- Was it possible that Mughniyeh helped plan the 9/11 attacks? Had he ever worked closely with Osama bin Laden and al-Qaeda?

- If Syria made early arrests, why were the suspects never named and what became of them? Is the joint Syrian Iranian investigation still actively seeking suspects?

- Was Mughniyeh receiving Syria's backing when he was killed? Were the country's security services protecting him at the time? Can any credence be given to the suggestion that the killing was carried out by Syria or Iran?

- Was Israel's Mossad secret service the most likely suspect considering their past successful record of assassinating terrorists? If so, did the CIA work closely with it to plan the car bomb? Was the pro-Western government of Beirut also involved?

142

KIDNAPPINGS

Any abduction of a child grips parents and communities with fear. Whether it happened for ransom, sex, or slavery, the result is often the victim's death. Adults can face the same fate when kidnapped for these reasons or political motives.

JUNE ROBLES

Robles Ranch, founded in 1885 by Bernabe Robles in Tucson, Arizona, was one of the first pioneer ranches in the southwestern United States. Robles's considerable wealth as a cattleman was known throughout the region and led to what newspapers would later label "the greatest manhunt ever staged in the West." The hunt was for 6-year-old June Robles, Bernabe's granddaughter.

June Robles (first row, far right) meets the press with her family after being rescued. After 19 days in a box, she was rescued unharmed, but her parents worried that the kidnappers would return.

At 3:00 P.M., on April 25, 1934, June was walking home from school when a shabby Ford sedan pulled up next to her, and the driver told her to get into the back seat. A witness described him as emaciated, dirty, and wearing sunglasses. The girl reluctantly did as she was told, and the car drove away.

Later that day a man paid a boy to take a note to June's father, Fernando Robles, who was across the street in the Robles Electric Company. The note demanded a $15,000 ransom and included instructions on how to deliver the money. It also said that June's life would be in danger if the contents of the note were revealed. Robles wrote a quick reply and gave it to the waiting boy, but the man had already disappeared.

The next day another note was delivered to June's grandfather. It said the child was safe and would be returned if he paid the ransom, which had now been reduced to $10,000. "Obey instructions," it ended and was signed, "Z."

The Investigation

The Tucson police leaped into action by blocking roads around the town, which at the time was just a small desert community. Hundreds of men, including 300 armed American Legionnaires, joined federal, state, and local forces to search every house in town and all the mailboxes in case other ransom notes had been left. While a plane searched the desert, police probed abandoned mine shafts and caves that once had hidden bandits.

False Clues. Erroneous "sightings" of the kidnapper with the child marred the investigation. Almost 100 people telephoned with tips in the first five days. Some claimed that June was being taken to Mexico, so police began to search the border canyons and mountains using Apache scouts. Tucson's frustrated police chief, Gus Wollard, lamented, "We have run down clue after clue, which has faded into nothing."

Meanwhile, June's father stole away alone to drop off the ransom money, following the directions he had been given in the note. He was told to dump the money on a particular road when he came to a white string that was stretched across it, but when he got to the road, there was no string to be found. On April 30 he publicly informed the kidnappers that he was having the police call off the search. He then asked for proof that June was still alive by publishing in the local newspaper questions that only she could answer. One of the questions was: "What do you do with your bunnies in the morning?"

A Third Ransom Note. The police ended their truce on May 7 when a third ransom note was shoved under the county attorney's office—nobody saw who delivered it. The message gave June's correct answers

TOO MUCH INFORMATION?

Does extensive press coverage aid or hinder the safe return of a kidnapped person? The media is often used by victims, such as June Robles's father when he published questions only his daughter could answer to verify that she was still alive. During the 1932 kidnapping of the aviator Charles Lindbergh's baby, a go-between, John Condon, communicated with the supposed kidnappers through a newspaper called the *Home News*. The kidnappers sent letters to the paper, and he placed ads. One promised, "Money is ready. No cops. No Secret Service. I come alone, like last time." Newspaper editors have also been known to address kidnappers directly, like the publisher of *The Las Vegas Sun* when he asked for a deal that would release Cary Sayegh (see page 157).

Unfortunately, media attention can also have negative effects on a case. Too much information about the search for a kidnapped victim can also help the abductor avoid capture, and blaring headlines can even risk turning a disturbed kidnapper into a murderer. When unfounded rumors or editorial speculation is published, an investigation can be seriously diverted. This happened during the 2007 hunt for Madeleine McCann's abductor (see page 178) after British and Portuguese newspapers ran hearsay stories that implicated the parents and another key suspect.

Searchers gather around the iron prison that held June Robles. Her chains are displayed by Clarence Houston, the attorney who spotted the box and rescued her.

to the newspaper questions and added that she would be released within 48 hours after the money was delivered. It was signed: "Now or never. XYZ. OBEY."

Discovered in the Desert. On May 14 a note bearing a Chicago postmark was sent to Arizona Governor Benjamin B. Moeur. It described a desert spot 9 miles (14 km) east of Tucson where June could be found, but added the chilling words, "You will find the body covered with a load of cactus." County Attorney Clarence Houston and his deputy, Carlos Robles, June's uncle, rushed to the area and searched for two hours. They were about to quit, assuming the tip was a hoax, when Houston stumbled over a mound of dirt and pushed aside the brush to find an iron box with the girl inside.

A Living Tomb. The living tomb was so small she could not stand, and one of her ankles was chained to an iron stake. The key to the padlock on her chain was lying on top of the box. The kidnappers had hammered nail holes in the metal box to let in air and had shoved food through a trapdoor. Two dirty cans held her water supply.

The padlock was unlocked and June pulled out—filthy and covered with insects and vermin. Incredibly, after spending 19 days in the metal sweatbox, she was bewildered and weak, but otherwise fine. She said two kidnappers, called Bill and Will, had left her there and visited only four times. Once, when she had cried, they threatened to stab her in the back unless she stopped.

The Suspects

FBI Director J. Edgar Hoover assigned his top assistant to track down the abductors. Only one person was arrested: Oscar H. "Buster" Robson, 31, a Tucson dance-hall operator, who was picked up in Phoenix by U.S. Department of Justice agents. The only evidence against him was that experts considered his handwriting a match to the writing on one of the ransom notes. Despite this, Hoover announced that the case had been solved.

An "Alleged Kidnapping."

A federal grand jury failed to indict Robson on January 11, 1935, but a new trial was quickly convened. After hearing the testimony of 30 officers and other witnesses and visiting the spot where the girl had been held in the desert, the jurors concluded on December 18, 1936, that they lacked the evidence to indict. They also called June's disappearance an "alleged kidnapping." Press reports said this meant they doubted the girl's story because she could not have survived 19 days underground in a metal box in the hot desert. Although the police promised to release their files on the case, they later refused to do so. Each piece of evidence to the grand jury was sealed, because no one was indicted.

New York's *Daily Mirror* gave full-page coverage to the kidnapping. Readers were hungry for more details about the shocking crime.

The John Dillinger Gang. The public, on the other hand, had other ideas about who had kidnapped the little girl. One theory suggested that the John Dillinger gang had taken her. The 30-year-old Dillinger, an infamous bank robber, had been captured in Tucson with his gang three months earlier, but they later escaped in Indiana. Locals believed that the kidnapping of June might have been revenge on the Tucson police. Another rumor suggested that a distant relative in Mexico had taken the girl to get even with her grandfather for a previous slight.

John Dillinger, America's notorious bank robber, was rumored to be involved in June's disappearance, but police spent little time hunting for evidence.

Lingering Doubts

- Who were Bill and Will? Was it just two men or were others involved? Who sent the letter from Chicago to the governor?

- Why did the kidnappers release June before her father, who was eager to give them the money, paid the ransom money?

- Was the kidnapping faked? Could a child survive 19 days in an iron box beneath the Arizona desert sand?

MEHDI BEN BARKA

Moroccan politician, Mehdi Ben Barka, was one of the leaders who helped bring about his country's independence from France in 1956. He then founded the left-wing party, the National Union of Popular Forces, in 1959. Although he had tutored Morocco's crown prince, Ben Barka opposed his former pupil when he took the throne in 1961 as King Hassan II. Ben Barka was accused of plotting against the king, so he exiled himself to Algiers in 1963, where he met Che Guevara and Malcolm X, among others. In his absence he was condemned to death by a Moroccan court. Nicknamed "The Dynamo," he later traveled to Cairo,

Mehdi Ben Barka gives a press conference in 1959 in Casablanca, Morocco. This was one of his many attacks on the government that preceded his disappearance.

Rome, Havana, Moscow, and Geneva, supporting Third World revolutions.

Ben Barka became head of the Tricontinental Conference that was scheduled for January 1966 in Havana to discuss and plot national uprisings. Meanwhile, back in Morocco, King Hassan blamed him for local riots against the monarchy, including one in Casablanca in March 1965 that resulted in hundreds of deaths.

On October 29, 1965, two French government agents stopped 45-year-old Ben Barka outside the Brasserie Lipp on Boulevard St. Germain in Paris. One told him, "You have a rendezvous with some politicians." Ben Barka got into their car, an unmarked Peugeot 403, and was driven off. He was never seen again. His disappearance caused a breakdown in diplomatic relations between France and Morocco for nearly four years.

One witness claimed that General Mohamed Oufkir (left), Morocco's interior minister, had stabbed Ben Barka to death. Seven years later, Oufkir was found dead.

The Investigation

The French president at the time, Charles de Gaulle, ordered a full inquiry into the disappearance of Ben Barka, since many people presumed the country's intelligence agency, the Service de Documentation Extérieure et de Contre-Espionnage (SDECE), was involved. Ben Barka's son, Bachir, 25, used French law to bring judicial proceedings against "unknown persons" for murder and complicity to murder, but the murderers were never found.

The Suspects

The investigation resulted in 13 suspects charged with crimes connected to the kidnapping, but most were never tried. Two French police officers were convicted of "illegally detaining" Ben Barka and served brief prison sentences. One witness testified that General Mohamed Oufkir, the Moroccan interior minister who controlled security, had stabbed the politician to death. The witness later died in what was officially recorded as a suicide. Oufkir refused to return to France and was convicted in his absence of illegal arrest and confinement, receiving an unenforceable sentence of life.

Another "Suicide." King Hassan made Oufkir his minister of defense after a failed coup in 1971 when the palace was attacked and more than

100 people were killed. A year later Moroccan fighter jets attacked the king's airplane as it returned from France, but he survived. Oufkir was accused of plotting this assassination and was now assumed to have been involved in the earlier palace attack. Oufkir was found dead in 1972, a "suicide" victim. However, his daughter's book (*Stolen Lives* by Malika Oufkir, 2001) she says this was impossible because she saw five

WHEN GOVERNMENTS KIDNAP

Mehdi Ben Barka is just one of the many high-profile people that have been allegedly kidnapped by authoritarian governments over the years, but headlines seldom name the ordinary victims taken from average families. An extreme example was "the disappeared" of Argentina, when up to 3,000 people were estimated to have been abducted and killed during the ruling regime of the military junta from 1976 to 1983. Many of the victims were buried in unmarked graves. In one cemetery searchers found approximately 600 "unknowns," and in 2007 officials collected relatives' blood to send to the United States to try and match DNA to the unnamed bodies.

Democracies have also engaged in kidnapping. Israel sent intelligence agents to Argentina in 1960 to kidnap Adolf Eichmann, the man who managed the logistics of deporting and exterminating millions in the Nazi death camps of Eastern Europe during World War II. He had escaped to Argentina and was working there as Richard Klement. As he walked home from work on May 11, 1960, the undercover Israelis knocked him unconscious, drove him to a safe house, and smuggled him out of the country heavily sedated and disguised as a Jewish union member. He was tried in Israel, convicted, and hanged in 1962. Argentina protested about the violation of its sovereign rights but did not pursue the matter for very long.

Adolf Eichmann was held in a glass booth surrounded by guards during his trial in Israel.

Governments have also been known to work with bounty hunters in kidnapping cases. In 1983, after prominent Canadian land developer, Sidney Jaffe, failed to appear in a Florida court on land fraud charges, two U.S. bounty hunters kidnapped him from his Toronto home. They flew him back to Florida, where the state successfully prosecuted him and sentenced him to 35 years in prison. When the Canadian government protested to Washington, D.C. about the activities of Florida, Jaffe was released, and Canada later convicted one of the bounty hunters for kidnapping.

The French
Marxist, Professor
Maxime Rodinson
(center), joins
others to praise
Ben Barka during
a service in his
memory in
October 1966.

bullet holes in her father's body. One account claims the king killed him personally. After Oufkir's death, King Hassan tried to remove suspicion of his involvement in Ben Barka's disappearance by blaming Oufkir.

Buried in Paris. In 1975 a decade after the abduction, sources told *Time* magazine that Oufkir had lured Ben Barka from Geneva to Paris to make an anticolonial documentary film. The meeting was supposed to be at the Brasserie Lipp, but two Moroccan agents kidnapped him and took him to a villa guarded by 30 men in Fontenay-le-Vicomte, a Paris suburb. Two nights later, they shot him. One source said the agents quickly buried the body at the villa's garden and 16 days later reburied it in another Paris suburb, Neuilly-sur-Seine.

Dissolved in Acid. A slightly different account was published in 2001 by the French newspaper *Le Monde*, using unnamed sources and hearsay. It stated that King Hassan had ordered Ben Barka's abduction back to Morocco, but Oufkir had accidentally tortured him to death at the villa. French officials then helped smuggle the body back to Rabat, where it was dissolved in a large vat of acid. This account claimed the CIA had given its approval of the abduction.

For its part, the CIA has acknowledged that it keeps files containing approximately 3,000 documents on the Ben Barka case, which cannot be released.

Ahmed Boukhari, a former member of the Moroccan secret service, confirmed that his group had interrogated Ben Barka in the villa and that he died during this harsh treatment. He also confirmed that the body was returned to Morocco and dissolved in an acid vat that was built under the supervision of a CIA agent.

Headless Body. A Moroccan-French dissident, Ali Bourequat, claimed a Moroccan secret agent confessed that he and other agents, led by Oufkir, had murdered Ben Barka in Paris. They had buried his body in cement outside the city, and Oufkir had carried Ben Barka's head back to Morocco in a suitcase to be buried on prison grounds.

Security Service Cover-up. Besides France's SDECE and the CIA, accusations were also made against Morocco's security service and Israel's Mossad, which had trained the Moroccan agency and, some sources claimed, helped track Ben Barka for Oufkir. Although the French government released documents in 2001 and 2004, Ben Barka's son said key information was withheld that would have implicated those three agencies along with King Hassan. Sources have stated that Ben Barka had been working for the SDECE, providing them with intelligence reports on North Africa.

A total of 37 people involved in this case have disappeared—some dying violently. They include three French criminals who were allowed to flee to Morocco to live under the protection of the security service, but they vanished mysteriously in the mid-1970s.

Lingering Doubts

- If a variety of sources agree that Oufkir had killed Ben Barka in a Paris suburb, why do they disagree about what happened to the body?

- Why would France's intelligence service, SDECE, work so closely with the CIA at a time when the country was distancing itself from the United States?

- What information lies in the CIA's massive file on the kidnapping? Why can none of it be released?

- Was Ben Barka working for the SDECE, as some claimed? If so, why would they participate in his abduction?

VIRGINIA PIPER

A wealthy socialite, Virginia Piper was the daughter of a pioneer advertising man in Minneapolis, Minnesota. She had married Harry C. Piper, who became chairman of the board of a Minneapolis investment company. Virginia had chaired the boards of Northwestern Hospital and the Minneapolis Medical Center. The couple had three children.

The Kidnapping

At about 1:00 P.M., on July 27, 1972, two husky men burst into the Piper's fashionable two-story colonial home in Orono, a suburb of Minneapolis. They both carried handguns and wore pullover sweaters, hoods, black nylon masks, and gloves. After tying up the housekeeper, they placed tape over Virginia's eyes, covered her head with a pillowcase and forced her into their two-tone green 1967 Buick sedan. They ordered the 49-year-old woman to lie down on the backseat and drove 140 miles (225 km) north to the wilderness area of Jay Cooke State Park near Duluth. During the ride, she was forced to tape-record ransom instructions.

Left in the Woods. Virginia was then marched to a secluded tree, handcuffed, and chained to its trunk. They did not harm or threaten her. One man remained and told her his name was "Alabama" and that he worked in construction. The next day, he abandoned her in the dark forest, leaving her with only some cheese, soggy bread, and soft drinks.

Ransom and Rescue

The kidnappers had left a note at the house confirming the kidnapping and demanding a $1 million ransom in $20 bills. Harry Piper, 54, appealed to them to get in touch, promising to cooperate fully. At about 9:30 P.M. on July 28 he received a call with his wife's recorded instructions for the drop-off.

Virginia Piper faced the press in Minneapolis a day after her rescue. The socialite said she had not eaten or slept during her confinement.

John Morrison, the brother-in-law of Virginia Piper, gives reporters details about her condition following her return, saying she was in good health.

> YOU GO SOUTH OF FOND DU LAC ABOUT ONE MILE. THERE IS A HIGH VOLTAGE POWER LINE THAT CROSSES THE ROAD AND A LITTLE BEYOND THE POWER LINE IS AN APPROACH THAT TURNS TO THE RIGHT ... YOU CALL HER NAME AND SHE CAN HEAR YOU.
>
> —KIDNAPPER SPEAKING BY PHONE TO LUTHERAN MINISTER KENNETH HENDRICKSON

The Drop-Off. Piper was able to secure the money and follow their directions late that same night. He was ordered to locate a radio transmitter at a signpost and follow its directions, transferring the money to a Monte Carlo car and driving it to the Sportsman's Bar in north Minneapolis. At that location he had to make phone calls from a phone booth while someone took the money from the car's trunk.

Piper later recalled that the package of bills was so heavy he could barely lift it. The ransom was, at that time, the largest ever paid in the United States and the third largest in the world.

Public Appeal. The kidnappers had promised to release Virginia on Saturday morning. When this did not happen, her husband appealed to the public to help find her. The FBI had 100 agents on the case and coordinated a police search in Minnesota, Illinois, Wisconsin, Iowa, South Dakota, and North Dakota.

The bureau also released a general description of the kidnappers (based on unconfirmed sightings) and revealed that the getaway car had stolen Minnesota license plates and was followed from the Piper home by a smaller "dirty yellow" car.

Anonymous Call. The breakthrough came from an anonymous telephone call at 9:00 A.M. to a Lutheran minister, who was informed that his number had been picked at random.

Following the directions, FBI agents found Virginia unharmed and still bound to the tree. They unlocked her handcuffs but were unable to release her from the chain strung around the tree. It was connected to both her hands but she had some mobility with a 3-foot leeway in the chain. She was eventually freed from the tree by four agents who bent the trunk to the ground until she could pull the chain over it.

During the press conference in Minneapolis in July 1972, the faces of Virginia Piper and her husband, Harry, express the joy of her safe return.

"They'll Find Me in November." At a press conference on Sunday, Virginia said she had not been in fear of her life until the kidnapper left her on Friday night. Then she thought, "I'm chained to a tree here and they'll find me in November."

She said she had dug at the ground with her bare hands, hoping to uproot the tree which was six inches (15 cm) thick. "I thought the only way I could ever get out was to uproot the tree and fell it and lug the tree out to the highway. At least it kept me busy." Only $4,000 of the ransom money was recovered, making this one of the most successful kidnappings ever.

UNLUCKY RANSOM MONEY

Most of the $1 million paid for Virginia Piper's release disappeared, as ransom money often does when nobody is convicted. If the police track down the kidnappers, however, the money might be around the corner. After 19-year-old Frank Sinatra Jr. was abducted in 1963, his famous father paid $240,000 in unmarked bills and had an FBI agent drop them off in Los Angeles. Within days, agents arrested three kidnappers, and they recovered virtually all of the money.

Ransom money, however, can be unlucky for careless kidnappers. In 1932 Charles Lindbergh paid a $50,000 ransom for the return of his infant son, who had already been murdered. Two years later, a gold certificate from the money was discovered, which had been used to write down the license number of Bruno Hauptmann's car. He was arrested the next day and later convicted and executed after $14,000 of the money was found in his garage.

A trail of money also solved another famous 1930s kidnapping. Nine-year-old George Weyerhaeuser was abducted in 1935. His wealthy lumberman father, J. P. Weyerhaeuser, paid $200,000, and his son was released. When the kidnapper, Harmon Waley, bought a train ticket with one of the marked bills, the FBI pounced. Waley had burned $3,700 of the money in his stove, but a laboratory at the FBI could still identify them as part of the ransom loot. Other money was discovered buried, and Waley and his wife, Margaret Waley, received long jail sentences.

Equal bad luck dogged the Somali pirates who received a reported $3 million in January 2009 to release a hijacked Saudi supertanker after two months in the Gulf of Aden. The eight pirates were transporting the cash in a small boat when a storm overturned it. Five died and three swam empty-handed for several hours to reach the shore.

Police can also trace known serial numbers on ransom money back to kidnappers.

The Suspects and Trials

The FBI employed 250 agents to explore leads, looking primarily at people with previous criminal records in Minnesota. On July 11, 1977, it arrested Kenneth Callahan, 50, and Donald Larson (age unknown). Amazingly, they were allowed to remain free on bail. Their lawyer, Ron Meshbesher, believed the police had allowed bail in the hope that they would lead the FBI to the ransom money.

Trials. Their first trial opened on October 11, 1977, and the evidence they presented was circumstantial—based mostly on a fingerprint from the Monte Carlo car linked to Callahan and a hair sample from the kidnap car. This proved to be enough for a jury to return guilty verdicts on November 2.

An appeal was successful, however, because the judge had improperly dismissed the testimony of a defense witness, Lynda Lee Billstrom. The defense had not acted on FBI information that the witness had implicated her common-law husband, Bob Billstrom, in the kidnapping, though she had earlier denied this claim.

During a second trial, a fingerprint expert from New York testified for the defense that someone had altered the fingerprint. The defense lawyer, Meshbesher, said it was the FBI. The expert used graphs, photographs, and simulations to make the case, and the prosecution did not call another expert to rebut the evidence. Both men were acquitted by the jury.

The Oldest "Lifer." Callahan died in December 2004 after suffering a heart attack while shoveling snow. Larson went on to murder five people in 1976, killing his estranged wife, her lover and his son, Larson's own son, and his wife's son from a previous marriage. He confessed and has been imprisoned in Minnesota for more than 30 years.

Lingering Doubts

- Since Donald Larson is serving a life sentence after confessing to murder, wouldn't he confess to the kidnapping if he was guilty of that crime?

- What happened to the ransom money? Is Larson hoping for release from prison with the possibility of recovering it despite the FBI's continued interest?

- Who was in the "dirty yellow" car that followed the kidnapper's Chevrolet? Was a third person or more involved in the crime?

CARY SAYEGH

Six-year-old Cary Sayegh was a brown-haired, brown-eyed boy with a slight gap between his front teeth. He was kidnapped on Wednesday, October 25, 1978, from the playground of the Albert Einstein Hebrew School in Las Vegas, Nevada, during the school's lunchtime recess. His classmates were the last to see him, climbing into a car in the school's parking lot on East Oakey Boulevard. He was wearing brown pants and a white T-shirt with "Las Vegas Quicksilvers" printed on the front.

Three hours later a man telephoned his wealthy parents, Sol and Marilyn Sayegh, to demand $500,000. He said he would call again in two days, at "midday Friday," to provide instructions on how the money would be paid, but he never contacted them again. Cary's parents, who also had a 13-year-old son and a 9-year-old daughter, offered a $50,000 reward for his safe return, making a tearful public plea in front of their two-story rambling home in a fashionable neighborhood 1 mile (1.6 km) from the Las Vegas Strip. However, Cary and his kidnapper have never been located.

Hank Greenspun, publisher of *The Las Vegas Sun*, put his reporters on the case and spent a large sum unsuccessfully trying to contact the kidnapper.

Investigation

Immediately after the abduction, police launched the most extensive manhunt ever held in Las Vegas. They were joined by the FBI, which brought in 23 agents from around the country to assist local staff. Agent Ed Gallagher, who directed the investigation, said, "We've used planes, helicopters, supersonic planes with infrared, hypnotists, and polygraph machines" and, he added, "We wish that somebody, including God, would come down and tell us what to do."

The Las Vegas Sun. Despite the massive search, the publisher of *The Las Vegas Sun* newspaper, Hank Greenspun, accused the FBI of bungling the case. Saying his reporters could conduct a better investigation, Greenspun wrote to the person who had abducted Cary, volunteering to

THE AMBER ALERT PROGRAM

Amber Hagerman, a 9-year-old girl from Texas, was abducted and brutally murdered in 1996. This event so shocked the nation that the AMBER Alert Program (America's Missing: Broadcast Emergency Response) was launched in 2001 by a group that included Amber's mother and the National Center for Missing and Exploited Children (NCMEC).

The International AMBER Alert Program has also been implemented across most of Canada, as well as in Australia, Britain, France, Germany, Greece, and the Netherlands.

The plan creates a partnership between law-enforcement agencies and broadcasters to send out urgent bulletins concerning serious child abductions. These broadcasts include a description of the abducted child and, if known, the suspected abductor. An entire community can be quickly alerted to assist in the search for the child and the apprehension of the suspect. "In 75 percent of child abduction homicides, the most serious cases, the child is dead within the first three hours," noted Ernie Allen, president and CEO of NCMEC. "We can't wait until tomorrow; we have to mobilize communities the instant the child is reported missing."

By July 2009 AMBER Alert bulletins had led to 467 successful recoveries of children.

be an intermediary for the boy's return and promising not to reveal the kidnapper's identity. He said, "Our line of communication will be totally inviolable and under no circumstance will law enforcement be involved or alerted in the process of bringing little Cary home." Greenspun's appeal went unheeded, however, and he was reportedly tricked out of $154,000 when he tried to buy information from a con man.

The Suspect

Detectives never suspected the parents or other members of the family. Cary's father, Sol Sayegh, 33, owned the Carpet Barn, a successful local company he started in 1971. At the time of the abduction, he was facing trial in federal court for allegedly attempting to bribe the chairman of the Nevada Gaming Commission to win approval for a new type of gaming device for the state's casinos. This charge was dropped for compassionate reasons following the kidnapping.

Former Employee. Investigators carefully reviewed people associated with Sayegh's business and targeted a former employee, Jerald "Jerry" Burgess, from nearby Henderson. Children who witnessed the kidnapping said he was the driver of the vehicle, which was never identified, and others said they recognized his voice on the ransom phone call. Burgess was able to show police the location of one of Cary's shoes off Mohave Road in Las Vegas, but he said the kidnappers had given this information to him when he tried to act as a go-between for them and Cary's family.

Lack of Physical Evidence. Burgess was arrested and tried in Clark County District Court on a charge of kidnapping. He claimed to be at the school delivering lunch to his girlfriend's son, a friend of Cary's. Despite strong circumstantial evidence, the jury brought back a judgment of innocence, citing the lack of physical evidence. Bizarrely, after being acquitted, Burgess stated that he believed the victim was alive and living in Israel.

Further Convictions. A week before the abduction, Burgess had sexually assaulted a woman in the same area from where Cary had been abducted. Arrested in 1978, Burgess was given a 15-year sentence the following year for this earlier attack and also served a concurrent 15-year term for fraud after he used a scheme to defraud a Texas couple out of $200,000. In 2001 Burgess was also convicted for selling a handgun equipped with a silencer, bullets, and rubber gloves to an undercover agent. He received an 11-year prison sentence.

The National Center for Missing and Exploited Children initially released these images of Cary in 2004 and continue to show them while updating his present age.

During the 18-month investigation that led to his arrest, he reportedly said he knew how to dispose of a body by welding it into a steel drum. It was also discovered that Burgess had rented welding equipment days before Cary was taken.

Reopened Case

FBI agents reopened the case in 1999 after officials received a tip that Cary was living in Boston, Massachusetts, in the 1990s. However, this lead was

Non-Family Abduction

CARY SAYEGH

Age Progressed

DOB: Nov 12, 1971
Missing: Oct 25, 1978
Age Now: 37
Sex: Male
Race: White
Hair: Brown
Eyes: Brown
Height: 4'2" (127 cm)
Weight: 65 lbs (29 kg)
Missing From:
LAS VEGAS
NV
United States

Cary's photo is shown age-progressed to 33 years. He was abducted from the grounds of his day school during lunch time. He has a small scar on the right side of his forehead, near his hairline. He has surgical scars on both feet near the little toes. He has a prominent space between his front teeth.

ANYONE HAVING INFORMATION SHOULD CONTACT
National Center for Missing & Exploited Children
1-800-843-5678 (1-800-THE-LOST)

NATIONAL CENTER FOR MISSING & EXPLOITED CHILDREN
www.missingkids.com

Las Vegas Metropolitan Police Department (Nevada) - Missing Persons Unit 1-
702-229-3111

unsuccessful. Detectives now believe he was killed and have continued to search for his body. Others say he may be alive and does not even know his real name anymore.

In 2008 an employee at Cary's private elementary school, who was working the day of his abduction, said he believed Burgess was guilty and that others were also involved. "I think he was a camouflage," he said, "a smokescreen for whoever really did this." The employee's name was not released because he claimed his life had previously been threatened after he gave details to detectives.

British jockey Walter Swinburn rode Shergar to a famous victory in July 1981 at the Ascot racecourse in England.

SHERGAR

Considered by many to be one of the best racehorses the world had ever seen, Shergar had a short, but incredibly successful, career. The Irish bay colt, nicknamed "the Wonder Horse," raced only eight times in one year, winning six times and earning nearly a million dollars (£500,000) in prize money. The champion jockey Lester Piggott rode him to victory in the Irish Derby. Shergar's most famous win came at the 1981 Epsom Derby (one of the most important races in the U.K.), which he won by 10 lengths, the largest margin in the long history of the race. Shergar was

named "European Horse of the Year" in 1981 and retired to stud that same year. The syndicate that owned him, headed by the Aga Khan, charged up to $160,000 (£80,000) a time for his stud fee, and his insurers, Lloyds of London, valued him at $20 million (£10 million) while at stud. Then, on the foggy evening of February 8, 1983, tragedy struck.

In the first kidnap of its kind in Ireland, just after 8:30 P.M. at the Ballymany Stud Farm in Newbridge, County Kildare, three armed men wearing balaclavas forced their way into the home of Shergar's 53-year-old head groom, James Fitzgerald. "We've come for Shergar," one said. "And we want two million quid [four million dollars] for him. Call the police and he's dead."

They locked Fitzgerald's family in a room and forced him at gunpoint to take the racehorse from his security stable behind a five-bar, wooden gate and latch. Five more men appeared, they loaded Shergar, with Fitzgerald, into a stolen horse trailer, and towed it away with a Ford Granada car, leaving two intruders behind to watch the family. After 40 miles (64 km), the gang released Fitzgerald, who returned home to find his family alone and safe.

Two days later on February 10, 1983, a man called the stables demanding a ransom of four million dollars. After having second

The Aga Khan, who owned six of the 40 shares in Shergar, greets the horse after it raced to victory in the 1980 Irish Derby in County Kildare, Ireland.

thoughts, the kidnapper called again later in the day to reduce the price to $80,000 (£40,000), but the horse's 34 shareholders still refused to pay. They knew that if they gave into the kidnapper's demands it would lay them open to threats of extortion and encourage more racehorse kidnappings.

Shergar, who had a distinctive white blaze and four white "sock" marks on his lower legs, has never been found, and the police have never officially identified the kidnappers.

The Investigation

The Gardaí (the Irish police) were not alerted for more than four hours, because phone calls were at first only exchanged between people directly connected with the stud farm. Another problem facing the Gardaí, and a cunning ruse by the kidnappers, was the number of horse trailers on the road since Ireland's largest racehorse sale was also being held on the day Shergar was taken. Officers questioned Fitzgerald for several hours and tapped his phone to intercept any future calls from the kidnappers.

> MR. FITZGERALD WAS ORDERED TO GET OUT OF THE CAR, TO KEEP WALKING. EVENTUALLY, HE WALKED TO THE NEXT VILLAGE AND RANG HIS BROTHER.
>
> —THE *DAILY TELEGRAPH*

Competing Forces. The investigation ran into problems because officers from two forces, Dublin and County Kildare, had been assigned to the case and they began to compete with each other. The competition between the two groups even reached the point of withholding information. Despite this, an extensive hunt was conducted, with mediums and psychics being consulted, too.

During the investigation the police had to deal with numerous hoax calls and erroneous sightings of the horse, which confused and complicated the investigation. But the Gardaí were aided by the Irish love of horses, an element the kidnappers had failed to consider, and the Irish Thoroughbred Breeders' Association put up a $200,000 (£100,000) reward for information leading to Shergar's safe return.

The Suspects

Most speculation centered on the Provisional Irish Republican Army (IRA), a paramilitary group that had previously kidnapped rich businessmen for ransom money, which it used to buy weapons. During the investigation, Gardaí raids were made on known IRA houses and several caches of weapons were seized.

IRA Members. Sean O'Callaghan, a former IRA member who became an informer on the organization, wrote a book in 1999 called *The Informer*, in which he stated that the group had kidnapped Shergar, believing the Aga Khan would pay a large ransom for him. They did not realize that all 34 members of the syndicate had to agree to pay up.

O'Callaghan, who admitted he had killed two members of the security forces and participated in a range of terrorist activities, named seven men that he claimed had carried out the kidnapping. These included Kevin Mallon, 44, a senior IRA leader that O'Callaghan alleged had planned the kidnap, and Nicky Kehoe, 26, who denied involvement and said the only reason he had not sued was because nobody believed O'Callaghan since he worked for both sides. Another source stated that the IRA's Army Council had sanctioned the kidnapping. Despite the allegations and strong suspicions about the IRA, however, the Gardaí found no direct evidence and were unable to charge anyone.

O'Callaghan also reported that Shergar was shot within hours of being taken, because he was hard to handle and had injured his leg. The kidnappers felt it would be impossible to move the horse because of the Gardaí that were swarming over the area. Shergar's burial place has never been located, though rumors say it is on a mountainside in Ballinamore, County Leitrim, about 100 miles (160 km) from the Ballymany Stud Farm. Because his remains have not been found, the life insurance policy on the horse has never been paid.

One rumor said Shergar was seized for the Libyan leader, Colonel Qaddafi, in return for arms to the IRA terrorists.

The Libyan Connection. The public and media had more theories about possible suspects. Colin Turner, the racing correspondent of a London radio station, suggested that the Libyan leader, Colonel Qaddafi, sent arms to the IRA in return for kidnapping Shergar—to damage the man he hated, the Aga Khan.

The Mafia. Another strange rumor targeted a French bloodstock agent, Jean Michel Gambet, who supposedly borrowed money from the Mafia to buy a champion horse from the Aga Khan. The deal collapsed, but Gambet had already spent the money.

His dead body was discovered in a burning car in Kentucky with a gunshot wound to his head. According to this theory, the Mafia kidnapped Shergar to recoup their financial loss. Regardless of the theories, Shergar's abduction remains an unsolved crime.

Lingering Doubts

- How reliable are the accusations of Sean O'Callaghan, a self-confessed murderer and terrorist? Since he was not part of the kidnapping, how reliable are his sources?

- British intelligence has been infiltrating the IRA for years, so why have no additional details of Shergar's abduction ever come to light?

- Where is Shergar's final resting place, and how could a racehorse be transported and buried without eyewitnesses?

Police search for Suzy Lamplugh's body in woods near "Dead Woman's Ditch" in Somerset, England. Several sites in different counties have been searched for years.

SUZY LAMPLUGH

British real-estate agent, Suzy Lamplugh, 25, disappeared on July 28, 1986, after driving to meet a caller who said he wanted to view one of her agency's houses in London. Her appointment diary listed a 12:45 P.M. meeting with "Mr. Kipper" outside the empty Victorian property on Shorrolds Road in the fashionable Fulham area. When she failed to return to the office, the staff notified the police, who launched a massive, but unsuccessful, hunt. She has never been found.

The Investigation

Detectives believed a stalker, who knew the area, had been keeping track of Lamplugh's daily movements as she worked, shopped, and socialized. He may have telephoned her office more than once to learn her schedule, then made notes on when she would be most vulnerable. Days before her abduction, a mystery man had delivered a bouquet of roses to her office at Sturgis Estate Agents.

Eyewitnesses. Eyewitnesses told police they had seen Lamplugh, who was wearing a gray skirt and dark jacket, arguing with a man in front of the house before getting into a car. Her white Ford Fiesta was discovered that night about 1.5 miles (2.4 km) away and outside another property that was for sale on Stevenage Road, also in Fulham. Her purse was inside the car, but the ignition keys were gone. A jogger reported seeing a blonde woman, who seemed to be screaming for help, in a black, left-hand drive (non-British) BMW that was parked outside the second address. Lamplugh's hair was naturally brown, but she had highlighted it the week before. Police, however, were not sure this sighting fitted the time frame of the abduction. However, they theorized that the name given by the man could have been a pronunciation of "Kuiper," a Dutch name. They traced people named Kipper and Kuiper but none had links to Lamplugh.

New Leads. In 1987 the police search for Lamplugh and her killer was scaled down, and in 1994 she was officially declared dead and the case was closed. But it was reopened in 2000 following new leads. In 1999 a new witness said he had seen who he had thought was Lamplugh being driven in her car shortly after her meeting at the Shorrolds Road house. Police originally believed she had been driven directly to Stevenage Road and her car abandoned within 80 minutes. The new information indicated a different route had been taken. Detectives felt this might mean she was dropped off at an address along the way, and more than one abductor was involved.

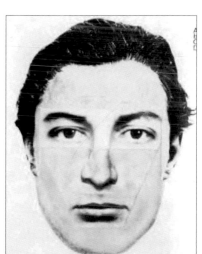

Suzy Lamplugh's name lives on in the Suzy Lamplugh Trust in London, England. It was founded by her parents in 1980 to offer advice on personal safety.

The Main Suspects

John Cannan, 32, was the prime suspect in the case, and he had served five years for rape. He was released from prison days before Lamplugh disappeared, and he was only a few miles from the house. Cannan was imprisoned again in 1989 for raping and murdering a woman; this time he was given three life sentences. He also bore a striking resemblance to the police picture the police had drawn up of

Police released a composite photo of a man seen with Lamplugh on the day she vanished. It bore a close resemblance to the suspect, John Cannan.

the suspect from eyewitness descriptions. Scotland Yard questioned him several times, but found no evidence that he was involved in Lamplugh's disappearance. Although he denied it to police, he liked to give others the impression he had been involved, even telling prison inmates his nickname was "Kipper." He also told one person that a businessman in Bristol, where he had lived at the time, had killed Lamplugh.

Possible Burial Sites. Cannan invented false leads about Lamplugh's burial site, telling a fellow prison inmate that he had placed her under the patio of his mother's home in the West Midlands. He also informed his girlfriend that he had raped and killed Lamplugh, and then disposed of the body at "Norton barracks." She passed this information to the police, but later retracted it.

Years later, Diana Lamplugh, the victim's mother, received the same information from private investigations, so in 2000 detectives reopened the case and began searching in Worcestershire, around the former Royal Air Force barracks that was by now covered with new houses. They worked with forensic archaeologists and divers, and also used cadaver-sniffing dogs. The next year they searched a similarly named Royal Marine barracks in Somerset. Neither site yielded the body or any clues.

Other Suspects

Another possible suspect was considered in 2008. While looking into Lamplugh's background, investigators discovered that she was employed in 1982 as a beautician on the *QE2* ocean liner. Steve Wright, who was convicted of murdering five prostitutes in 2008 in Ipswich, England, was one of the ship's stewards at the time. After he was sentenced to life, detectives went over the prosecution's files, but found no evidence that Wright had any contact with Lamplugh.

Another murderer was briefly considered after the 1995 book, *Unmasking Mr. Kipper: Who Really Killed Suzy Lamplugh?* authored

Police notices appealed for help in locating Lamplugh, and her disappearance was featured on the BBC's *Crimewatch* television program to no avail.

METROPOLITAN POLICE

Appeal for Assistance
ABDUCTION

Susannah LAMPLUGH, aged 25, was last seen outside 37 Shorrold's Road, Fulham, SW6, at about 1pm on Monday July 28.

Her car, a white Ford Fiesta Reg No. B396 GAN, was later found unlocked in Stevenage Road, Fulham.

Police wish to trace this man, who was seen with Susannah that day. He is white, aged 25-30, 5'7" – 9" tall, with dark, swept back hair.

DID YOU SEE SUSANNAH, THIS MAN, OR THE CAR ON MONDAY AFTERNOON, JULY 28?

Please contact the Incident Room at
KENSINGTON POLICE STATION
Tel: 741 6357
All information treated as strictly confidential

KIDNAPPED OR MISSING?

When a child disappears, has he or she been kidnapped, or did the child just wander off? Does a teenager's sudden absence indicate abduction, or did they run away from home? Is a missing adult being held captive, or just enjoying a private adventure? American organizations for missing children have become worried that the public is becoming less sensitive to AMBER Alerts because many turn out to be false alarms.

In 2007 the Canadian Missing Children's Report showed a total of 60,582 missing cases, of which 46,189 turned out to be runaways and 576 were children who had wandered off and had not returned when expected. In California when people are reported missing as juveniles they are recategorized as "emancipated juveniles" when they are still missing past the age of 18.

Although serious crimes do occur, most missing people are quickly found. Almost 35,000 people are reported missing each year in Australia, with 20,000 under the age of 18. Ninety-five percent of these are found within a short period of time, usually less than a week, while most children are located safe and well within 24 hours.

A bulletin board in Schenectady, New York, shows photos of missing children.

by Christopher Berry-Dee, was published. He claimed that Michael Sams, who killed the prostitute Julie Dart in 1991, also murdered Lamplugh, based on interviews with Sams and his wife. Police dug for Lamplugh's body in the garden of Sams's former house in Peterborough, Cambridgeshire, but found nothing and later discounted this theory.

Hope for DNA Evidence

During the investigation police investigated thousands of lines of inquiry, took statements from hundreds of witnesses, and compiled documents more than a million words long. They still hope DNA advances may someday lead them to the killer, because forensic scientists recovered DNA from her car.

In 2000 police also traced a car that had been loaned to Cannan around the time Lamplugh vanished. Although it had been parked for years at a used-car dealership, forensic experts said they recovered some DNA after examining it for microscopic traces of hair, skin, and body fluids.

Sharon Wills wore a man's shirt and was wrapped in plastic garbage bags when Mr. Cruel released her after 18 hours.

"MR. CRUEL"

Between 1987 and 1991, in the suburbs of Melbourne, Australia, an unknown sex offender raped four young girls. One was attacked in her home, and three were kidnapped. He released his first three victims, but murdered the last one. At first he was called "the Hampton Rapist," but the newspapers quickly dubbed him "Mr. Cruel."

The Victims

- **An 11-year-old girl (unnamed).** The intruder broke into the victim's house around 4:00 A.M. on August 22, 1987, in the suburb of Lower Plenty. Armed with a handgun and knife, he forced her parents to lie on their stomachs and bound their hands and feet before locking them in a wardrobe. The girl's 7-year-old brother was tied to a bed. The man then raped the girl and, before leaving, cut the telephone lines.

- **Sharon Wills, 10.** Mr. Cruel kidnapped his next victim more than a year later, on December 27, 1988. Wearing a mask, and again armed with a gun and knife, the man forced his way through the back door of a home in Ringwood at 5:30 A.M. He again forced the girl's parents to lie on their stomachs so he could bind and gag them, and cut the phones. This time he also demanded money. He then put tape over Sharon's eyes and placed a ball in her mouth before taking her to an unknown house. About 18 hours later, he left her outside a local high school.

- **Nicola Lynas, 13.** The rapist repeated his crime in Canterbury on July 3, 1990. In a similar style to his earlier attacks, he entered the victim's house through a window at 11:30 P.M. and forced the girl to lie on her stomach as he tied and gagged her. He searched for money and cut the phone lines, before placing tape over her eyes and taking her to a house where he imprisoned her for 50 hours. He released her outside a power substation in Kew.

- **Karmein Chan, 13.** The final, and most tragic, attack was on April 13, 1991, in Templestowe. Wearing a mask and carrying a knife, he cut through a screen and opened a window. Inside he found Karmein and her two younger sisters alone as their parents worked in their Chinese restaurant. He ordered the younger girls into a wardrobe and blocked the doors with a bed. He kidnapped Karmein at 9:15 P.M., but this time he did not let her go. The girl's body was discovered a year later in Thomastown with three gunshot wounds to her head.

The Investigation

Detectives put together a task force with the code name Operation Spectrum. The staff of 40 checked approximately 30,000 houses in an attempt to find the one where Mr. Cruel had taken his victims. In the 29 months that the task force was in operation, it investigated almost 27,000 suspects, narrowing it down to 20 with six strong suspects. Spectrum questioned about 150 men who subscribed to child pornography by mail and investigated 10,000 tips offs.

Although nobody was arrested for Mr. Cruel's crimes, the search led detectives to arrest 73 other people for various other crimes, including pedophilia, rape, and blackmail. In total, this long search cost almost

four million Australian dollars. Besides the four known rapes, police believe Mr. Cruel may have carried out at least eight more attacks.

Lost Evidence. The investigation found that crucial forensic evidence had been lost in the murder case because the crime scene was improperly secured. The first police officer to arrive at Karmein Chan's home had set up a command post inside the house. Other evidence was later lost or thrown out, such as criminal records and the tape Mr. Cruel had used to bind the victim that may have revealed his DNA.

Fanatical Habits. Spectrum's work found that Mr. Cruel had used a camera to film his attacks in the secret house. One victim recalled a tripod and camera at the end of the bed—to which the girls had been shackled with a rough neck brace. The house was never located, although two girls gave details of it. One had heard airplanes landing, so police searched homes on flight paths to Melbourne's airport.

The victims also told detectives that Mr. Cruel was fanatical about erasing clues. He wiped sinks and other surfaces to remove fingerprints and covered the floor with a sheet to avoid leaving footprints. He even bathed two victims before releasing them. Worried about leaving traces of evidence on the victims' clothes, he released Sharon Wills wearing plastic garbage bags; another victim was released in different clothes he had taken from her bedroom.

Victoria Police Commander David Sprague, head of "Operation Spectrum," holds a poster with photos of three of Mr. Cruel's victims, Sharon Wills, Nicola Lynas, and Karmein Chan.

The Suspects

The FBI joined Spectrum to create a profile of Mr. Cruel, stating that he would have homemade and commercial pornography. The profile suggested that he would not fit the stereotype of a child molester, but

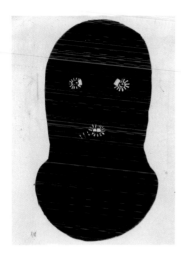

was probably "a good neighbor, polite, quiet, somewhat introverted, but may be involved in certain community-minded projects." It added that he probably spent a great deal of time with children, and perhaps was even employed in a school.

Strong Circumstantial Evidence.

Police identified 10 suspects in Victoria during the next decade but withheld their names, hoping to find more concrete evidence. "Having interviewed some of them," said Victoria Police Commander Dave Sprague, "I can tell you they are bloody scary."

Then in 2003 detectives revealed that their best unnamed suspect was still living in Victoria. They lack a strong case against the man but continue to keep tabs on his movements. Commander Sprague said a good circumstantial case existed against the key suspect, but the evidence was not strong enough to charge him. Officers had interviewed him for 14 hours, and it seems that this close attention may have stopped his attacks.

The police continued to watch all of the suspects' movements. Also in 2003 Detective Senior Sergeant Chris O'Connor, head of the sexual crime squad, stated that he suspected Mr. Cruel might have moved abroad in order to continue abusing minors.

The case has yet to be solved, and detectives continue to withhold some facts from the public in case they help the suspect to avoid capture, and they are also helpful in eliminating suspects and people who falsely confess to the crime.

Police released a sketch of the dark green balaclava worn by Mr. Cruel when he kidnapped Nicola Lynas. He also wore gloves, as he did in the other abductions.

Lingering Doubts

- Why did Mr. Cruel murder his last victim? What made him use the execution style of gunshots to the head, which is not typical of pedophiles?

- If the police have strong circumstantial evidence pointing to one suspect, why haven't they charged him?

- What facts are detectives withholding from the public?

MICHAELA JOY GARECHT

At 10:20 A.M., on the sunny Saturday morning of November 19, 1988, in Hayward, California, Michaela Joy Garecht and her friend were riding their scooters three blocks from Michaela's home to Rainbow Market, a neighborhood store on Mission Boulevard. The 9-year-old girls left their scooters outside the store, but when they came back out her friend's scooter had been moved to the parking lot. Michaela went over retrieve it, but as she bent over to pick up the scooter a man jumped out of the car that was parked next to it. He grabbed her from behind, forced her into his vehicle as she screamed, and sped away while Michaela's friend ran into the store for help.

Local police were immediately on the scene, but Michaela has never been found or the kidnapper identified.

The Investigation

Since Michaela was abducted in plain sight, many eyewitnesses were available. They told police the man was driving an older model U.S. sedan that was burgundy and had a battered front bumper. It was last seen speeding down Mission Boulevard, a busy highway, toward Union City.

Instead of immediately interviewing Michaela's friend, who had seen the abduction, the police chose to interview a member of staff from the Rainbow Market, who had seen the car drive past earlier in the day. This produced some disagreements, such as the car's color and the fact that the store worker said the man had a moustache while Michaela's friend said he did not.

An age-progressed image of Michaela Joy Garecht released by the National Center for Missing and Exploited Children shows what the blonde, blue-eyed girl might look like at the age of 29 in 2008.

Witnesses. Other onlookers described the abductor as being slender, between 18 and 25 years old, with dirty shoulder-length blond hair, and a pimpled or pockmarked complexion. He was also wearing a white T-shirt. Witnesses helped police to put together a composite sketch.

One woman had witnessed the car weaving past her and tried to memorize the licence plate in case there was an accident. She later watched the news and realized it had been the kidnapper's car, but she did not come forward at the time. Three months later, she saw a man in a grocery store that resembled the police sketch. Fearing he had recognized her and would come after her, the woman finally told police. Although she underwent hypnotherapy, the woman could not recall the license plate number.

Open Case. Soon the FBI joined the investigation, and in the first year the police already had five file cabinets full of leads. By 2008, the twentieth anniversary of the abduction, they had received almost 15,000 tips but had made no arrests. The case remains open and is still being actively investigated. Sergeant Mark Mosier of the Hayward police said, "We'll go anywhere, clear across the world, to try and track down new information that might solve this case."

The Suspects

- **Timothy Bindner, 42.** The married sewage-plant worker had once been arrested for trying to lure two small girls into his van, but the charge was dropped. He also sent birthday cards and letters to young girls and offered assistance to the mothers of missing girls, referring to himself as a "good Samaritan" who thought about the kidnapped victims as his children. On one bizarre occasion, Bindner asked a reporter to interview him at 4:30 A.M. in Oakmont Cemetery, where a 5-year-old girl who had been kidnapped and murdered in 1983 was buried. He told the reporter how he guessed various missing girls would have reacted during their abductions, saying some would have been submissive, but "Michaela was harder. She was a fighter." Shortly before nine-

year-old Michaela disappeared, Bindner wrote to the police telling them that the next victim's age would be nine. Detectives never found any hard evidence against Bindner so he was never charged, but authorities thought he may have had connections to three other missing girls in the area, all blonde with blue eyes and similar facial appearances. Bindner denied all the allegations and won a defamation suit against the city of Fairfield, California, in 1999.

> SHE ACTUALLY GAVE A DESCRIPTION OF THE CAR AS BEING A BUTTERSCOTCH COLOR, AND WHEN THE POLICE GOT MY DAUGHTER'S FRIEND CALMED DOWN, MUCH LATER THAT DAY, AND ACTUALLY TALKED TO HER, IT ACTUALLY TURNED OUT TO BE MORE OF A BURGUNDY COLOR.

—IN AN INTERVIEW ON OCTOBER 7, 2007, MICHAELA'S MOTHER WAS QUOTED WHEN REFERRING TO THE STORE CLERK

Only after police interviewed the friend of Michaela Joy Garecht, were they able to release a composite of the suspect and this did not match earlier descriptions.

- **A 49-year-old sex offender.** In 1995 two Hayward detectives traveled to Oklahoma to question a convicted sex offender for the second time. The man had lived only two blocks from the kidnapping site and a year before had been convicted of a felony assault with intent to commit rape. Police decided he was not involved and never named him.

- **James Daveggio, 28.** Convicted with his girlfriend, Michelle Lyn Michaud, of the 1997 kidnap, rape, and murder of a 22-year-old California woman, they are both now on death row. Despite police suspicions, no link was found to Michaela.

STOCKHOLM SYNDROME

When police rescued Elizabeth Smart from the religious fanatic Brian David Mitchell in 2003, in Utah, she seemed reluctant to leave him. Police had previously stopped Mitchell and a woman with Elizabeth, but the 14-year-old failed to identify herself. When they finally rescued her she was discovered wearing a wig, veil, and sunglasses, and at first denied that she even was Elizabeth Smart. After nine months of accompanying Mitchell on his preaching tour, she seemed to have developed Stockholm Syndrome and was identifying with her kidnapper.

Natascha Kampusch recently purchased the house where she had been held captive.

The syndrome acquired its name in 1973 when bank robbers held hostages for six days in a bank in Stockholm, Sweden. Beginning to sympathize with their captors, several victims even resisted rescue attempts and afterward refused to testify against their captors.

America's most-famous example of Stockholm Syndrome involved the 19-year-old heiress Patty Hearst, who was kidnapped in 1974 in California by the radical Symbionese Liberation Army. She soon became their accomplice, assisting in armed bank robberies and once firing 27 bullets into a storefront. She went on the run and was arrested in 1975 in San Francisco. When asked her profession, she said "urban guerrilla."

More recently, 10-year-old Natascha Kampusch was kidnapped in Austria in 1998 by Wolfgang Priklopil and held in a small cellar for more than eight years. Later he allowed her to venture outdoors, but she never sought help. She finally escaped in 2006 and her captor quickly committed suicide. Natascha cried when she was told, saying that she felt sorry for him and had not missed anything during her captivity, since Priklopil had kept her from bad habits and bad company.

- **Curtis Dean Anderson, 27.** Named as a possible suspect, he was convicted of the abduction and molestation of a young girl in 2000, but again, no evidence pointed to Michaela.

- **Steven Shane, 21.** This convicted felon resembled the composite picture and was briefly detained, but no evidence could be found to link him to Michaela.

- **Brian David Mitchell, 35.** He kidnapped Elizabeth Smart in 2002 and was living in California when Michaela and the three other girls disappeared. Blonde Elizabeth, who was rescued unhurt, resembled the other missing victims, but no link could be matched to Michaela.

Lingering Doubts

- How can a screaming girl be kidnapped in a public parking area without witnesses pursuing the car or writing down the license number? Why did one witness wait three months before reporting that she had seen the kidnapper's car?

- Since Timothy Bindner showed morbid interest in girls being kidnapped, correctly predicted the next victim would be nine years old, and then said Michaela would have been a fighter, why did the police not consider this to be enough evidence to charge him?

SABRINA AISENBERG

Four-month-old Sabrina Aisenberg disappeared from her family's home in Valrico, Florida, on November 24, 1997. Her mother, Marlene Aisenberg, 38, said she checked on the infant around midnight and then discovered she was missing at 6:42 A.M. She immediately called the 911 emergency number. Sabrina, who had been wearing a lavender sleeper with a floral pattern and sleeping with a handmade blue and yellow blanket with animal images, was missing from her crib. A massive search began and despite 2,000 tips to investigators, no trace of the infant has ever been found.

The Investigation

The Aisenbergs had left the garage door unlocked that night, and investigators found that the door from the garage into the house was unlocked. The parents said an intruder had obviously entered the house silently and kidnapped the child, but investigators soon suspected the parents, assuming they had killed or sold their daughter. Sheriff's investigators said Marlene had failed their polygraph test a day after the kidnapping. At the time of the disappearance, Marlene was running Playtime Pals, a program for toddlers and their mothers. Her husband, Steven, 37, was a real estate agent.

Search and Surveillance. FBI agents and Florida detectives arrived the next day to join the search conducted by the sheriff's department, which used dogs in nearby woods and sent divers to probe the pond behind the subdivision. In the Aisenbergs' house, investigators discovered an unidentified blond hair and a shoe print on a dust ruffle used to cover the space from a crib to the floor. Forensic scientists also found seven unidentified fingerprints in the house; five were on the inside of a sliding glass door, one on a screen door and one on the washing machine. About three weeks after the disappearance, detectives bugged their home, placing one listening device in the bedroom and one in the kitchen.

The Grand Jury

In May 1999 the Aisenbergs moved to Bethesda, Maryland. On September 9, a federal grand jury used recordings from the listening devices to indict the Aisenbergs on charges of conspiracy and lying about the kidnapping. FBI agents arrested them that day, forcing their front door open after Marlene refused to admit them.

Marlene and Steven Aisenberg walk to the courthouse in Tampa, Florida, on December 15, 2000, where hearings were held concerning their missing daughter.

Tape Recordings. Federal prosecutors claimed that the tapes had picked up more than 2,600 conversations and some had recorded the parents talking about their daughter's death, while others had references to violence and cocaine use. The indictment claimed that Steven Aisenberg had said, "I wish I hadn't harmed her. It was the cocaine." Another quoted conversation accused Marlene of saying, "The baby's dead and buried! It was found dead because you did it! The baby's dead no matter what you say—you just did it!" To this, he supposedly replied:

"We need to discuss the way that we can beat the charge." Yet not enough evidence was found to bring a murder charge.

Possible Intruder. During the grand jury hearing, statements from neighbors backed up the possibility of an intruder. One couple with an infant heard their alarm going off one morning a few days before Sabrina disappeared and discovered an open window. Another found a window screen bent back near where their infant son slept. At a house close to the Aisenbergs', the owner said his dog barked that morning, and when he walked outside about 1:00 A.M., he heard what sounded like a baby crying.

Strange Behavior. Other neighbors, however, thought the parents had acted strangely after the kidnapping. A next-door neighbor, Martha Jones, said Marlene knocked on her door that morning saying "My baby's missing, my baby's missing," but was not crying and drew back when she put her arm around her. Jones also noted that the parents began to have backyard parties after the sheriff's surveillance ended.

Claims Dismissed. Prosecutors put little value on evidence suggesting an intruder. Despite testimony about the neighborhood disturbances, they pointed out that neither the Aisenbergs' two other children or their dog had been disturbed. They downplayed the fingerprints that they said were lifted four days after the disappearance and could have been made by relatives, friends, and reporters. They claimed that the unidentified hair came from a toy bunny and the shoe print on the dust ruffle could not have been made the night the infant disappeared because it was off the floor.

Prosecution Abandoned. In October 1999 the investigators moved 35 miles (56 km) from the Aisenbergs' home to a subdivision where Steven once worked, using sniffer dogs, a ground-penetrating sensor, and drilling equipment to search for Sabrina's body. However, their efforts were unsuccessful. By the next month, however, a judge ruled that the tapes were of such poor quality they were "largely inaudible," adding that those he had listened to had no incriminating comments

> I THINK THEY (THE SHERIFF'S INVESTIGATORS) CAME IN WITH A PRECONCEIVED IDEA OF WHAT HAD OCCURRED. SOMETIMES IT'S EASIER TO FOLLOW PRECONCEIVED IDEAS AND THROW AWAY THE FACTS THAN TO CHANGE YOUR PRECONCEIVED NOTION AND FOLLOW THE TRUTH.
>
> —STEVEN AISENBERG

that could be heard clearly. He also said the sheriff's detectives had made up facts to get permission for the listening devices. By February 2001 federal prosecutors dropped the case, saying conviction was virtually impossible without the tapes as evidence. In 2004 an appeals court ruled that the government should pay the Aisenbergs $1.3 million for their lawyer's fees.

A New Development

Another suspect arose in 2008 when Dennis Byron, a prisoner, said his cell mate, Scott Overbeck, 44, had confessed to involvement, claiming Marlene Aisenberg killed the child on his boat, and he had chopped up the remains and put them in crab traps. Byron secretly recorded Overbeck for a reduction in his sentence. Detectives showed photos of Overbeck to the Aisenbergs' neighbors, but no one recognized him. The U.S. Attorney's office said it no longer was investigating the kidnapping case and did not believe it would be reopened.

Lingering Doubts

- Why didn't investigators target the Aisenbergs immediately? How incriminating were the failed polygraph test and the parents' behavior?

- If the fingerprints and other evidence can be discounted, why was no real evidence of an intruder found? How important were the neighbors' reports of prowlers?

- How could the prosecutor report such detailed conversations from the listening devices, yet the judge rule they were too unclear to understand?

- Was Scott Overbeck lying about Marlene Aisenberg killing her daughter? Why has the federal attorney closed the case instead of investigating?

MADELEINE McCANN

Gerry and Kate McCann, both doctors from Leicester, England, took a spring vacation to Portugal's Algarve region in 2007 with their children, Madeleine, almost 4, and younger twins, 2. On May 3 the McCanns left the children in their Ocean Club resort apartment at Praia da Luz to join seven friends for an evening meal at the resort's tapas bar and restaurant about 130 yards (119 m) away. The friends took turns checking on the children, and to facilitate this, the McCanns left their apartment back door unlocked. Just after 9:00 P.M., Gerry checked on the children, and found nothing out of the ordinary. But around 10:00 P.M., Kate looked in and found Madeleine gone and the bedroom window open. The police were quickly called and arrived within 10 minutes. They conducted an all-night search of the complex and were joined by the staff and guests.

The Investigation

The head of the case was Chief Inspector Olegário de Sousa, whose local force was eventually joined by the Portuguese secret service, Serviço de Informações de Segurança (SIS), and detectives from Britain's Scotland Yard.

Portuguese police study a map of the area after Madeleine's disappearance. They would later name her parents as suspects and be criticized for their haphazard investigation.

The Search Begins. Because friends and resort personnel walked through the apartment soon after the abduction, forensic evidence was immediately compromised. The Portuguese police looked at photographs taken by tourists, but these failed to reveal anything suspicious. Based on interviews officers began searching for a brown-haired man, about 5 ft. 7 in. (1.7 m) tall, who was seen wearing a blue coat.

Possible Sighting. The morning after the abduction Jane Tanner, one of the McCanns' friends who was with them at the restaurant on the night Madeleine disappeared, told police she had seen a man carrying a sleeping child away from the apartments 45 minutes before Kate discovered Madeleine was missing. She said the girl's pajamas were the same as Madeleine's, but she had not realized the significance of the sighting. The police never issued an image of the man she claimed to see, and, although they warned witnesses not to release any details to the public, Tanner told the news media about her sighting in November 2007.

The Search Widens. Police brought in sniffer dogs and widened the search into the surrounding area until May 11. Their first assessment was that either a pedophile ring or an illegal adoption syndicate had

kidnapped Madeleine. They also speculated that the child might already be dead. On June 1 forensic work uncovered a DNA sample in the bedroom that did not match the family or anyone else in the immediate area. Throughout their investigation, the police received several reported sightings of Madeleine as well as letters and telephone calls purporting to know her whereabouts, both living and dead. Many of these came from clairvoyants.

The McCanns were staying in this apartment when Madeleine was abducted. It is part of the Ocean Club resort in the village of Praia da Luz, Portugal.

Media Criticism

The British media severely criticized the Portuguese police for not securing the crime scene sooner, for their slow action in collecting forensic evidence, their failure to secure roads and borders, and their three-month wait before accepting British assistance.

Maintaining Public Awareness. The McCanns conducted their own investigation, hiring a Spanish detective agency. They have worked hard to keep Madeleine's plight in the news by distributing posters and traveling to many countries for interviews and meetings, including a

Kate and Gerry McCann display a photo of their daughter during a press conference in Rome on May 30, 2007, after an audience with Pope Benedict XVI in the Vatican.

KIDNAPPED BY FAMILY MEMBERS

While it seemed unlikely for the Portuguese police to believe the McCanns abducted their own daughter, statistics prove that family members are often involved. In the United States family members abduct more than 354,000 children each year. And in the United Kingdom, the number is approximately 150,000. Most abductors are parents engaged in custody disputes. The FBI can issue a criminal arrest warrant if an abducting parent flees across a state line or outside of the United States. The Missing Children Registry of the Royal Canadian Mounted Police recorded 60,582 missing children in 2007, but only 56 of these were abductions by individuals other than parents or guardians.

Karen Matthews, shown with her boyfriend, Craig Meehan, had her daughter kidnapped.

In one bizarre case in Britain, the mother of schoolgirl Shannon Matthews, 9, was sentenced in 2009 to eight years in prison for kidnapping and drugging her own daughter. Karen Matthews, 33, had devised a plot to "rescue" the girl and collect the $80,000 (£50,000) reward offered by *The Sun* newspaper for information. The kidnapping was carried out by Shannon's stepfather's uncle, Michael Donovan, 40, who was also given an eight-year prison sentence. The girl's ordeal ended after 24 days when police, who were working their way through interviews of relatives, visited Donovan and found the terrified Shannon hidden in a drawer in a bed. The search for Shannon was one of the largest for a missing person in Britain in the last decade. It cost nearly $5.2 million (£3.2 million), with 60 detectives assisted by hundreds of officers and several thousand volunteers.

U.S. appearance on the Oprah Winfrey show and an audience with Pope Benedict XVI. Gerry McCann returned to the Ocean Club in 2009 for a television reenactment. Their fundraising organization, Madeleine's Fund: Leaving No Stone Unturned, maintains a constantly updated website, "Find Madeleine" (www.findmadeleine.com).

The Suspects

- **Robert Murat, 33.** The first official suspect was a British expatriate who lived in his mother's villa near the crime scene. He had drawn the attention of the police by hanging around investigators, trying to act as a translator and asking questions. A forensic team searched his villa, took away computers, mobile phones, and other items, and then drained its swimming pool. No evidence was

Britain's Forensic Science Service (FSS) carried out tests on samples of blood, fluids and hair found in the McCanns's vacation apartment and rented car.

found, and police said on July 21, 2007, that Murat was no longer a suspect.

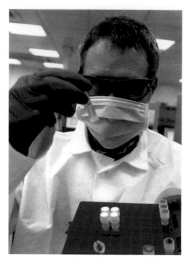

- **Gerry and Kate McCann (both 39).** In a shocking move, the police turned their suspicions on Madeleine's parents. On September 7 detectives interviewed the couple all day before naming them as formal suspects. It was based on traces of Madeleine's DNA that was found in the trunk of the McCann's rental car, which they had rented 25 days after their daughter's disappearance. Forensic experts, however, said that contamination had probably occurred from Madeleine's clothing or toys. Detectives speculated that, after Madeleine had complained about being left in the apartment the previous night, Kate had given her sedatives, or even hit her too hard, and accidentally killed her. She and Gerry then concealed the body and disposed of it. Officers seized Kate's diary and Gerry's laptop computer. However, after finding no evidence, and after news media in Portugal and Britain had headlined these charges, the McCanns were officially removed as suspects on July 21, 2008.

- **Sergey Malinka, 22.** A minor suspect of Russian origin, he frequently telephoned Murat and set up a website for him, as well as two pedophiles (see below). He was soon ruled out of the case.

- **Urs Hans Von Aesch, 67.** A Swiss national, he had been vacationing in the area when Madeleine disappeared. He has since committed suicide after Swiss police questioned him about another child abduction.

- **Raymond Hewlett, 64.** A convicted British child rapist who looked similar to police sketches of the suspect. Living in Germany at the time, he gave a DNA sample to German police, but refused to see detectives in 2009 and would not provide an alibi, although he admitted to being in the Algarve on the day Madeleine was taken.

Lingering Doubts

- How could the kidnapper enter the apartment and then carry Madeleine away through the evening crowd without being noticed? Does it seem more like a crime of opportunity or a carefully planned and professional abduction?

- Since there is virtually no circumstantial evidence, why did the Portuguese police name the McCanns as formal suspects?

- Why would Raymond Hewlett provide a DNA sample to police, but refuse to talk with British detectives or give them an alibi?

NATALIA ESTEMIROVA

By 2009 the Russian human-rights activist Natalia Estemirova, 50, had documented hundreds of cases of abuse in Chechnya, the breakaway Muslim republic that was crushed by Russian troops in 2000. She also worked with Amnesty International and Human Rights Watch. Estemirova, of Russian-Chechen parentage, had taught history in the republic's capital, Grozny, before becoming a journalist. She was a friend of Anna Politkovskaya, the Moscow journalist assassinated in 2006. Estemirova had received the inaugural Anna Politkovskaya Award in 2007 in London from the Reach All Women in War organization. She also was given an award in 2005 for her work from members of the European Parliament.

Natalia Estemirova received death threats and spent several months in England, but her dedication to human rights drew her back to the dangerous region of Chechnya.

The Kidnapping

Estemirova, known as Natasha to her friends, left her small apartment in Grozny at about 8:30 A.M., on July 15, 2009, to go to the bus stop for the 20-minute ride to her office where she worked for Memorial, a Russian human-rights organization. However, four gunman were waiting. They forced her into a white Russian-made Zhiguli car and sped off as she cried out that she was being kidnapped. The car was waved through several police checkpoints as it headed for the neighboring republic of Ingushetia.

Execution-Style Killing. Once over the border, the kidnappers stopped near the city of Nazran, marched

Dozens of demonstrators hold placards bearing Estemirova's photo during a rally commemorating her life in Moscow in August 2009.

Estemirova off the road with her hands tied and shot her execution-style twice in the head at close range. Her body was found at 5:20 P.M., in the woodlands beside the road. Estemirova's husband had been killed in the First Chechen War (1994–96). She is survived by their daughter, Lana, who was 15 when her mother was murdered.

The Investigation

Ramzan Kadyrov, the Chechen president installed by the Kremlin after he switched sides from the rebels, announced that he was taking charge of two separate investigations of the murder: one that would be official and one unofficial "according to Chechen traditions." Kadyrov, who is also suspected of ordering the abduction and assassination, said he would bring Estemirova's "cynical" killers to justice.

Russian Reaction. In Russia, President Dmitri Medvedev expressed outrage over the killing and said he would have Russia's chief prosecutor lead a top-level

Estemirova's death is lamented at a press conference in Moscow on July 16, 2009, by human-rights leaders (left to right) Alexander Cherkasov, Allison Gill, and Oleg Orlov.

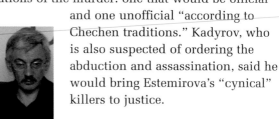

investigation from Moscow. Remaining silent was Prime Minister Vladimir Putin, who had appointed Kadyrov in 2004 as Chechen Deputy Prime Minister to suppress disorder. Official investigations of human-rights murders in the region have seldom produced arrests or any important results.

Suspects

Those who knew Estemirova agree that she was killed because of her coverage of human-rights abuses. Memorial, Estemirova's employer, believes that the Chechen government's security services were involved, because she had exposed crimes by the militias it sponsored. In recent months, she had discovered that militia members in masks and uniforms had torched the homes of those who had spoken against Kadyrov's government.

NOVAYA GAZETA

Natalia Estemirova worked with Anna Politkovskaya to investigate human-rights abuses in Chechnya for Russia's leading opposition newspaper, *Novaya Gazeta* (New Newspaper). Since 2003 three reporters have been murdered. One of the owners, Alexander Lebedev, said his journalists are being targeted for assassination in order to force *Novaya Gazeta* to close. He added that the Kremlin "didn't give a damn" about the deaths and had not even offered its condolences. The paper now assigns bodyguards to reporters and publishes articles without reporters' names or uses pseudonyms. *Novaya Gazeta* was founded in 1993, partly financed by former Soviet President Mikhail Gorbachev, who used money awarded from his 1990 Noble Peace Prize. He has a 10 percent stake, Lebedev holds 39 percent and the staff has the remaining 51 percent. Ironically Lebedev is a former KGB agent who also purchased London's daily *Evening Standard* newspaper in 2009.

Besides the Chechen investigations, *Novaya Gazeta*'s staff have uncovered corruption within Russia and various scandals in institutions, such as Russia's International Industrial Bank. "Somebody has to call a spade a spade," said Yulia Latynina, one of the columnists, "and it will be much more dangerous to live in Russia without doing this."

In 2007 *Novaya Gazeta* was awarded the prestigious Henri Nannen Prize for outstanding journalism. The paper's importance was recognized in July 2009 when President Barack Obama granted an exclusive interview before his visit to Moscow.

In 2007 in Paris, France, "Reporters Without Borders" commemorated the 18 journalists killed in Russia since former President Putin took office, on the first anniversary of Anna Politkovskaya's murder.

People gather in Koshkeldy, Chechnya, for the funeral of Estemirova. Earlier that day, weeping mourners had carried her body through Grozny.

Militia Atrocities. For a longer period, Estemirova had gathered information on torture, kidnappings, and killings by the militias and Russian troops. The Kremlin had lifted security restrictions in April 2009, transferring more power to the militias. The militias increased the climate of fear by hunting indiscriminately for Islamist fighters among the population, often taking their victims from their homes at night. Memorial estimates that at least 86 people were kidnapped in the first nine months of 2009, with nine found dead, but most simply vanished.

Threats. Individual threats, possibly from members of the militias, had put stress on Estemirova and her daughter. Estemirova admitted that "there are moments when I feel scared." However, she considered her work too important to discontinue it, never traveling with bodyguards or giving much attention to her own safety. But she felt it was a good idea in 2008 to leave Chechnya for several months, spending the summer with her daughter in Oxford, England, where she studied English, practiced yoga, and took long walks. Her daughter and friends said these were the happiest days of her life.

"Ramzan Kadyrov Is Responsible." Estemirova had recently published a report saying Kadyrov's government had carried out revenge killings. Although it is virtually impossible to prove, human-rights journalists and campaigners believe the orders for her death must have come from the top. "Ramzan Kadyrov is responsible," claimed Memorial's director, Oleg Orlov. Estemirova had recently received threats from Kadyrov's senior aides, and in March 2008, the President summoned her to complain about her opposition to his edict forcing women to wear headscarves. At that meeting, he is alleged to have admitted: "Yes, my hands are up to the elbows in blood. And I am not ashamed of that. I will kill and kill bad people."

Seventh Victim in 10 Months. Estemirova had documented and publicized other abuses carried out by the Chechen law enforcement and security agencies controlled by Kadyrov. In fact, she was the seventh person opposing Kadyrov to be killed in 10 months. The Chechen leader was careful to respond furiously to her death, saying those who had organized the crime were a greater threat than terrorists. He added that he respected Estemirova, never directly threatened her, and he would never kill women.

Putin Blamed. The finger was also pointed at Vladimir Putin. Just hours before the journalist's death, human-rights activists had demanded that Putin be prosecuted over alleged atrocities committed in Chechnya when he was President of Russia. During a press conference in Moscow, Lyudmila Alekseyeva, head of the Moscow Helsinki Group, the oldest human-rights organization in Russia, said she blamed both Kadyrov and Putin for the killing. Putin's spokesman denied his involvement, saying he had spent a decade "bringing peace, stability, and rule of order to the troubled land of Chechnya."

Lingering Doubts

- If the Chechnyan government ordered Estemirova's death, was the Kremlin aware of this? If its investigation implicates Kadyrov, will it remove him? Why did Russia transfer more power to him in 2009?

- Western governments have condemned the killing, but can they bring pressure on Russia to protect human-rights activists in the region?

- What did Kadyrov mean by saying he would conduct an unofficial investigation "according to Chechen traditions?"

- Why did Vladimir Putin appear unconcerned about Estemirova's death, as he had about the shooting of Anna Politkovskaya?

ROBBERY

Robberies range from personal thefts of purses, cars, and household items to million-dollar heists at banks and art museums. At their worst, thieves may not hesitate to kill to get what they want. Police can be baffled by clever robbers or professional gangs, who may spend years planning and rehearsing a big-time job.

THE "CROWN JEWELS" OF IRELAND

On July 6, 1907, four days before the planned state visit of King Edward VII to Ireland, the country's so-called crown jewels were discovered missing. The infuriated monarch immediately postponed a ceremony to invest a new knight into the Order of St. Patrick.

The jewels associated with this order included pieces studded with rare gems. The highlight of the collection was the star and badge of the Order of St. Patrick. The star was formed of Brazilian diamonds with a central shamrock of emeralds and a cross of rubies; the badge also was composed of diamonds, emeralds, and rubies. The estimated worth of these jewels today would be at least $1.4 million. However, their historical value made them priceless, since they previously had been the property of Queen Charlotte, King George IV, and King William IV.

King Edward VII and Queen Alexandra visited Dublin, Ireland, for an exhibition on July 10, 1907, but the monarch called off an investiture ceremony.

Amazingly, the jewels were taken from a tower in Dublin Castle, which was considered the most secure building in Ireland. Police and soldiers were on duty around the clock, and police thoroughly inspected the premises each night. The theft was discovered by Sir Arthur Vicars, who was the Ulster King of Arms in the castle and responsible for the jewels. He had asked a messenger to return a gold collar to the safe in the library, but the man had found it unlocked. The theft was very tidy—the silk ribbon that was attached to the star had been carefully removed and replaced in the box.

A reward of $1,000 was offered for information leading to the capture of the thief, or thieves, and to the recovery of the jewels. The gems were never seen again, and it is generally feared that the ceremonial objects were broken up, and the separate jewels were sold on the black market. The safe was taken to a local police station for further examination in 1908 and returned to Dublin Castle in 2007 to be displayed in the Gardaí (police) Museum.

The Investigation

The Dublin Metropolitan Police made an extensive search of the tower, but they were unable to determine how the robbery had occurred. Detectives contacted all the Dublin locksmiths to make sure no duplicate keys had been made. They also asked the manufacturers of the safe, Radcliffe and Horner, if there was any other way the safe could have been opened, because it had not been forced. But no leads came from these investigations.

The police asked for Scotland Yard's assistance and circulated details about the stolen pieces to law enforcement agencies around the world. Scotland Yard's Detective Chief Inspector John Kane arrived in Dublin on July 12 at the request of the Royal Irish Constabulary, which had also joined the case. His investigation named the probable thief, but Kane left after the chief commissioner of the Dublin Metropolitan Police refused to accept his identification. The information Kane submitted has subsequently been lost.

The Suspects

The police immediately suspected an inside job, because the safe had been simply opened with a key and the doors had not been forced. The safe had been installed in the library rather than the secure strong room, because it was too large to fit through the door.

- **Sir Arthur Vicars, 43.** Vicars held the only two keys to the safe and had stored some of his mother's jewels in the safe, which were also stolen. The king wanted him suspended, and on October 23 officials informed Vicars that his services were no longer required. The royal commission (a public body) launched a sworn inquiry on January 10, 1908; Vicars refused to take the stand because the inquiry was not held in public, but other members of his staff were among the 22 individuals who did testify. However, Vicars was never charged with the theft, but the inquiry decided that he "did not

The Irish "Crown Jewels" were kept in the eighteenth-century Bedford Tower in the Upper Court Yard of Dublin Castle, supposedly the safest place in Ireland.

Sir Arthur Vicars was responsible for the jewels' safety. He claimed the royal commission had made him a scapegoat, and he later became a bitter recluse.

exercise due vigilance or proper care as the custodian of the Regalia." Although no evidence was found against him, he was dismissed on January 30, 1908. Vicars lived his remaining life dishonored and under suspicion until he was shot and killed in 1921 by the Irish Republican Army (IRA) who viewed him as an important member of the establishment.

- **Francis Shackleton, 31.** Vicars's will named the robber as Shackleton, who, at the time, was his second in command. Vicars wrote that he "was made a scapegoat to save other departments responsible" and added that they had shielded the real culprit while his own life was ruined by "the wicked and blackguardly acts of the Irish Government." The potentially explosive nature of these accusations meant that they were excluded from probate in 1922 and not made public until 1976. At the time of the robbery, however, Shackleton had been visiting friends in England, so he could only have masterminded the heist. Some people believe the theft was actually committed by his friend and former army buddy Captain Richard Gorges, who was in Dublin at the time. Gorges later served time in prison for manslaughter. When Sir Arthur Conan Doyle, the creator of Sherlock Holmes, investigated the crime in 1907, he came to the conclusion that Shackleton and Gorges were guilty. But the fact that Conan Doyle was Vicars's second cousin does cast some doubt on his intentions.

There is, however, some evidence that Shackleton was involved. Before the robbery, Shackleton and Vicars had shared a house. When someone took the keys as a joke during a party in Vicars's office, removed the jewels, and mailed them back to him a few days later, Shackleton would have seen how easy it was to steal them for real. If Shackleton had pulled off the robbery, the police and government would have a quandary: His older brother was Ernest Shackleton, the famous Antarctic explorer. And to add to the situation, the suspect led a life that apparently involved homosexual activities with members of the British colonial establishment in the castle.

The regalia of the Order of St. Patrick was representative of that society's prestige. It was founded in 1783 but ended in 1922 when the Irish Free State was established.

FBI NICKNAMES FOR UNIDENTIFIED ROBBERS

Once a criminal has been given a nickname, such as Jack the Ripper or the Zodiac Killer, people are more inclined to remember him. Working on this assumption, the FBI gives clever nicknames to unknown robbers to keep them in the public mind. The Los Angeles bureau has been one of the most creative. In 2007 it asked people to be on the lookout for the "Mutton Chops Bandit," who wore a fake goatee beard and sideburns to rob several banks; and for the "Manicured Nails Bandit," who was a female Hispanic bank robber. In previous years the FBI has also pursued the "Mummy Bandit," who wore gauze over his face; the "Miss America Bandit," who was thought to be beautiful; the "Micro-Optic Bandit," who blinked a lot; and the "Michael Jackson Bandit," who wore a glove on his left hand.

California has also had the obviously named "Bad Breath Bandit" and the "Neck Brace Bandit," as well as the "Armada Bandit," who wore a U.S. Navy hat and the "Two-Dollar Bandit," who always asked for small bills.

Not to be outdone, Chicago's branch came up with memorable nicknames such as the "Bandage Bandit," who held up 13 banks with a scarf or wrap over his head; the "Lunchtime Bandit," who preferred to rob around lunchtime, the "Quick-and-Quiet Bandit," who was just that; the "Foul-Mouthed Bandit," and the "Cross-Dressing Bandit," a man who robbed banks wearing a pink and black dress with a sun hat and carried a black purse.

An FBI poster shows the "Starlet Bandit," who wore movie star sunglasses in a Hollywood robbery.

A Modern Review of the Evidence. Irish historian Sean J. Murphy reviewed the evidence and in 2008 published his conclusion that "Shackleton was able to dangle that threat of exposing a scandal over his interrogators." He was the only person that the inquiry absolved by name, calling him "a perfectly truthful and candid witness." But in 1913 he was convicted in England of defrauding a rich widow and served several years in jail for fraud.

Murphy also believes that a strong second suspect is Francis Bennett Goldney, 32, who had joined the office five months before the jewels disappeared. Goldney's evidence at the inquiry seems to give a poor impression of Vicars's character. After Goldney's death in 1918, several stolen items were found among his possessions. Like Shackleton, he was away from Dublin during the theft, but he could have organized the robbery.

Republicans vs. Unionists. The two sides of the Irish political question did not escape suspicion. Some Unionists, who supported the continuous rule of Britain, placed the blame on those fighting for an Irish republic (Republicans), since a homosexual scandal would have severely wounded the colonial establishment. Republicans, on the other hand, suggested that Unionists, who were trying to wreck Ireland's chance of self-rule, stole the jewels.

Lingering Doubts

- Was there another reason for Vicars's refusal to take the stand at the inquiry? Since he was the most important witness, why didn't the commission agree to his request for a public hearing?

- How many people knew where Vicars kept the keys to the safe? Why was he so certain Shackleton was the thief? Why was the accusation in his will kept secret for so many years?

- Why did the inquiry praise Shackleton instead of questioning his decadent lifestyle? Was this a cover-up to protect officials within the government from homosexual charges?

- What happened to the jewels? Were they sold to a wealthy collector, broken up, and distributed on the black market, or are they still hidden in England or Ireland?

D. B. COOPER

One of America's most heroic and mysterious robberies happened on November 24, 1971, when a plain-looking man wearing a dark suit, black tie, and dark raincoat approached the counter of Northwest Orient Airlines in Portland, Oregon. He identified himself as Dan Cooper and paid cash for a one-way ticket on Flight 305 to Seattle, Washington. The passenger settled into seat 18C, in the last row of the Boeing 727, and waited for the 30-minute trip to begin. He ordered a bourbon and soda and smoked a cigarette.

Authorities believe that the rugged Cascade Mountain region of Oregon was the probable landing ground of D. B. Cooper. Mount Hood towers in the background.

Shortly after 3:00 p.m., when the plane was airborne, he called a stewardess over and handed her a note indicating that he had a bomb in his briefcase and wanted her to sit with him. After she sat down with him, he opened up his cheap attaché case and showed her that it was filled with wires, a battery, and six red sticks. In a polite voice he demanded $200,000 in $20 bills by 5:00 p.m., along with four parachutes. Finally, he wanted a fuel truck ready to refuel the plane when they landed in Seattle.

The stewardess wrote the information down and conveyed the note to the pilot, who contacted Seattle airport. FBI agents met the plane with the ransom in twenty dollar bills, as requested, and the parachutes. The hijacker then exchanged all 36 passengers and 2 stewardesses for the money and instructed the pilot to fly to Mexico City. As the plane passed over southwest Washington, just north of Portland, Oregon, the hijacker strapped on two parachutes, climbed down the rear stairway that he had lowered, and—just after 8:00 p.m.—he leaped, clutching the bag of money, into the dark freezing wind and rain, falling toward the rugged woodland below.

The man who would become lionized as D. B. Cooper in folklore, film, books, and songs had pulled off one of the most famous crimes in American history. He disappeared forever into the black night, and his fate is still unknown.

The Investigation

Federal authorities and personnel from Fort Lewis, an army post in western Washington, searched hopelessly for days seeking Cooper or his remains, his parachutes, or the money. The FBI immediately put agents

Crime writer Dirk Summers holds an FBI photograph of Jack Coffelt, one of 933 suspects named through the years. Coffelt supposedly told a prison cell mate that he was Cooper.

on the investigation, code-named Norjack (Northwest hijacking). They soon learned that Dan Cooper was a bogus name. The mythical name D. B. Cooper was created as the result of a miscommunication between the police and the press.

Available Evidence. The FBI had a good physical description of the hijacker from the two stewardesses and other witnesses. He was in his mid-40s with brown eyes, standing about 6 feet (1.8 m) or just under, and weighing between 170 and 180 pounds (77 and 82 kg). In 1980 an 8-year-old boy walking along the bank of the Columbia River near Vancouver, Washington, came upon a rotting package filled with $20 bills totaling $5,800, which matched the serial numbers on the ransom money. The FBI have searched the area in vain for Cooper's body or more money, but nothing else has been recovered.

An Inexperienced Parachutist. Thanks to advances in DNA technology, the bureau reopened the case in 2007 because samples of Cooper's DNA were found on the necktie he left on the plane. This new evidence was investigated by Special Agent Larry Carr in the Seattle office. Although the FBI originally thought Cooper was an experienced parachutist and could have even been a paratrooper, Carr is convinced that Cooper was inexperienced, since he wore loafers and a trench coat to make the jump.

Cooper also failed to note that his reserve chute was sewn shut and the parachute he chose could not be steered. And jumping into a 200 mile per hour (322 kph) wind on a pitch-black night is not the typical actions of an experienced parachutist.

> FOLKS ARE ACTUALLY PULLING FOR THIS MAN. THAT'S ALL ANYBODY WANTS TO TALK ABOUT. I HEAR IT ALL DAY LONG. "HOPE HE MADE IT, HE DESERVES IT, HOPE HE GETS AWAY WITH EVERY NICKEL." LIKE HE'S SOME KIND OF ROBIN HOOD CHARACTER.
>
> —A LOCAL OREGON RESIDENT

The Mystery Continues. Over the years the public has given the FBI 10,000 possible names. The agency has also followed thousands of leads across America and interviewed hundreds of sources. The files on the case now occupy several long shelves in the basement of the FBI's Seattle field office, and they continue to grow.

Suspects

In the first five years after Cooper's jump, the FBI considered more than 800 suspects.

- **Richard Floyd McCoy, 28.** A main suspect, this former Vietnam helicopter pilot pulled a similar skyjacking less than five months

---

THE CULT OF D. B. COOPER

The steel nerves needed to leap out of a commercial jet with stolen cash into the unknown night sky quickly caught the imagination of ordinary Americans. Therefore, D. B. Cooper has risen from the ranks of ruthless hijacker to become a cult hero, ranking somewhere between the daredevil Evel Knievel and the outlaw Jesse James.

Cooper's great adventure has not been missed by commercial ventures. At least five books have retold the story—J. D. Reeds's 1980 novel, *Free Fall,* was turned into a movie the year after it was published. *The Pursuit of D. B. Cooper* tells the story of how Cooper landed safely, rejoined his wife, and headed for the Mexican border pursued by an insurance investigator, played by Robert Duvall. In 2004 the story also became a movie comedy in *Without a Paddle,* in which three men canoe down the Columbia River hunting for the elusive Cooper.

Songwriters have also penned at least a dozen tributes to Cooper. Todd Snider envisioned a pleasant ending for the hijacker in his 2000 song "D. B. Cooper," imagining him settled near Portland, Oregon:

> *Not far away from the City of Roses,*
> *A light shined from a house out in the rain.*
> *It was D. B. Cooper*
> *Drinking champagne.*

But surely the most whimsical tribute is an annual remembrance in the small town of Ariel in southern Washington state. D. B. Cooper Days take place each November at the Ariel Store and Tavern on State Highway 503. Confident that Ariel was on the flight path and that Cooper bailed out nearby, townspeople drink to his health, hold a look-alike contest, and wear special T-shirts.

This FBI composite sketch of D. B. Cooper was one of several the agency created and distributed widely. Some suspects have resemblances to the features shown in the sketch.

after Cooper's disappearance. McCoy demanded $500,000 and four parachutes, escaping in a dive over Provo, Utah. FBI agents tracked McCoy and the money down and arrested him, but he did not fit the description and had a solid alibi. He received a 45-year prison sentence for his Utah skyjack, but escaped and was killed in a shootout. The 1991 book, *D. B. Cooper: The Real McCoy* claimed that McCoy was Cooper because he kept newspaper clippings of the hijacking, and McCoy's family claimed the mother-of-pearl tie clasp left in the Northwest Orient plane by Cooper belonged to McCoy.

- **Duane L. Weber, 47.** According to Weber's wife, he confessed to being Cooper on his deathbed in 1995, although she only went public with the story in 2000. She claimed to be able to recall evidence to back up the claim. The FBI analyzed his DNA and fingerprints and dropped Weber as a suspect when the samples did not match Cooper's.

- **Kenneth Christiansen.** In 2004 Lyle Christiansen told the FBI that his brother, Kenneth, was Cooper "without a doubt." On Kenneth's deathbed in 2004, he had told his brother, "There is something you should know, but I cannot tell you." Kenneth was a former paratrooper who first worked as a Northwest Orient flight attendant and later as a purser. Agents were impressed by his similarity to their composite sketch, but he was shorter and did not have brown eyes.

Lingering Doubts

- After planning the hijack details carefully, wouldn't Cooper select a drop zone in advance? Did he have an accomplice waiting on the ground to meet him at a designated place?

- Why was it so difficult to uncover Cooper's real identity, since the FBI had an accurate composite sketch, his DNA, and his fingerprints?

- Kenneth Christiansen had many similarities to Cooper but not height and eye color. Could witnesses have gotten these descriptions wrong?

- Why was the parachute or a body never found? Why was only some of the money recovered? What happened to the rest of the money?

BRITISH BANK IN BEIRUT

One of the largest bank heists in history occurred on January 20, 1976, when a commando team blasted into the headquarters of the British Bank of the Middle East in Beirut, Lebanon. At the time Beirut was in the throes of a civil war between Christian and Muslim militants, and gunmen were roaming the dark battle-ravaged streets of the city's financial district. The commandos knew that Syria was mediating a truce that would halt the urban jungle conditions, so they had to move quickly. They attacked a bank located on Rue Riad al-Sohl, commonly known as Bank Street.

Eight soldiers, dressed in military fatigues with no rank or unit identifying marks, blasted through a wall that the bank shared with the Catholic Capuchin Church. The soldiers were each armed with a high-powered Browning pistol and an American-made M16 assault rifle with an attached grenade launcher.

The attack on the bank involved mortars and grenades. Once inside, the robbers bypassed the vault's thick metal door, using plastic explosives to blow through a wall adjacent to the vault. Some accounts say that Corsican safecrackers and locksmiths assisted them. In the fourth hour of the attack, the robbers used crowbars to raid the safe-deposit boxes, where jewelry dealers and wealthy Lebanese kept their jewels, gold, and large amounts of cash. One single box reportedly

The bank was badly wrecked by the explosion and resulting fire. The robbers blasted a gaping hole in the wall of the vault four hours after the raid had begun.

contained $8 million in jewels and cash, while another, overlooked by the robbers, held $400,000 in Lebanese money.

Because of the general chaos on the streets at the time, the gang was able to load up three trucks over two days with the bank's riches—mostly gold bullion but also cash, jewels, and stocks and bonds. Various guesses have been made at the value of the robbery, but Lucien Dahdah, a former Lebanese finance minister, estimates the total value to be around $50 million (more than £100 million today). None of the stolen items has been recovered, and no one has been arrested.

The Suspects

The warring groups quickly blamed each other. Muslim forces claimed the Christian Phalangist militia had carried out the operation, while the Christian forces put the blame on the Democratic Front for the Liberation of Palestine (DFLP), a Muslim militia. Despite these counter-accusations, some Lebanese believed the Christians and Muslim foes had put aside their differences to pull off the caper together.

- **The Palestine Liberation Organization (PLO).** A common theory is that the robbers were from Yasser Arafat's PLO. Neil Livingstone and David Halevy, who believe the amount stolen was actually

$850 million, put this forward in their 1990 book, *Inside the PLO*. The PLO has also been named by the Lebanese Forces, a Christian organization. That theory, although it has never been proved, is that Arafat's bodyguards, known as Force 17, hired Corsican safecrackers and flew them to Beirut to break into the vault. The riches are said to have been divided, with the PLO taking two thirds and the Corsicans keeping one third. The DFLP supposedly made an effort to control the riches, but the book alleges in March 1976 the PLO loaded its takings onto a charter aircraft, along with Arafat and other officials, and flew to Geneva, Switzerland. At this point the PLO presumably deposited their loot in secret bank accounts. Some of it was also supposedly placed in accounts in Nicosia, Cyprus; Athens, Greece; Düsseldorf, West Germany; and even Beirut. In the months following

IDENTIFYING BANK ROBBERS

Security cameras are the quickest way to identify bank robbers. Even blurred images captured on closed-circuit television (CCTV) cameras have led to identifications. Few robbers are able to disable or turn them off. In October 2004 Kevin O'Donoghue, 33, the security supervisor for a Japanese bank in London, England, used his inside knowledge to tamper with CCTV cameras. He did this to help the computer hackers whom he had brought in to steal $343.5 million (£229 million), but he failed to eradicate all their images. All seven gang members were arrested, and after all their efforts, their illegal computer transfers failed.

Marked money has been the downfall of many robbers. Recorded serial numbers help lead police to those who spend the bills. Invisible marks can also be placed on the money, but dye provides a more spectacular way of marking it. Police in Montreal, Canada, arrested two men in March 2000 after the bank they robbed gave them a bundle of money with an exploding dye pack inside it. Less than two hours later, the robbers tried to pay at a motel with the ink-stained bills, and the desk clerk called the police.

Bank robbers today also have to contend with modern technology, such as the Global Positioning System (GPS), which uses navigation satellites. When a robber hit a bank in Cincinnati, Ohio, in May 2005, the teller dropped a GPS device into the bag of money, and police found the robber in just 42 minutes. He was apprehended at a car dealership, returning the car he had taken for a test drive and had used for his getaway. When he was arrested, police said money began spilling out of his pockets.

CCTV cameras have become a common fixture along the streets of Britain.

British writer Damien Lewis said he was told about the SAS's role in the bank robbery by an aging SAS solder who met him in a cafe in London.

the robbery, it is alleged that the PLO sold many of the stocks and bonds back to the original owners for 20 or 30 cents on the dollar. The Lebanese Forces account claimed that Arab governments and officials were eager to buy them back because the original owners had obtained them illegally in the first place. The disclosure of such large amounts and the companies that were connected to those governments would prove to be a source of great embarrassment.

- **The British SAS.** An unusual suspect is Britain's Special Air Services (SAS), a small, elite, and clandestine force that is used for unconventional warfare, special reconnaissance, and counter-terrorism. Damien Lewis, journalist, documentary filmmaker, and author, has written a novel called *Cobra Gold* that has the SAS robbing the British Bank of the Middle East. According to Lewis, a source within United Kingdom Special Forces (UKSF) contacted him and claimed that a nine-man SAS unit had been sent from its Cyprus base to infiltrate Beirut and rob the bank. The source alleged that the bank was holding terrorist documents that were valuable to the British government because they detailed the finances of several terrorist groups, including the PLO and the Popular Front for the Liberation of Palestine (PFLP).

  Besides taking the documents, it is said that the soldiers also emptied the vault and transferred the loot into a landing craft that took it to a waiting ship. Although it was delivered to the base, he alleges in the book that the SAS members kept a small amount of gold hidden for themselves. But, after pulling off such a difficult and dangerous operation, the men received no significant disciplinary action. Lewis claims that two other members of the raid later verified the story. He believes this is why very little news has even been released about the world's largest bank robbery, which he said might total 10 times the $50 million estimate.

- **Various criminal and political groups.** Among other groups that have been suspected of the heist are the Russian Mafia, the Irish Republican Army (IRA), the Sicilian Mafia, the Corsican Mafia, and the Israeli intelligence agency, MOSSAD.

THE ISABELLA STEWART GARDNER MUSEUM

St. Patrick's Day revelers were still celebrating in Boston, Massachusetts, at 1:00 A.M., on March 18, 1990, unaware that the biggest art robbery in history was just getting underway at the Isabella Stewart Gardner Museum. On duty inside were two inexperienced guards: one making his rounds, and the other sitting in an office next to the museum's side entrance. At 1:24 A.M., two men wearing Boston police uniforms pressed the buzzer and told the guard they were responding to a reported disturbance. He opened the door, which was contrary to museum regulations, and called the other guard, as the "policemen" requested. The robbers, who showed no weapons, told the guards they were under arrest and handcuffed them before revealing their plans to rob the museum. They took the victims into the basement and used duct tape to bind their mouths and eyes before handcuffing them to pipes.

The thieves then took a leisurely 81 minutes to roam around two of the museum's three floors and select 11 artworks and two ornaments. Today

A security guard stands outside the Dutch Room of the Isabella Stewart Gardner Museum, where robbers stole treasured art objects early in the morning.

BOSTON POLICE SPECIAL OPERATIONS DO NOT CROSS   BOSTON POLICE

the total heist is thought to be worth approximately $500 million. The artworks included five drawings by Degas, three paintings by Rembrandt (including his only seascape), a Vermeer, a Govaert Flinck, and a Manet. The ornaments were a Chinese Ku, or beaker, and a gilded eagle taken from a Napoleonic banner.

The robbers handled the canvases roughly, smashing frames and glass and leaving shreds of canvas behind. When an alarm beeped as they took down the Rembrandt, the thieves smashed the device. Its purpose was to warn when visitors came too near the paintings, and no other alarms existed to warn that the masterpieces were being removed. The only panic button was behind the guards' desk, and this remained inactivated.

Before they left, the raiders removed the videotapes that the security cameras had taken both inside and outside the building. Although they also ripped out a computer printout from a motion detector, their movements remained on the computer's hard drive and showed that it took them two trips to carry out the art and that they finally left at 2:45 A.M. The following morning a security officer and maintenance worker arrived, found the guards, and called the police at 8:15 A.M.

An empty frame is all that remains of one of the stolen Rembrandts. The robbers smashed many of the frames and damaged parts of the valuable paintings.

The Investigation
The FBI began looking into the heist without requesting assistance from the Boston or Massachusetts police. However, this soon changed, private detectives came on the case, and even Interpol has added its European expertise over the last several years. These efforts are supported by a $5 million reward offered by the museum and its insurance companies for the safe return of all the objects in good condition. A portion of the reward is offered for individual items.

Myles Connor, a suspect, was the son of a policeman and the brother of a priest. A known thief, he was often seen around art galleries and museums admiring the paintings.

FBI agents have kept on searching for both the suspects and artworks without success. "All logical leads have been followed through to conclusion," the agency stated, "with no positive investigative results." Their agents still visit museums and galleries to make sure the missing paintings are not on display, and they even go into private homes. "I've been all over the country," said FBI Special Agent Geoffrey J. Kelly, including trips to Ireland and France. Another agent was dispatched to Japan.

A Possible Lead. Investigators have tracked hundreds of leads and dealt with dozens of fake intermediaries who said they knew where the art was located. Perhaps the best lead was an anonymous letter sent to the museum in April 1994, saying the writer would give back the paintings in return for $2.6 million and full immunity from prosecution. The letter included accurate details about the paintings and the international art world. It told museum officials to publish a code in the *Boston Sunday Globe* newspaper if they were interested, which they did. Then a second letter arrived expressing anger over police reaction to the first letter, and no more was heard from the anonymous correspondent.

Dead End. Agents and detectives also interviewed numerous people, including past and current employees of the museum. Many were given

> THE IMPOSSIBLE THING ABOUT THE CASE IS THAT THERE WERE SO MANY POSSIBILITIES. IT WAS ABSOLUTELY BAFFLING. I LITERALLY WORKED DAY AND NIGHT. IT WASN'T A TASK; IT WAS A PASSION . . . YOU GET INVOLVED IN SOMETHING LIKE THIS. IT'S A PART OF YOUR LIFE. . . .
>
> —FBI AGENT DAN FALZON

THE FBI'S ART THEFT PROGRAM

The FBI estimates that the black market for stolen art is worth an annual $6 billion, with 50,000 heists a year. It has an entire team dedicated to finding stolen objects under their Art Theft Program, located in the bureau's headquarters in Washington, D.C. This was a two-person operation until the 2003 looting of 14,000 works from the Baghdad Museum in Iraq. The bureau then realized that international art thefts required more attention, so the rapid-deployment Art Crime Team (ACT) was established in 2004 and now has 13 members assigned to different U.S. regions.

Bonnie Magness-Gardiner views stolen terra-cotta figurines that were recovered.

These special agents receive training in art and art recovery, which includes learning the difference between an engraving and an etching, as well as how thieves place stolen works in the international art market. "Art easily moves across state and international boundaries," said Bonnie Magness-Gardiner, manager of the Art Theft Program. "Having this network of agents has been very effective."

By 2009 the program had recovered more than 1,000 items with a value over $222 million (£135 million). These have ranged from a painting by the Spanish artist Goya to almost 700 pre-Columbian artifacts. An impressive cold case solved by the team was reclaiming North Carolina's Bill of Rights, which was stolen by Union soldiers in 1865 in the final days of the Civil War. When two antiques dealers offered the work for $4 million in 2003, an undercover FBI agent posed as a millionaire philanthropist and recovered the valuable document, thus closing the 138-year-old case.

The program also maintains the National Stolen Art File (NSAF), which is a computerized index of stolen art and cultural property in the United States and worldwide. This record consists of images, descriptions, and investigative case histories. Law enforcement agencies in the United States and other countries can search the NSAF files.

polygraph exams that yielded no positive results. The FBI lab also holds the forensic evidence recovered by the Boston Police Department, including latent fingerprints that were exposed by fingerprint powder and other means on the broken frames. These did not match any in the national database, and the guards said the robbers wore gloves.

The statute of limitations for prosecuting the thieves ran out in the mid-1990s, and the U.S. attorney in Boston now says he will not charge anyone who offers to return the paintings.

The Suspects

Passersby on the night of the robbery saw the car waiting outside the museum and provided descriptions of the two men seen in police uniforms. One was in his late 20s or early 30s, between 5 feet 7 inches (1.7 m) and 5 feet 10 inches (1.78 m) tall, with short black hair, a mustache (which seemed false) and glasses; the other man was in his 30s, approximately 6 feet (1.8 m) tall, with black hair and also an apparently false mustache.

- **Myles Connor, 47.** This Boston thief was a serious suspect. Although he was in jail during the robbery, Connor claimed in 1997 to have thought the idea up and passed it on to another criminal, Bobby Donati, 50, who hired robbers for the job. Donati was murdered in 1991.

- **William Youngworth, 33.** A career criminal who was associated with Connor, Youngworth claimed in 1997 that he held the stolen art and showed a rolled-up canvas to a *Boston Herald* reporter as proof. He also provided paint chips from what he claimed to be one of the stolen paintings, but an FBI analysis proved these were fake.

- **The Irish Republican Army (IRA).** Boston has a strong connection with the IRA due to its large Irish-American community; also this terrorist group had previously stolen valuable paintings in 1974 from an estate outside Dublin. The FBI followed this hunch without success.

Lingering Doubts

- Was the museum heist an inside job? Why didn't the guards press the panic button or offer resistance to the unarmed thieves?

- What happened to the artworks? Have they been sold or destroyed? Is this indicated by the letter writer breaking off contact with the museum?

- Why did the museum hire inexperienced guards? Why weren't there alarms installed to protect their masterpieces from theft?

- Does the rough handling of the paintings indicate that the thieves were not used to dealing with works of art?

SECURICOR ARMORED VAN

On July 3, 1995, two employees in a blue armored van were making a delivery to the Midland Bank's check-clearing center in Salford, part of Greater Manchester, England. The van was operated by Securicor, a company that transports cash and other valuables. As a guard entered the building at 8:05 A.M., an armed gang of three robbers wearing black ski masks swooped on the van, knocked on the window, and pointed a pistol at the driver's head, forcing him to open the door. They directed him to drive them to a nearby dead-end street where they blindfolded him, bound him with tape, and handcuffed him to a lamppost. Next they transferred 29 bags and some boxes of cash into their white Ford Transit Connect van, which was driven away by a fourth robber. The raiders' loot totaled $6.6 million (£4.4 million) in cash and $3.3 million (£2.2 million) in checks—making it the largest robbery ever carried out in Europe at that time.

The same day, Securicor offered a $375,000 (£250,000) reward for information leading to the arrest and conviction of the gang members.

The Investigation

A workman who witnessed the guard being handcuffed alerted the police, and they soon found the abandoned van with its license plates removed. The witness described one of the thieves as 5 feet 7 inches

The armed gang targeted a Securicor van similar to this one. The extremely professional raid was planned for a morning when the van held a large amount of money.

LAUNDERING STOLEN MONEY

Money laundering is the classic way to disguise stolen or illegally obtained money as legal funds. Bank robbers, con men, drug rings, and the Mafia, to name but a few, are known for money laundering. When money is laundered electronically, actual cash is never touched. Instead the illegal money is passed through multiple electronic transactions, which is often done by setting up shell companies or overseas bank accounts.

An international example of this activity came to a head in May 2009 when a federal court in Las Vegas, Nevada, sentenced two former managers of the Bank of China and their wives for money laundering and other crimes, including passport fraud. The Chinese men devised a scheme to defraud their bank of $485 million and laundered it through a dummy corporation in Hong Kong and bank accounts in Canada, the United States (as well as Las Vegas casinos), and other countries. Next, they immigrated to the United States on false passports.

Criminals are also now using the Internet to launder money, asking citizens in other countries to "transfer funds" or "process payments" that they cannot carry out as a foreign national. These appeals ask for the victim's bank account number and promise a payment that never arrives.

Xu Guojun was one of the Bank of China managers convicted of money laundering in 2009.

(1.7 m) tall, with an Irish accent and wearing a blue parka; another man was almost 5 feet 10 inches (1.78 m) tall and was wearing a black parka and black trousers; while a third man was of mixed race, about 6 feet (1.8 m) tall and spoke with a northern English accent.

Operation Volga. The Greater Manchester Police investigation, known as Operation Volga, lasted four years. Officers said the robbery was well planned and daring, since it was pulled off during the morning rush hour. However, the gang left another $1.5 million (£1 million) behind as they hurried to escape.

The Suspects

- **Graham Huckerby, 42.** The main suspect at the time was the Securicor driver. Detectives believed that Huckerby, a former policeman from Prestbury, Greater Manchester, was the inside man who had accepted $3,600 (£2,400) from the gang to provide them with information. An undercover policeman joined Securicor and found out that Huckerby had failed to carry out normal emergency procedures for a robbery and let the raiders break into his van. Huckerby told police that the gang had said they had taken his colleague hostage and if he did not let them into the van, they would "blow his head off." He also thought the raiders had bundled his coworker into the back of the van. Although Huckerby insisted he was a terrified victim, detectives noted that soon after the robbery he made a series of bank deposits and took a three-week vacation in the United States.

- **James Power, 60.** Also labeled a suspect, Power, from nearby Bury, was thought to be Huckerby's "handler" and an accomplice in setting up the raid.

The Trials

Four years after the robbery, police arrested 12 people living in Greater Manchester and London's East End. Their ages ranged from the 30s to mid-50s. Seven were charged in connection with the robbery. Three people were released and the other four were tried in 2001. Two were found not guilty and the other two, Huckerby and Power, were freed because no verdicts were reached.

Graham Huckerby was supported by his partner, Luci Ropert. She insisted that he was as much of a victim as the bank. "If Graham can be convicted," she said, "then anyone can be."

Huckerby and Power's Retrial.

In 2002 Huckerby was retried along with Power. The prosecution's case centered on the driver giving the gang access to the van and not operating the security system. Huckerby claimed this happened because he feared for his life and that of his colleague. He also said he was still suffering psychologically from a raid five months earlier, when a coworker was hit on the head with a sledgehammer and stabbed in the chest. The prosecution also said Huckerby often telephoned Power. No transcripts existed, and both men testified that the calls only involved social plans like meeting at a pub for drinks.

"Jet-Set" Lifestyle. The Greater Manchester Police claimed Huckerby had had financial problems before the raid, and the gang had paid him to help. The prosecution in the 2002 trial noted he had deposited $3,600 (£2,400) into his bank account to pay debts and live a jet-set lifestyle with foreign vacations. The money's source could not be traced, and Huckerby claimed his mother gave him $900 (£600) to buy furniture and the other $2,250 (£1,500) was repayment of money he had lent to a friend. The friend was called as a defense witness and produced records of the repayments. Huckerby also proved his "jet-set lifestyle" consisted of two vacations—a trip to stay with his cousin in Los Angeles and one week in Corfu.

Investigative journalist Don Hale and Susan Kelly, the sister of Graham Huckerby, successfully campaigned for Huckerby's release. This also resulted in James Power being freed.

Found Guilty. Seven years after the crime, in March 2002, Huckerby and Power were both convicted and given 14-year sentences. They were also ordered to pay $75,000 (£50,000) or serve an additional 15 months. The judge said he had "no doubt this offense was masterminded by more criminally sophisticated people than you two" and noted that Power had links to criminals and the ability to manipulate Huckerby.

Justice Prevails. Huckerby and Power were granted an appeal in 2004. During more than two years in jail, Huckerby suffered from depression and required medication to control it. It was only after the trial that Huckerby was diagnosed as suffering from Post Traumatic Stress Disorder (PTSD) from the first attack, and during the appeal, three judges considered new medical evidence from expert witnesses about his state of mind during the robbery. Both Huckerby and Power had their convictions overturned, and the $75,000 (£50,000) confiscation payments were also set aside.

No one else has ever been convicted of the robbery, and the money has not been recovered.

Lingering Doubts

- Why did the police and prosecution base most of their case on Huckerby's understandable fear that the armed gang would kill him if he refused their demands?

- Why didn't the police investigate Huckerby's valid explanations about the money he deposited and his telephone calls to Power?

- Huckerby explained the stress he had suffered from the first attack, so why did medical experts diagnose his Post Traumatic Stress Disorder only after he was convicted?

THE NORTHERN BANK OF BELFAST

At 10:00 P.M., on Sunday, December 19, 2004, three masked men arrived at a house in the Poleglass housing project on the outskirts of Belfast, Northern Ireland. This was the home of Chris Ward, 24, an official at the Donegall Square West branch of the Northern Bank of Belfast. One of the men took Ward away at gunpoint, while the other two remained behind with Ward's parents, brother, and girlfriend, holding them hostage for more than 24 hours.

Ward was driven to Downpatrick in County Down, to the house of his supervisor, Kevin McMullan, 28, who had already been tied up along with his wife, Karen, by two masked men pretending to be police officers. At 11:30 p.m., Karen was taken away and held, blindfolded, for more than 24 hours in nearby Drumkeeragh Forest Park.

The next morning at 6:30 A.M., the masked men left McMullan's house after giving the two bank officials precise orders about what to do to save their loved ones— McMullan was told that if he did not comply, they would damage his wife "beyond repair." The two men went to work as normal at the bank, and at 6:00 P.M. Ward carried a gym bag containing $1.8 million (£1.2 million) in

Police tape off the side of the Northern Bank on Wellington Street in Belfast the morning after the robbery. They were told of the raid 15 minutes before midnight.

THE "INSIDE JOB"

Police know that the easiest way for robbers to enter a building is through an insider. When robbers walked casually into the Northern Bank of Belfast and took their time loading cash, investigators figured that there must have been an inside contact—so they targeted Chris Ward, an innocent kidnapping victim. Another wrongful arrest of an "inside man" involved Graham Huckerby, 42, the driver of a Securicor van robbed in 1995 in Greater Manchester, England (see page 208). He served three years before his conviction was overturned.

Despite this, detectives have used the inside job theory to capture many guilty robbers, including those involved in three famous heists in England. In November 1983 six robbers stole more than $39 million (£26 million) in gold bullion and gems from the Brinks Mat warehouse at London's Heathrow Airport, after a security guard gave them the key to the main door along with details of the security system. Two of the robbers were convicted. Arguments over the loot led to the murder of six people linked to the robbery and the suicide of two. Eight other robbers tried to rob another warehouse at Heathrow of $50 million (£33 million) in May 2004, again aided by an inside informant, but this time police were tipped off and more than 100 officers were waiting. In July 1987, in a fashionable London district, $40 million (£26.7 million) was stolen from safe-deposit boxes at the Knightsbridge Safe Deposit Center with the help of the managing director, who was heavily in debt.

Inside jobs are sometimes more audacious. The Soboba Casino in San Jacinto, California, was robbed of $1.5 million in August 2007, when an armed casino worker, Rolando Ramos, 25, bound five other employees with duct tape. He escaped but was soon apprehended.

CCTV footage captures the Brinks Mat robbery at Heathrow Airport in London.

cash outside and handed it to a gang member at a bus stop. This was apparently a trial run.

Afterward, they let the gang into the bank and vaults. McMullan waited in the bank's loading bay, where crates full of bills totaling millions were stored—he even had a discussion with one of the security guards who came by. An hour later a white truck pulled up to collect the money and then returned for a second pickup. The money that was taken out in garbage bags was mostly uncirculated Northern Bank bills and also pounds, dollars, and Euros. The total take was $39.75 million (£26.5 million) and is one of the largest cash robberies in British history.

Security footage revealed the image of Chris Ward as he left the bank carrying the gym bag full of cash. He turned this over to a gang member in a trial run.

At about 8:10 P.M., a couple out shopping saw two men, who appeared to be wearing wigs, hanging suspiciously around a van next to the bank. They reported this sighting to a parking-meter attendant, who told the police. Two police officers arrived at the bank at 8:18 P.M., just missing the gang who had left, so they decided that nothing was wrong. Roadside closed-circuit TV cameras, however, captured the van leaving Belfast.

That night, at around 11:00 P.M., Karen McMullan, who was suffering from exposure and shock, stumbled out of the forest park after being released and sought help at a nearby house. Her car was later found burned out in the park. Police were alerted to the bank raid 45 minutes later and immediately started hunting for the robbers. However, six hours had passed since the robbery, and the gang had disappeared.

The Investigation

In January 2005 Northern Ireland's Chief Constable Hugh Orde announced at a press conference that the Irish Republican Army (IRA) was guilty, a view that was shared by both the British and Irish governments. Orde said the police were considering the IRA theory only because this made "operational sense." The terrorist organization had previously been blamed for, but denied, a similar robbery in May 2004 of a large store, where hostages were held and around $8 million (£5.3 million) was stolen.

Chief Constable Hugh Orde told the press that the IRA was behind the robbery. During the trial of Chris Ward, however, this alleged connection was never mentioned.

Police Raids. In February 2005 police conducting raids on IRA money-laundering operations in the Republic of Ireland discovered more than $3 million (£2 million) in unmarked bills that they believed was from the Northern Bank robbery, but they could not confirm this. Seven suspects were arrested during the raids. That same month, $100,000 (£67,000) was found in the bathroom of the Newforge Country Club, which was run by the police athletic association. The money proved to be from the heist, and detectives decided it was most likely planted there to throw them off the real trail.

In March 2005 the Northern Bank redesigned the style and color of their bills to prevent the robbers from spending their loot.

The Suspects

Police arrested 10 people during their investigations, but only one person was ever accused of the robbery—Chris Ward, the bank official kidnapped from Poleglass. The police released Dominic McEvoy, 23, who was accused in November 2005 of taking the McMullans hostage, and Martin McAliskey, 40, who was charged in the same month for being responsible for the robbery van. The Public Prosecution Service withdrew both charges against these men within days due to lack of evidence.

The white truck (front left) used in the bank robbery was captured on CCTV as it neared the city center heading for the bank. It took two trips to collect the cash.

Circumstantial Evidence. Ward's trial began on September 9, 2008, and never mentioned any alleged IRA involvement. The evidence that the robbery was an inside job was circumstantial and involved a suspicion that Ward had arranged a late shift at the bank on the day of the robbery. CCTV had also captured him handing over the gym bag to one of the robbers. While providing testimony, his boss McMullan said the masked men had told him it did not matter if they were jailed for 30 years for murder or 30 years for kidnapping. "They made clear if the robbery did not go to plan, if they did not get away with it, they would kill Karen."

Acquittal. The trial lasted exactly a month, and on October 9, Ward was cleared of any involvement. His lawyer said Ward should have been a witness for the prosecution instead of being accused, and members of Sinn Féin—the political party associated with the IRA—and his lawyer claimed he had been scapegoated because he was a Catholic.

Review of the Suspects. With Ward's acquittal, the police have turned to other suspects. On May 12, 2009, they arrested Tom Hanlon, 42, and George Hegarty, 62, for offenses connected with the robbery, based on "suspicion of being a member of an unlawful organization [the IRA]."

Lingering Doubts

- Why weren't workers at the bank, including the security guard, not suspicious of the millions being prepared for the robbery?

- What made the policemen on patrol ignore the couple's suspicions, and why did it take so long to inform police of the robbery?

- Why would the police chief announce that his force was only interested in IRA suspects? If they were, why did they arrest Ward and not an IRA member, and then not mention the organization during his trial?

- Why was an amount of stolen cash planted at the police club? Did the robbers believe this would throw investigators off their trail?

This French miniature snuff box is similar to those stolen from Waddesdon Manor. The gold boxes, the rarest in the world, are considered irreplaceable.

WADDESDON MANOR

One of England's stately homes, Waddesdon Manor near Aylesbury in Buckinghamshire, was built at the end of the nineteenth century by Baron Ferdinand de Rothschild. He designed it to resemble a sixteenth-century French chateau to house his impressive collections of French furniture, English portraits, and other items of fine art. Its famous visitors include Queen Victoria and Winston Churchill. In 1957 the property was bequeathed to the National Trust, which preserves historic buildings and opens them to the public. Waddesdon Manor now welcomes 400,000 visitors each year. In 1990 the present Lord Rothschild, who still lives in a part of the building with his family, restored the house's ornate gardens.

The Robbery

At about 2:00 A.M. on June 10, 2003, five men wearing coveralls and wearing balaclavas pulled off a spectacular robbery, using a scaffolding pole attached to their car to smash a window in the west wing. In less than four minutes the thieves broke the glass of a cabinet and filled their bags with 100 French miniature gold boxes, some of which had belonged to the French Queen Marie Antoinette, and other precious items, such as French miniature paintings, gold flasks, and a gold watch studded with diamonds. The box collection is considered the rarest in the world, and the overall loss from the robbery was valued at $13.1 million (£8 million). The robbers did set off the manor's alarm system, but they got away too fast to be caught. After the heist, new alarms were installed as well as CCTV cameras at the property's gates.

The Investigation

Police realized that the burglars had meticulously planned the raid. They were certain that members of the gang had toured the house on guided tours during the weeks before the robbery. This was evident in the way they went straight to the priceless gold boxes in the tower drawing room. Officers speculated that the items were stolen to order for particular clients. The robbers had escaped in two stolen cars, and one, a blue Toyota, was discovered burned out in a nearby village.

The Reward. The devastated Lord Rothschild offered a $82,000 (£50,000) reward for the safe recovery of the items and for information leading to arrests. None of the irreplaceable boxes have been found, and detectives believe they have disappeared into the black market or were melted down for their gold value.

Waddesdon Manor in Buckinghamshire, England, is 20 miles (32 km) from Oxford. All revenue from admissions goes toward the upkeep of the house, collections, and garden.

Lord Jacob Rothschild, a member of one of Europe's most influential dynasties, accepted the help of a criminal in an effort to recover the stolen items.

Key Suspects

The police were almost certain they had identified the Waddesdon gang when they arrested a family that was allegedly notorious for plundering mansions of the wealthy from 2003 to 2006. The Johnsons were Irish-born "travelers" who had stolen approximately $131 million (£80 million) from homes, antique shops, and other sites. In 2006 they pulled off Britain's largest burglary ever when they robbed Ramsbury Manor in Wiltshire of museum-grade objects—including porcelain busts, paintings, and several clocks—valued at $48 million (£30 million). Their crimes were so audacious, that it took five police forces to pursue them in "Operation Haul."

Cleared of Waddesdon Raid. Twelve members of the 15-strong gang were found guilty in December 2007 at their trial in Bristol. Despite evidence covering more than 100 separate crimes, the prosecution could not prove their involvement in the Waddesdon robbery. Three family members who were charged—Ricky Johnson, 54, Chad Johnson, 33, and their nephew Danny O'Loughlin, 32—were found not guilty after the judge ruled some evidence could not be included. In a second trial in August 2008, the three were among five members of the gang imprisoned for other burglaries.

"Jimmy" Johnson. In January 2009 the leader of the family, Alan "Jimmy" Johnson, 56, continued to deny the group's involvement in the Waddesdon robbery. He has been in and out of prison for years, and was arrested for everything from murder and armed robbery to stealing trailers. Police blamed him for the Waddesdon theft and passed his name to Lord Rothschild as the man most likely behind the robbery. Although Johnson was in jail when it happened, detectives interviewed him there several times about his family's involvement, and 200 officers raided a trailer encampment where 60 of the Johnson clan lived in the beautiful Cotswolds area in south-central England.

Denial. Johnson was released in August 2008 after serving nearly two years for robbing post offices. Although he confessed to being an "antiques expert" who targeted grand homes for valuable items, Johnson singled out Waddesdon as a place his family never touched, saying they had been blamed by "dirty, gutless people."

Suspect Turns Detective

To clear his name, Johnson declared that he had not forgotten about Lord Rothschild's stolen gold boxes "because I'm coming for them." He also claimed to know where they were, and in a surprising move, drove to Waddesdon Manor and asked to speak with Lord Rothschild. According to *The Guardian* newspaper, the staff served Johnson, still wearing his probation tag, tea in bone china cups as he protested his innocence and promised to recover the antiques.

Ricky Johnson was the leader of the Johnson gang. He and other members were charged with the Waddesdon robbery, but found not guilty. All were later imprisoned for other burglaries.

Johnson's Search. Lord Rothschild decided to join forces with the notorious thief and worked with him through Charlie Hill, a leading private art-theft investigator. "I decided that I had to fight back," Johnson declared, adding that "the only thing I could do was find out who actually did this, get the stuff, and give it back to Lord Rothschild." Johnson, carrying letters of support from the police and Rothschild, began a search that has covered the seedier streets of several English cities, including London, Liverpool, Birmingham, and Manchester, and even traveled to Alicante, Spain. Besides proving his innocence, another incentive for Johnson is the reward, which is still being offered.

His efforts and those of the police have been futile, with officers admitting that the stolen items may never be recovered. Lord Rothschild has images and descriptions of the stolen items on the Waddesdon website (www.waddesdon.org.uk).

Lingering Doubts

- Are the police correct about the gang taking guided tours of Waddesdon or did the thieves receive inside help? Was there any forensic evidence found in the room or getaway car?

- When the three gang members were not convicted for the robbery, what evidence was thrown out by the judge and why has it been kept confidential?

- Although "Jimmy" Johnson was in jail during the burglary, was he involved in the raid as police thought? If he confessed to robbing other stately homes, why does he deny the Waddesdon crime? If he knows where the gold boxes are, has he passed this information to the police?

THE CHACARA DO CEU MUSEUM

On February 24, 2006, the first day of Rio de Janeiro's famous carnival, huge crowds of people were dancing to feverish samba rhythms in masks and fancy costumes. This provided the perfect chaos for one of Brazil's most audacious art robberies. The target was the small Chacara do Ceu Museum in what was once a hillside mansion in the Santa Teresa district. That afternoon at least four gunmen pulled off a $50 million heist.

The raiders stormed the museum shortly before closing time and took the guards by surprise, disarming them. They threatened staff and visitors with a hand grenade and briefly took several tourists hostage. The thieves then forced the staff to turn off security cameras and the alarm system. This simple act overcame a security upgrade that had been installed the previous year, when the government had spent $44.4 million to protect artworks throughout the country.

The robbers then grabbed four of Brazil's most prized paintings: *Two Balconies* by Salvador Dali, *The Dance* by Pablo Picasso, *Luxembourg Gardens* by Henri Matisse, and *Marine* by Claude Monet. The Dali and Matisse paintings had been among 10 that had been stolen from the same museum in May 1989, but they were recovered in two weeks after a tip led police to the home of an antique dealer with a long criminal record. No robbery had occurred at the museum since. The Dali was the only work by that artist on public display in Latin America, and the Matisse was one of his best early works. The gang also took *Toros,* a book of etchings by Picasso.

One museum guard who tried to stop the thieves was hit in the face. Another guard, who attempted to grab the Picasso from a robber's hands, was hit on the head with a weapon. Then, to add insult to injury, the thieves stripped the five hostage tourists of their wallets,

Rio's wild and joyful carnival was a good cover for the thieves who raided the famous museum. Approximately 100,000 people were crammed along the city streets at that time.

The Chacara do Ceu Museum, called "the mansion in the sky," sits on a hill in the Santa Teresa district, a quiet neighborhood where many artists have their studios.

cell phones, and digital cameras. "The robber who spoke to us was very calm," said David Gee of New Zealand. "I was surprised by the speed of the robbery."

No one was seriously injured during the siege, and the thieves calmly walked out into the street and disappeared among the revelers, following a passing samba parade. The museum quickly alerted the police who sent two cars to drive through the crowd searching for anyone carrying a painting. They also examined a videotape taken of the procession, but they have not been able to identify the thieves.

The Investigation

The police and museum officials believed this was a "made-to-order" contract job that was planned by mastermind specialists, probably from an international crime ring, and carried out by professionals who knew exactly what they were stealing and how to take the artworks without damaging them.

Immediate Alert. Brazilian authorities quickly went on the alert to stop the pieces from leaving the country, because the police feared the paintings would be smuggled out by air or taken overland into

FINDING THE *MONA LISA*

On August 21, 1911, one of the most-famous paintings in the world, Leonardo da Vinci's *Mona Lisa*, was simply removed from the wall of the Louvre Museum in Paris and stolen. The thief, Vincenzo Peruggia, had previously worked at the museum and was an Italian patriot who wanted the masterpiece returned to its native country. To accomplish this, he hid in the museum overnight and early the following morning took the painting off the wall. He took the painting, which was painted on wood, out of its frame. He hid it under his smock and walked out, passing an unattended guard station.

When the museum employees arrived, they saw only four iron pegs where the *Mona Lisa* had been hanging for five years, and assumed it was being cleaned or photographed. When the section head arrived, however, he was horrified to see it missing, and a resulting search found the frame and glass on a staircase. Police were summoned and a longer search revealed that the painting had vanished. They found one thumbprint on the frame, but it did not match any on file.

People gather around the *Mona Lisa* the day it was returned to Paris.

Peruggia kept his prize hidden in a trunk in his Paris apartment for two years, while police went through a useless list of suspects including the Spanish painter Pablo Picasso. The thief finally took the painting to a hotel in Florence, Italy, and offered it to a local art gallery. The owner informed the director of the city's famous Uffizi Gallery, who verified the painting and had the police arrest the thief. The *Mona Lisa* was exhibited around Italy before being returned to the Louvre on January 4, 1914. Peruggia received only a short jail sentence after explaining his motive: "Why should an Italian painting hang in a French museum?"

Argentina, Paraguay, or Uruguay—the three countries closest to Rio. "They will not be very easy to sell in Brazil," said Jean Boghici, a Brazilian art dealer, "because they are so well-known." The victims gave descriptions of the thieves to the police, who issued computer-generated images. Descriptions of the missing artworks were also sent immediately to Interpol and relayed to 182 countries. The FBI Art Crime Team has listed this heist as one of the top 10 art crimes. Meanwhile, Brazil's National Historic and Cultural Heritage Institute and friends of the museum have put up a $5,000 reward for the paintings' safe return.

A Link to Drug Traffickers. On March 6, 2006, during a reconstruction of the heist, police announced that burned fragments of three of the frames had been discovered near a bar close to the museum in the shantytown of Morro dos Prazeres. Also in March 2006, a week after the robbery, Interpol launched an unsuccessful probe after the stolen Matisse was put up for sale in an auction on the Russian website MaStak.com for four hours, where it was offered for $13 million. The Brazilian police suspected this was a collaboration between Brazilian drug traffickers and foreign buyers. Isabelle Vasconcellos, the police chief heading the investigation, said she believed the stolen works were still in Rio.

The Suspects

Detectives have never named suspects and continue to seek tips, keeping a special telephone line for the public to provide information anonymously. The Brazilian press has speculated that the heist might have been carried out by an unnamed Frenchman, who once resided in a beachside apartment in the expensive neighborhood of Ipanema.

> EVEN THE TIME OF THE THEFT WAS CALCULATED—THE CARNIVAL MADE IT EASIER TO ESCAPE AND MORE DIFFICULT TO TRACE THE WORKS. IT IS NOW VITAL TO MAKE WIDELY AVAILABLE PICTURES OF THE STOLEN PAINTINGS TO PREVENT THEIR BEING SOLD.
>
> —JOSÉ DO NASCIMENTO JR., DIRECTOR OF IPHAN (BRAZIL'S BUREAU FOR CULTURAL PATRIMONY PRESERVATION)

Lingering Doubts

- Why is a reward of only $5,000 (£3,500) being offered for such valuable paintings?

- Are the artworks still in Rio de Janeiro, as the police suspect? Since the robbery alerts remain at airports and land routes, how could they have been smuggled abroad?

- Did the museum do everything in its power to protect these pictures, their most valuable possessions? Was there an alarm button connected to the police department? Can any security work if thieves force employees to deactivate it?

- Who planned and coordinated the heist? Why have no true suspects been named and charged? Who is the mysterious Frenchman suspected by the press?

- Why was Interpol unable to trace the criminals through the Russian website that offered the stolen Matisse for sale?

FRAUD

As time goes by, methods for swindling the public have become more complex. From high-tech techniques to steal identities to illegal cash transfers and viral e-mail hoaxes, the web of deceit has grown to worldwide proportions. And even in modern times, we still have age-old frauds, such as fake products and counterfeit money.

THE VATICAN BANK SCANDAL

COUNTERFEIT "SUPERNOTES"

PIETRO PSAIER

POISONOUS PHARMACEUTICALS

HACKING INTO THE PENTAGON

THE VATICAN BANK SCANDAL

Shady dealings within the Institute for Religious Works, commonly know as the Vatican Bank, came to light in 1982 when Italy's largest private bank, Banco Ambrosiano, collapsed. The Vatican Bank was the fourth-largest shareholder in Ambrosiano, a Milan bank with operations in 15 countries. Its demise revealed that $1.3 billion was missing. The money had been lent to 10 shadowy shell (dummy) companies in Latin America, that were controlled by the Vatican Bank.

Founded in 1942, the Vatican Bank manages the Pope's investments and is a clearinghouse for donations raised by charitable orders of the church. All depositors must have a Vatican connection, and the Pope maintains a personal account. Vatican officials steadfastly denied any wrongdoing, but they did acknowledge "moral involvement" and eventually paid $244 million to the creditors of Ambrosiano as a "goodwill gesture."

Roberto Calvi, 62, Ambrosiano's secretive chairman, who was also known as God's Banker, was convicted of fraud by the Italian authorities and sentenced to a four-year suspended sentence and a $19.8 million fine for taking $28 million out of the country illegally. He attempted suicide during his short stay in jail. While he was on bail awaiting an appeal, he fled from Rome—at first to Venice and then to London via a private jet. A passing postman found him on June 18, 1982, the day after he had been stripped of his post at Banco Ambrosiano by the Bank of Italy, hanging from scaffolding beneath Blackfriars Bridge. His pockets were stuffed with bricks and $14,000 in three different currencies.

When Roberto Calvi died in London, he was living there on a bogus passport with a false name. In another effort to disguise his identity, he had shaved off his mustache.

Suicide

The day before, on June 17, his secretary, Graziella Corrocher, 55, had leaped to her death from the fourth floor of the bank's Milan headquarters. She left an angry note that accused Calvi of ruining the bank and its employees. Calvi's death was first ruled a suicide, but foul play was suspected. Five men, including three Mafia members, were tried in October 2005 for Calvi's murder and acquitted in June 2007. An Italian movie, God's Bankers, which was released in 2002, explored Calvi's ties with the Vatican Bank.

The missing money has never been recovered, and no official at the Vatican Bank has ever been prosecuted.

The Investigation

Investigators were faced with a complex web of international fraud and intrigue. They found that Calvi, after becoming director general (the company's most senior position) of Banco Ambrosiano, had the bank set up a holding company in Luxembourg to avoid Italian banking regulations. He then used it to establish banks in Switzerland, Peru, Nicaragua, and the Bahamas. He also set up shell companies in Panama, Luxembourg, and Liechtenstein. Although the companies were tiny, large loans were funneled into them—by 1982 the shell companies owed Ambrosiano approximately $1.2 billion.

"Letters of Patronage." Detectives also discovered that the Vatican Bank had given Calvi documents called letters of patronage that vouched for his good credit by stating that the Vatican Bank controlled the shell companies that were receiving the loans from Banco Ambrosiano. The letters acted as a way of guaranteeing the loans, and Calvi also used them to reassure the directors of Banco Ambrosiano's bank in Peru, who were worried about the financial strength of the companies.

Calvi had also written a letter to the Vatican Bank, relieving it of any responsibility. This letter was kept secret from Banco Ambrosiano's banks in Latin America, which were the institutions actually lending out the money. Detectives investigating the case were never able to establish that the Vatican Bank actually owned the shell companies and were involved in the fraud.

A Masonic Link? During the investigation, the police also raided the villa of Licio Gelli, who served as the grand master of a Masonic lodge called *Propaganda Due*, or P2, that was intent on taking control of Italian institutions, including banks. Police found

Scaffolding was used to remove Calvi's body from under London's Blackfriars Bridge. A postman was the first to see him hanging there at 7:30 A.M. on June 18, 1982.

Calvi's name on a secret membership list, and unconfirmed suspicions grew that P2 was involved in his death. Symbolic links were made to Blackfriars Bridge, the place where Calvi's body was found hanging, because P2 was known as the *Frati Neri* (Black Friars). The Masons also figured prominently in David Yallop's 1997 book, *In God's Name,* which was "an investigation into the murder of Pope John Paul I." The pontiff had died in 1978, only 33 days after being elected. Yallop's best seller claimed Pope John Paul I was murdered because he failed to excommunicate 100 top-ranking Vatican officials who were also Masons. These included several members of P2 who were thought to be some of the masterminds involved in the Vatican Bank scandal.

Special Panel. Pope John Paul II quickly established a 15-man panel, which had the impressive title of the Council of Cardinals for the Study of the Organizational and Economic Problems of the Holy See, to look into the scandal and other financial issues. Although the Pope's panel never released the findings of its investigation into the scandal, it still publishes an annual Consolidated Financial Statement for the Holy See and the Vatican City State Governorate.

Cover-up for the Mafia. In 2003 Italian investigators traced $70 million of the missing Ambrosiano money to banks in the Bahamas. The

Italian businessman Flavio Carboni (second from left), one of the five alleged murderers, stands with his lawyers at his trial in Rome in 2005. All defendants were judged innocent.

following year, files were stolen from the London coroner Paul Matthews who was reexamining the death of Calvi. Although he claimed that no witness statements or investigative reports were included in the stolen information, Italy's anti-Mafia police believe Matthews could have been targeted by the Mafia and covered up the theft.

Legal Action

In June 2007 a court in Rome cleared five people who had been accused of conspiring to murder Calvi. The defense said that murder had never been proven beyond a reasonable doubt.

The Innocent Archbishop. In 1987 Italian courts ruled that three Vatican Bank officials, including Archbishop Paul Marcinkus who was the American-born president of the bank from 1971 to 1989, could not be prosecuted because of the Lateran Treaty of 1929, which recognizes the Vatican as a sovereign state. This means that arrest warrants cannot be served by Italian authorities and extradition treaties cannot be enforced.

Archbishop Marcinkus had been associated with the bank for more than 20 years and was a friend of Calvi's. In 1989 Marcinkus became governor of Vatican City before retiring in 1990 to do parish work in Chicago. In 1999 he noted, "I may be a lousy banker, but at least I'm not in Jail." The archbishop died in 2006 at the age of 84 at his home in Sun City, Arizona.

The Guilty Banker. Officials at Banco Ambrosiano did not fare quite so well. Its former chairman Carlo de Benedetti was sentenced to four and a half years in prison for corruption in May 1981. Although he had only been the deputy chairman of Banco Ambrosiano for 65 days, Benedetti had invested $42 million for a 2 percent stake in the bank. He then made an illicit profit of $22.4 million when he sold his shares in January 1982, upon resigning. But in 1998 an Italian court threw out the conviction due to lack of evidence.

Carlo de Benedetti, the former chairman of Banco Ambrosiano, holds a press conference in Milan, Italy, on January 26, 2009. His prison sentence for corruption was overturned.

Lingering Doubts

- Why did the Vatican Bank admit to "moral involvement" in the scandal and pay millions to the creditors if they claimed to have done nothing wrong? Why would the Catholic Church be so involved in international finances?

- Did the Vatican Bank own the Latin American dummy companies? Why couldn't investigators determine this? Why are Italian courts forbidden to interfere in the Vatican's secret dealings? Should this be changed, and will the Vatican become more open and public about its financial details?

- How much power did the P2 Masonic lodge exert in these banking transactions? Is it possible that 100 high Vatican officials were also Masons?

- Was Pope John Paul I murdered?

- What happened to the missing money?

- Was there any symbolism in the three currencies, the bricks, the amount of money found on Calvi's body, and the Blackfriars Bridge location?

To the untrained eye, these counterfeit $100 "supernotes" resemble real bills. Despite security upgrades, the false money continues to turn up to this day.

COUNTERFEIT "SUPERNOTES"

In 1989 counterfeit American $100 bills began turning up that were copied with absolute perfection. Some had details that were even sharper than those found on real money. The first counterfeit note was discovered in a bank in Manila, the Philippines. Large batches of these "supernotes" or "superdollars" then started to appear around the world. For years the dollar has been the most counterfeited currency in the world, but this copied version was exceptional. It had just one hidden flaw: the lack of magnetic and infrared security features. This meant that special devices in American banks could automatically identify these bills as counterfeit.

Confronted with the possibility that millions of bogus bills were being released into circulation, the U.S. government seriously considered the possibility that a hostile nation or group was attempting to destabilize the

dollar as an act of economic warfare. To counter this possible threat, the U.S. Bureau of Engraving and Printing issued a new dollar series—the first changes in the appearance of the greenback since 1928—with a new style of $100 bill released in 1996. The alterations included the addition of "optically variable ink" in one corner, which changes from green to black when the bill is held at different angles.

Despite these security precautions, new supernotes continued to appear. In 2003 the bureau produced new $20 and $50 bills, with a colored background, but these were also perfectly copied. Most recently, an even higher security $100 bill has been developed. It is expected to incorporate a "motion" device containing 650,000 microlenses, which would make the image of Benjamin Franklin move depending on how light strikes it. But few expect this new feature to stop counterfeit $100 supernotes from reappearing.

Investigation

Experts from the Bureau of Engraving and Printing analyzed the workmanship on the phony bills to understand how they had been produced. They noted that the special cotton fiber paper used in the supernotes is the same as that used for real dollars. They also found the same proportion of embedded red and blue fibers in the paper that is used for security by the Treasury Department in genuine U.S. dollar bills. The special security ink used by the U.S. Bureau came from the same manufacturer, SICPA. The raised intaglio printing was an exact duplicate of the bureau's and done on the same type of expensive machine made by De La Rue Gioro in Switzerland. This type of press forces paper into ink-filled grooves on an engraved plate at very high pressure to create tiny ridges.

Suspects

U.S. Secret Service agents immediately began tracking counterfeiters across the world.

> # NOTHING THAT WE CAN PRODUCE IS PERFECT TO THE POINT NO ONE ELSE EVER COULD PRODUCE IT. WHAT WE WANT TO DO IS TO MAKE IT SO DIFFICULT THAT THEY WON'T TRY. BUT WE WOULD NEVER CLAIM THAT THIS DESIGN . . . WOULD BE PERFECT.
>
> —TOM FERGUSON, DIRECTOR, U.S. BUREAU OF ENGRAVING AND PRINTING

- **Stasi secret police.** When the Berlin Wall fell in 1989, the same year the first $100 bill appeared, the West German police discovered a precision printing plant in East Berlin that had been used by the Stasi secret police, supposedly for counterfeiting documents and personal identification. The incriminating intaglio printing machine had vanished from the plant, and experts who had worked there claimed that the supernotes had never been produced. However, detectives were convinced that the Stasi had trained printers from other Communist nations in the art of counterfeiting money.

- **North Korea.** Britain's BBC program *Panorama* aired a report in 2004 that featured a North Korean defector saying he had worked on counterfeit supernotes. Also appearing on that program was Sean Garland, a member of the Irish Republican Army (IRA), who may have been involved in carrying up to $1 million counterfeited North Korean bills into Western Europe. A year later, the U.S. Justice Department officially accused the North Koreans of producing supernotes and brought charges against Garland, saying he had wrongly told co-conspirators that Russia had produced them. After the United States requested Garland's extradition, he was arrested in Great Britain in 2009. He remains in British custody fighting extradition to the United States.

- **Iran.** U.S. authorities suspected Iranians early on of printing supernotes on equipment purchased by the Shah two decades

LAUNCHING REDESIGNED MONEY

The redesign of currency is a major undertaking for any country. It involves the design and approval of new security details on the bills, adjustments to the printing machinery, and a careful mass circulation of the replacement notes. To reassure the public, the new money needs to look familiar, but also be slightly different. The government can help the transition by launching a media campaign to explain the changes and why they are necessary.

The new U.S. $5 bill unveiled in 2007 added purple and gray to President Lincoln's image.

Since 2003 the U.S. government has distributed 80 million pieces of information about the new bills. When the new $5 bill went into circulation on March 13, 2008, the U.S. Bureau of Engraving and Printing put the word out early and often. Besides press releases and television appearances, the bureau promoted the change on its website, *www.moneyfactory.gov/newmoney,* where a video featured interviews with consumers who approved of the changes.

The first-day launch was done with flare to attract viewers. The very first redesigned $5 bill was spent at the historic site of President Abraham Lincoln's summer retreat, the Cottage at the Soldiers' Home in Washington, D.C. Michael Lambert, an assistant director of the Federal Reserve Board, spent the $5 at the Cottage's gift shop on a book of Lincoln's speeches. President Lincoln had established the U.S. Secret Service on the same evening he was assassinated. The agency's primary mission was to safeguard the nation's currency from counterfeiters.

The new $5 bill, like the other redesigned money, features the Great Seal of the United States printed in purple on the front. Small yellow 05s were added on the front and a large 5 was placed on the back in purple. When the bill is held to the light, two watermarks and a security thread can be seen.

earlier and then shipping the bills to Lebanon via Syria. In February 1996 Kenneth R. Timmerman, editor of *The Iran Brief* (a newsletter for policymakers dealing with Iran), presented this view to the congressional subcommittee that investigates banking. He said intelligence sources believe that the Iranian engravers had been trained by the U.S. Treasury Department in the 1970s, or working with the Stasi, had recruited master engravers from East Germany in the late 1980s. Timmerman revealed that one European intelligence official had told him: "The U.S. government knows it's Iran. They just don't want to admit it publicly."

- **The CIA.** One conspiracy theory even suggests that the CIA could be the source of supernotes. In *Moneymakers: The Secret World of Banknote Printing,* by German financial journalist Klaus W. Bender, the author points out that supernotes tend to show up in countries in which the United States has encountered problems and wants to influence leaders and important groups. "Could it be that they are being paid for their services in counterfeit dollar notes?" he asks, adding that the bogus money could be used by leaders in areas such as the Middle East and Africa to buy weapons from North Korea, which then funnels the supernotes back to the West. Bender also cites a rumor that just north of Washington, D.C., the CIA runs the same type of printing presses used by the U.S. Bureau of Engraving and Printing.

Lingering Doubts

- Will the United States or any other nation ever halt the flow of supernotes? Does this illegal money really threaten to destabilize American currency?

- How have counterfeiters been able to duplicate every security measure devised for dollar bills?

- Why has the United States been unable to extradite the IRA's Sean Garland? Does he actually know the original source of the false currency?

- Is it conceivable that the CIA would print supernotes and flood other countries with bogus American bills? Wouldn't Congress or other government agencies be aware of this if it were true?

- Do the isolated North Koreans have access to such sophisticated printing presses, since experts note that they have trouble printing their own currency?

PIETRO PSAIER

When the massive tsunami devastated Sri Lanka on December 26, 2004, among the thousands reported to have died was Pietro Psaier, an Italian pop artist closely associated with Andy Warhol. His reputation peaked in the 1990s when his works were sold around the world by famous auction houses such as Sotheby's, Christie's, and Bonhams. Psaier's fans, who include the actor Jude Law, made his work more famous and newsworthy. After his death, a British auction raised $180,000 (£123,000) for 235 of his works. He has become another success of Warhol's art-producing studio, the Factory—if Psaier existed.

Some art experts have cast doubts. Not one of Warhol's surviving staff say they ever heard of Psaier. He is not mentioned in any Warhol biography, and the Warhol Museum in Pittsburgh, Pennsylvania, has no documentation of him. "Warhol saved hundreds of thousands of bits and pieces and recorded conversations," said the museum's archivist, Matt Wrbican. "We have found no evidence of Pietro Psaier."

The 2004 Indian Ocean tsunami is estimated to have killed at least 230,000 people in 14 countries. Conveniently, Pietro Psaier's body is said to be among the many bodies never recovered.

The Evidence

Were the art lovers who purchased original Psaier paintings the victims of a clever hoax? One person trying to prove Psaier's existence is dealer and auctioneer John Nicholson of Fernhurst, Surrey, England, who since 2004 has sold some 1,500 works attributed to Psaier, including a painting of Marilyn Monroe, for $16,000 (£10,000). In one press release, he claims, "Psaier was a skilled artist with watercolors, oils, and pencils. Some critics say without Psaier...Warhol could never have maintained the production of the Factory commercial output."

Suspect Therapy. Nicholson received most of the paintings from Peter Psaier, who claims to be the painter's son. Nicholson also has a letter from Dr. Carlos Langelaan Alvarez, who is said to be Psaier's therapist, that states he treated him between 1979 and 1992 for "drug psychosis"

Andy Warhol is standing in front of a piece of his own art, "Statue of Liberty." Not one from his group or staff claim to have ever met Psaier.

and saw Psaier and Warhol together in Madrid in 1983. In a 1990 interview in a Madrid newspaper, a man calling himself Psaier gave his age as 26, which is far too young to have joined Warhol's group. Finally, only a grainy photograph of the two men exists as proof (see page 238).

Bogus Biography? It is reported that Peter Psaier has also put together a slim biography of the artist for Nicholson, the auctioneer. It says Psaier was born near Rome on August 21, 1936, and was the son of an automobile designer. In 1960 he immigrated to New York and had a chance meeting with Warhol in a café where Psaier was working. The two began to produce joint works and became lovers, but in 1963 Psaier fathered Peter with an unknown mother. In 1969 the artist was imprisoned in Spain for producing pornographic pictures. In 1974 he was a guest at the Italian-American Institute of Art's 56th annual award in New York. He joined Warhol in his exhibition in 1983 in Madrid, Spain. His life then ended 20 years later with the tsunami in 2004.

A closer look at this brief evidence reveals serious flaws. Most of Psaier's life, including his education, is unknown. The existence of the Italian-American Institute of Art cannot be traced. Critics have dismissed as a fake the only known photograph of the two artists. And Psaier's body was never recovered after the tsunami.

It is understood that Nicholson plans to publish a book about Psaier, but crucial archival material may be missing, such as birth and death certificates, exhibition catalogs, and other primary sources. Furthermore, doubt has been cast on some statements by Nicholson. For example, he claimed that Psaier had exhibited 16 acrylic pictures in September 2004 at the Passion of the Christ at Our Lady of Malibu Church in California. However, the pastor who has been at the church for 12 years, said he had never heard of Psaier or the exhibition.

PROTECTING YOUR IDENTITY

Identity theft is possibly the largest white-collar crime in the United States. The U.S. Federal Trade Commission (FTC), which maintains a database of such cases, estimates that one in six Americans (50 million people) became a victim of identity theft in 2009. In the previous year, approximately 10 million people suffered from identity-theft crimes, forcing them to spend an average of $1,200 and 175 hours to correct the problem.

Large corporations are prime targets for identity-theft gangs. However, individuals can also make themselves easy victims by discarding documents containing personal information that could be used to access their bank accounts, purchase goods, apply for loans or government benefits, and obtain jobs. Information protection agencies around the world recommend shredding a range of documents, including medical records, credit-card statements, telephone bills, bank statements, and old mailing labels from magazines.

They also offer other tips, advising you to remove your name from mailing lists, do not carry personal information unless needed, order a copy of your credit report regularly, and avoid giving out personal information in the mail, over the telephone, or on the Internet.

Safe surfing includes looking for the lock icon on Web pages and not responding to spam, phishing messages (a process where a site masquerades as a trustworthy entity to gain passwords or credit card details), and other unsolicited e-mails.

The FTC makes the following suggestions in the case of identity theft:

- Place a fraud alert on your credit reports, and review your credit reports.
- Close the account that you know or believe to have been tampered with or opened fraudulently.
- File a complaint with the Federal Trade Commission.
- File a report with your local police or the police in the area where the identity theft took place.

Ned (name and face disguised) demonstrates how items stolen from Dumpsters are used for identity theft.

Investigations

The strongest arguments against Psaier's existence comes from the Andy Warhol Foundation for the Visual Arts, which is supported by funds from Warhol's estate and the Warhol Museum. They were responding to queries by warholstars.org, a private research project that has been called "Warhol on the Web." Officials at the foundation stated they have never encountered Psaier's name. Curators at the Warhol Museum searched through their extensive archives and found no trace of Psaier's name, a fact that they consider "extremely unusual."

The only known photo showing Psaier (left) with Warhol has not convinced many critics, and the supposed photographer remains unknown.

Newspaper Search. Journalists have also been on the trail of the invisible Psaier. Investigative work in 2009 by the *Sunday Times* of London could not find any Warhol experts or friends who were aware of Psaier. Its reporters also scrutinized Studio Psaier, Inc., the Los Angeles company that owns the backlog of Psaier's works. It is run by Peter Psaier and Nadia Fairchild, the daughter of John Fairchild, a British man convicted in 1992 of selling counterfeit paintings and artifacts. In 2001 John Fairchild started a company, Factory Additions, which supposedly authenticated many of Psaier's works. When the newspaper went to Peter Psaier's home in Los Angeles to ask if the artist had existed, he replied, "What do you know, what do you think?"

Art for Art's Sake

Reports about Psaier's possible nonexistence have delayed some sales and apparently dampened prices. Authentication has caused other problems. One picture of Marilyn Monroe was auctioned with a "probate clearance" document from California's secretary of state. However, this type of document does not exist and the office labeled the claim fraudulent. However, though fraud is suspected by sellers and buyers, they still express interest in the art works. "I buy them on artistic merit alone," said Peter Barham, an antiques dealer in Nottinghamshire, England, who purchases them at auctions. "I wouldn't mind if they were by Fred Bloggs."

POISONOUS PHARMACEUTICALS

When U.S. and Canadian consumers were warned in 2007 to avoid all toothpaste made in China, the precaution highlighted yet another example of Chinese companies using diethylene glycol, a syrupy poison ingredient of antifreeze, in consumer products.

The tainted toothpaste was first found in New York, New Jersey, Massachusetts, Pennsylvania, and Maryland. Some of it had entered the United States as counterfeit Colgate, with a label saying it was manufactured in South Africa. However, Colgate-Palmolive, the world's largest toothpaste maker, stated that it did not import toothpaste from South Africa and had never used diethylene glycol as an ingredient in its products. The tubes were therefore clearly counterfeit, complete with misspellings like South African Dental *Assoxiation*. Besides the United States and Canada, 32 other countries—including Australia, Nicaragua, Honduras, and Costa Rica—discovered and recalled tens of thousands of tubes of the tainted toothpaste.

Chinese regulators say they have investigated the allegations and found that the toothpaste manufacturers had done nothing wrong. They insisted that small

Relatives of those who died in 2007 after treatment with diethylene glycol protest in Panama City on March 31, 2009, demanding compensation.

amounts of diethylene glycol could be used safely in toothpaste but added that they would introduce new, more rigorous controls.

Cheap Substitute. Counterfeiters increase their profits by replacing the safe additive glycerin with the highly toxic diethylene glycol because it is cheaper. This practice has caused deaths around the world, including an incident in Panama in 2007 when a Chinese-manufactured substance labeled as 99.5 percent pure

Counterfeit purses, some labeled Dior and Burberry, are sold in Hong Kong, China.

CHINESE FAKES

Despite government efforts to stem the flow, fake products from China are constantly being unloaded in American ports and around the world. The Chinese are known for copying virtually any popular item, including drugs, cigarettes, electronics, handbags, carpets, sneakers, golf clubs, and liquor. Estimates for 2009 suggest 200 trillion counterfeit cigarettes were produced in China alone, while its fake and possibly dangerous pharmaceuticals will grow into a $150 billion industry.

Raids and arrests make dents in the traffic, but it quickly recovers. In March 2009 Italian police raided 17 warehouses in Rome and seized more than $28 million worth of counterfeit electronics, clothes, and around 150,000 children's toys labeled as Disney and other brands. The year before, Interpol announced "Operation Storm," a coordinated police crackdown across Southeast Asia that discovered 16 million doses of counterfeit drugs valued at $6.6 million.

In recent years, the West has pressured the Chinese government to clamp down on counterfeiters. In January 2009 a court in Shenzhen handed down prison sentences to 11 ringleaders of the world's largest software-counterfeiting syndicate. They had manufactured an estimated $2 billion worth of counterfeit Microsoft products in at least 11 languages and distributed them in 36 countries on five continents.

Consumers in China are also victims of fake merchandise. The European Spirits Organization estimates that a quarter of all liquor labeled as European brands are fakes. Investigators discovered Cabernet Sauvignon purported to come from a nonexistent winery in British Columbia, Canada. The label featured a red maple leaf and the words *Friendship from Canada*. Counterfeit electronics are another internal problem. In August 2009 the World Trade Organization ruled in favor of the United States against China's restrictions on importing American DVDs and other media products, a move that may slow the production of Chinese fakes in that area.

glycerin was mixed with cold medicine. Two hundred and sixty thousand bottles were released onto the market, and more than 100 people died. The same year, 18 people died in China after taking similarly poisoned medicine.

Decades of Deception

Incidents like this have been occurring for more than a decade. In 1992 a health supplement containing diethylene glycol killed 29 people in Argentina.

In 1995 at least 88 Haitian children, most under the age of five, died after taking a fever medicine with a lethal concentration of the poison. When officials from the U.S. Centers for Disease Control (CDC) went to Haiti to provide assistance to other victims, they found the children suffering from facial paralysis, respiratory failure, and brain damage.

The same year, Dastech International, Inc., a company based in Great Neck, New York, bought 284 barrels of "glycerin" from Sinochem, a Beijing-based company owned by the Chinese government. The barrels were labeled 98 percent pure glycerin, but Dastech soon received a complaint from a customer and ran a test on the syrup, which proved to be diethylene glycol. Diethylene glycol poisoning is extremely painful. Death occurs from rapid kidney failure, but the poison can also cause nausea, vomiting, high fever, and swelling of the limbs.

In 1996, 36 children died the same way in Delhi, India, after a local druggist unwittingly mixed the poisonous ingredient from China into acetaminophen (paracetamol) syrup.

The Investigation

After the Haitian tragedy, investigators from the U.S. Food and Drug Administration (FDA) were concerned that the same poison could be shipped into the United States or other countries. They asked Chinese officials for the name of the state-owned company that had produced the poisonous syrup and had exported it as a safe ingredient, but their request was ignored.

An FDA agent then traveled to China to investigate further, only to be told that the companies were not responsible for the deaths, and that the plant involved in supplying the ingredient had been shut down.

> CHINA IS TURNING INTO ONE OF THE MAJOR BULK PHARMACEUTICAL PRODUCERS IN THE WORLD. UNLESS THEY HAVE AN OPEN, TRANSPARENT, AND PREDICTABLE SYSTEM FOR DEALING WITH PROBLEMS AND OTHER COUNTRIES, IT IS GOING TO BE ROUGH SLEDDING IN THE YEARS AHEAD.
>
> —MARY PENDERGAST, DEPUTY COMMISSIONER, U.S. FOOD AND DRUG ADMINISTRATION

The Hidden Source. The investigation into the source of the diethylene glycol was hampered because the poison had been passed along a distribution chain, within the global economy, involving many different companies. The initial Chinese company, which was not registered to make pharmaceutical ingredients, labeled the poison as a pharmaceutical-grade substance. It was then transferred to a state-owned exporter, who shipped it to European traders where it changed hands several times (five times in the Panama case and six in the Haiti case).

The original source did not appear on shipping labels, other documents, or product packages. This practice, called neutralization, assures that the final buyer never knows who actually manufactured the substance. To add to the confusion, European middlemen often hide the origin of a shipment by photocopying their own letterhead onto a copy of the Certificate of Analysis. This document needs to come from the factory that made the product and attest to the contents of the shipment and who manufactured it. Chinese certificates often disappear as the product moves through new hands. This practice makes it impossible to trace the manufacturer if problems occur.

The Chain Is Revealed. Despite the complications, in 1996 the FDA discovered that the lethal ingredient had been sold to Haiti by a Dutch company called Vos BV, who was acting for a German broker called

Chemical Trading and Consulting. The barrels of poison had come from Sinochem. Sinochem first refused to reveal the manufacturer of the lethal ingredient, but after constant pressure from the United States, it eventually named the Tianhong Fine Chemicals Factory. No address was available, they said, only a telephone number. Sinochem's plant manager, who also refused to reveal its address, told American officials that their own tests had found no diethylene glycol.

Chemical Manufacturing Plant. In November 1997 U.S. investigators again questioned Sinochem managers, who simply said that the product had passed through several other companies. They told the Americans to look at every link in the supply chain to find the source of the poison. The 18-month-long investigation hit a dead end in December 1997, when an FDA agent gained access to the Tianhong plant in Xingang. Unfortunately it had already been shut down, and the records had been destroyed. The manager claimed that his company had never produced the poison. Dr. Suzanne White Junod of the FDA reported in 2000 that the poison was not produced in a pharmaceutical plant but rather in a chemical manufacturing plant. She particularly blamed uncooperative local officials for hampering the initial investigation.

Compensation. A 10-year compensation claim against the Dutch seller, Vos BV, resulted in Dutch authorities assessing a $250,000 fine against the company. It had tested the counterfeit product and discovered that it was impure, but it failed to warn anyone in Haiti.

Counterfeiters are still seldom identified, much less face prosecution. No international authority exists to pursue leads across foreign borders, leaving it up to individual countries to trace the source of poisonous consumer products.

Lingering Doubts

- Since tests by the Dutch company successfully identified the poison diethylene glycol, why aren't more official tests required for Chinese imports?

- Why are there no international regulations to check the movement of goods along the global distribution chain? Why are so few middlemen prosecuted and fined?

- Should the U.S. Government put more pressure on Chinese authorities to reveal the names and addresses of illegal manufacturers?

HACKING INTO THE PENTAGON

The F-35 Joint Strike Fighter (JSF) jet program, at a cost of $300 billion, is the most expensive project ever developed by the U.S. Department of Defense. The department calls the aircraft "the world's foremost stealthy supersonic, survivable, lethal, supportable and affordable multirole fighter." Lockheed Martin has led the plane's development by nine countries: the United States, United Kingdom, Italy, Canada, Australia, Norway, Denmark, the Netherlands, and Turkey. JSF aircraft have had many test flights, and more than 2,400 of the jets will be built.

A computer system is tested during the Ethical Hacking class at the InfoSec Institute in Manassas, Virginia. The class helps identify security holes.

The Hack

Beginning in 2007 and continuing into 2008, hackers broke into the Pentagon computer system to copy and steal several terabytes (trillions of bytes) of data concerning the jet fighter's design and electronics systems, which diagnose the aircraft's maintenance problems during flights. The spies used technology to encrypt data while it was being stolen, so investigators could not pinpoint what information was taken. The breaches were made through computers belonging to defense contractors working on the project.

Failure to Supervise. A Pentagon report said the Department of Defense had failed to oversee the 1,200 contractors enough and was working more closely with them to improve cybersecurity. It said one hacking had occurred in Turkey and also named BAE Systems, the British arms company, as one victim. However, BAE said no information had been compromised.

Program Compromised. According to the *Wall Street Journal,* which reported the story in April 2009, the spies were unable to access the most sensitive data, such as flight controls and sensors, because it is kept on military computers that are not connected to the Internet. However, the officials explained that the thefts would make it easier for potential enemies to defend against the fighter. American counterintelligence chief Joel Brenner added that warplane programs have been compromised in the past.

Similar Attacks

Attacks on Pentagon computers had escalated dramatically in the six months before the JSF incident. One involved a serious breach of the U.S.

Air Force's air-traffic control system. This particular stolen information might allow enemies to disrupt the system, even to the point of confusing or damaging aircraft. Brenner, who warned that "our networks are being mapped," suspected the Chinese government.

First Breach. In June 2007 the first very sophisticated cyberattack on the Department of Defense occurred with a breach of a noncritical area of the Defense Secretary's office after the Pentagon had staved off the hacker attempts for several months. Investigators assumed this had come from within the Chinese government because of the advanced technology used to break through the computer firewalls. The Pentagon took its computers off line for more than a week.

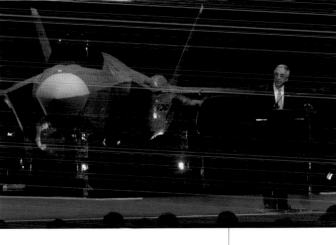

U.S. Deputy Secretary of Defense Gordon England speaks at the inauguration ceremony of the Joint Strike Fighter program at the Lockheed Martin plant in Fort Worth, Texas, on July 7, 2006.

Other Targets. Commenting on this breach, Britain's MI5 intelligence organization said up to 20 foreign spy agencies were involved in hacking operations against Britain, with China and Russia posing the greatest concern. Around the same time, Germany's *Der Spiegel* reported that spying was detected on the computer systems at the office of the Chancellor, foreign ministry, and other government agencies.

Suspects

The U.S. Air Force is conducting an investigation into the breach. Although authorities cannot discover the origin or identity of the JSF hackers, some say the attacks possibly did come from China since the web addresses seem to be the same previously used in Chinese attacks.

The Chinese. A Pentagon report a month before the breach said the Chinese military has made "steady progress" in developing computer hacking techniques. Its military also sponsors competitions for hackers and chooses the most skilled for undisclosed contract assignments. One former Department of Defense official said the Chinese military has been testing the Pentagon's networks hundreds of times a day. China's state-run *Global Times* claimed its hackers could not be guilty since "from a

DEFENDING U.S. MILITARY SECRETS

Hackers have been targeting the Pentagon since the dawn of the digital age. In 1986 five West Germans working for the Soviet Union's KGB began hacking Pentagon sites. By 1998 Vice President Al Gore had announced a new federal encryption policy for the Internet to block terrorists from acquiring defense secrets. At that time, the Defense Department began removing sensitive information from its web pages. This move was necessary because the military sent 95 percent of its communications over public networks. By 2009 the department had approximately 90,000 personnel defending its 15,000 networks.

In May 2009 U.S. President Barack Obama announced the creation of a cybersecurity coordinator who would oversee defense against computer hacking and have regular access to the White House. Plans were also underway for the Pentagon to establish a new cybercommand to organize and train personnel for digital warfare. The U.S. Department of Defense now operates a Cyber Crime Center to coordinate responses to hackers threatening the defense industry. The Center has 277 employees, mostly contractors, who work together to thwart the growing attacks. Alongside this team, military contractors individually fight the problem. After Lockheed Martin officials notified the government about hackers who had stolen data about the Joint Strike Fighter, the company began its own investigations at its Security Intelligence Center.

Also in May, the U.S. Air Force announced it would establish its own Cyberspace Command, the 24th Air Force, at Lackland Air Force Base, in Texas. It is focused on protecting the Air Force's crucial websites, but it also has the ability to attack hostile computer networks. "If they want to fight with us in cyberspace," said the command's head, Lt. Gen. Robert Elder, "we're willing to take them on there, too." He called the command's personnel "cyberspace warriors."

A representative from the Department of Defense Cyber Crime Center offers advice at the IACP Annual Conference.

technical point of view on the global scale, hackers in the United States, Russia and Israel are at a higher level than those in China." For its part, the Chinese Embassy in Washington, D.C., said its country "opposes and forbids all forms of cybercrimes."

Other Governments. The Chinese are not alone as possible suspects. According to Deputy Defense Secretary William Lynn in December 2009, more than 100 foreign intelligence agencies, including those of North Korea and Iran, are trying to hack into the Department of

Defense's seven million computers "So our defense networks are under threat each and every day," he added. "They are probed thousands of times a week. They are scanned millions of times a day, and the frequency and sophistication of these attempts and these intrusions are increasing exponentially."

Amateur Hackers. Besides hostile governments, Pentagon officials are aware of breaches by terrorists, organized crime groups, and disgruntled employees. Some recreational hackers try to crack the Department of Defense systems just for fun, including:

- **Gary McKinnon, 43.** A Briton accused of what Americans called "the biggest hack into military computers ever detected." McKinnon, who broke into the computer networks of nearly 20 U.S. military and six NASA facilities, confessed but said he was only searching for evidence of UFOs. He was arrested in 2002 and was still fighting extradition to the United States in 2009, where he would be brought to trial and face up to 60 years in prison.

- **Ehud Tenenbaum, 18.** An Israeli who hacked into unclassified material on the Pentagon, NASA, and Israeli parliament sites in 1998, Tenenbaum received only a suspended sentence and a fine.

- **Chad Davis, 19.** A man from Green Bay, Wisconsin, Davis was arrested in 1999 and sentenced to six months in jail for hacking into a U.S. Army page on the Pentagon site and modifying its contents.

Lingering Doubts

- Why does the Department of Defense keep any critical secrets on the Internet if it maintains a separate computer system unconnected to the Web?

- If the Pentagon believes that the Chinese may have stolen data about the Joint Strike Fighter, why can't its technology trace the source for definite proof?

- Since the enemy has apparently gained information to help it defend against the fighter, will modifications be made to the warplane?

- Is it possible that spies are in the Pentagon or among its civilian contractors and tell hackers how to breach their systems?

ADDITIONAL READING

Anderson, Andrew. "John Ward: 'If I Could Solve This, Then I Could Grieve.'" *Daily Telegraph* (London), September 7, 2008.

Bakri, Nada and Graham Bowley. "Top Hezbollah Commander Killed in Syria." *New York Times*, February 13, 2008.

Balakrishnan, Angela. "What Happened on the Day Madeleine Disappeared?" *The Guardian* (London), April 11, 2008.

Banks, Leo W. "The Girl in the Desert Cage." *Tucson Weekly*, November 27, 2003.

Bascomb, Neal. *Hunting Eichmann*. Boston: Houghton Mifflin Harcourt, 2009.

Bazley, Thomas. *Crimes of the Art World*. Westport, CT: Praeger Publishers, 2010.

Bennetto, Jason. "Great Unsolved Crimes: The King, the Conman and a Millionaire's Murder." *The Independent* (London), January 19, 2006.

Bird, Steve. "Theories: So Who Did Kill Jill Dando?" *The Times* (London), August 1, 2008.

Blanford, Nicholas. *Killing Mr. Lebanon: The Assassination of Rafik Hariri and Its Impact on the Middle East*. London: I. B. Tauris, 2006.

Bogdanich, Walt. "F.D.A. Tracked Poison Drugs, But Trail Went Cold in China." *International Herald Tribune*, June 16, 2007.

Bondeson, Jan. *Blood on the Snow: The Killing of Olof Palme*. Ithaca, NY: Cornell University Press, 2005.

Boser, Ulrich. *The Gardner Heist: The True Story of the World's Largest Unsolved Art Theft*. Washington, D.C.: Smithsonian Books, 2008.

Brandt, Charles. *I Heard You Paint Houses: Frank "The Irishman" Sheeran and the Inside Story of the Mafia, the Teamsters, and the Last Ride of Jimmy Hoffa*. Hanover, NH: Steerforth Press, 2004.

Brooks, Richard and Georgia Warren. "Andy Warhol Acolyte May be Artistic Illusion." *The Times* (London), August 30, 2009.

Burrough, Bryan. "Missing White Female." *Rolling Stone*, January 2006.

Butterfield, Fox. "'The Fugitive Didn't Do it.'" *New York Times*, February 9, 1997.

Cathcart, Brian. *Jill Dando: Her Life and Death*. London: Penguin Books, 2001.

Chivers, C. J. "A Fearless Activist in a Land of Thugs." *New York Times*, July 17, 2009.

Chivers, C. J. "Colleagues Honor Slain Russian Journalist with a Book and Demand Justice." *New York Times*. May 31, 2007.

Church, Robert. *Murder in East Anglia*. London: Robert Hale, 1987.

Collins, Danny. *Vanished: The Truth About the Disappearance of Madeleine McCann*. London: John Blake Publishing, 2008.

Coloradoan (Fort Collins). "Peggy Hettrick Murder Case Timeline," January 20, 2008.

Cooley, John. *Currency Wars: How Forged Money Is the New Weapon of Mass Destruction*. New York: Skyhorse Publishing, 2008.

Corchado, Alfredo. "Pancho Villa Assassin's Kin Say U.S. Goverment Still Owes Reward." *Dallas Morning News*, March 9, 2008.

Coreno, Catherine. "D. B. Cooper: A Timeline." *New York Magazine,* October 22, 2007.

Crimaldi, Laura and Tom Mashberg. "Step by Step, Retrace Art Thieves' Path." *Boston Herald*, March 16, 2009.

Daily Record (Glasgow, Scotland). "Suzy Lamplugh Cops Ponder Steve Wright Link," February 22, 2008.

Deflem, Mathieu. "Top Hezbollah Commander Killed in Syria." *Washington Post*, February 13, 2008.

Delventhal, Ivan. "Michaela Kidnapping A Mystery Years Later." *Oakland Tribune* (California), October 10, 2004.

Dennis, Brady. "Search for Sabrina Redoubled." *St. Petersburg Times* (Florida), October 20, 2000.

Dimanno, Rosie. "The Boy Who Never Returned." *Toronto Star*, December 20, 2006.

Edwards. Richard. "Poison-tip Umbrella Assassination of Georgi Markov Reinvestigated." *Daily Telegraph* (London), June 19, 2008.

Fenton, Ben. "What is Polonium 210?" *Daily Telegraph* (London), November 25, 2006.

Freed, Anne. "Dissecting Murder: Bone by Bone." *Toronto Star*, September 4, 2008.

Gavron, Jeremy. *Darkness in Eden: Murder of Julie Ward*. London: HarperCollins, 1993.

Gill, Charlotte. "DNA Breakthrough Could Solve Britain's Oldest Murder Case." *Mail on Sunday* (London), November 5, 2008.

Gleadell, Colin. "Andy Warhol's Mystery Acolyte Pietro Psaier." *Daily Telegraph* (London), September 16, 2008.

Gordon, David. "The Winter's Night They Took Shergar." *Belfast Telegraph* (Ireland), May 31, 2003.

Gorman, Siobhan, August Cole and Yochi Dreazen. "Computer Spies Breach Fighter-Jet Project." *Wall Street Journal*, April 21, 2009.

Graysmith, Robert. *The Murder of Bob Crane: Who Killed the Star of Hogan's Heroes?* New York: Crown Publishing Group, 1993.

Graysmith, Robert. *Zodiac*. New York: Berkley Publishing Group, 1996.

Harding, Luke. "Who Shot Natalia Estemirova?" *The Guardian* (London), July 23, 2009.

Hodel, Steve. *Black Dahlia: The True Story*. New York: Arcade Publishing, 2003.

Holloway, Beth. *Loving Natalee: A Mother's Testament of Hope and Faith*. New York: HarperOne, 2007.

Hussain, Zahid. *Frontline Pakistan: The Path to Catastrophe and the Killing of Benazir Bhutto*. London: I. B. Tauris, 2008.

Hunt, Swanee. "Russian Roulette: The Murder of Journalist Anna Politkovskaya Ripples Worldwide." *Sojourners*, January 2007.

Katz, Friedrich. *The Life and Times of Pancho Villa*. Palo Alto, CA: Stanford University Press, 1998.

Kelowna Daily Courier (British Columbia, Canada). "Man Cleared in Tran Murder Settles Suit with Mounties," December 31, 2000.

Kunstler, William. *The Hall-Mills Murder Case: The Minister and the Choir Singer*. New Brunswick, NJ: Rutgers University Press, 1980.

Lang, Holly. *The Notorious B.I.G.: A Biography*. Westport, CT: Greenwood Publishing Group, 2007.

Las Vegas Sun. "Where I Stand—Classic Hank: An Offer for Return of Cary Sayegh," August 3, 2001.

Leville, Sandra. "The Lord, the Lag and the Stolen Antiques." *The Guardian* (London), August 28, 2004.

Lewis, Damian. "Soldiers of Fortune." *Daily Mail* (London), June 2, 2007.

Lohr, Steve. "Palme Case: A Field Day for the Conspiracy Set." *New York Times*, September 28, 1989.

Long, Bruce. *William Desmond Taylor*. Lanham, MD: Scarecrow Press, 1991.

Louvish, Simon. "Silent Victim." *The Guardian* (London), October 24, 2003.

McDonald, Henry. "Employee Cleared of £26.5m Northern Bank Robbery." *The Guardian* (London), October 9, 2008.

McGrath, Darrin. *Hitching a Ride: The Unsolved Murder of Dana Bradley*. St. John's, Newfoundland, Canada: Flanker Press, 2003.

McKittrick, David. "Ireland's Crown Jewels: the Case of the King, the Courtiers and the Gay Cover-up." *The Independent* (London), November 12, 2003.

McVicar, John. *The Belfast Bank Robbery*. London: Artnik Books, 2006.

Martin, John. "Major Events in the Aisenberg Case." *St. Petersburg Times* (Florida), February 22, 2001.

Masood, Salman and Carlotta Gall. "Bhutto Assassination Ignites Disarray." *New York Times*, December 28, 2007.

Mihm, Stephen. "No Ordinary Counterfeit." *New York Times Magazine*, July 23, 2006.

Miletich, Steve. "Five Years Later, FBI Still After Wales' Killer." *Seattle Times*, October 12, 2006.

Mosedale, Mike. "The Killer Inside." *Minneapolis News*, November 9, 2005.

Moyes, Jojo. "Robbers Grab Pounds 5m from Security Van." *The Independent* (London), July 4, 1995.

Nakashima, Ellen. "Defense Department Joins Forces with Industry Against Cybercrime." *Washington Post*, May 25, 2009.

Neff, James. *The Wrong Man: The Final Verdict on the Sam Sheppard Murder Case*. New York: Random House, 2001.

New York Times. "Brazil Art Heist Is Cloaked by Carnival," February 25, 2006.

New York Times. "Strangling of a Little Girl Who Had Everything Stuns Boulder," January 1, 1997.

Punch, Rachel. "ACCENT: The Unsolved Murder of Renee Sweeney—Questions, But No Answers." *Sudbury Star* (Ontario, Canada), January 23, 2010.

Puod, Ric R., and Johnna Villaviray. "Ninoy's Death a Triumph for the 'Invisible Group.'" *Manila Times*, August 20, 2003.

Reed, J. D. *Pursuit of D. B. Cooper*. New York: Dell Publishing, 1981.

Rhys, Steffan. "Sion Jenkins: I Saw Who Killed Billie-Jo." *Western Mail* (Cardiff, Wales), August 2, 2008.

Roberts, Genevieve. "Billie-Jo Jenkins Died Minutes After Attack, Court Told." *The Independent* (London), November 2, 2005.

Rubin, Paul. "The Bob Crane Murder Case Part Two." *Phoenix New Times*, April 28, 1993.

Samuel, Henry. "French Secret Services Accused of Link to Murder of Ben Barka." *Daily Telegraph* (London), October 16, 2009.

Seale, Patrick. "Who Killed Rafik Hariri?" *The Guardian* (London), February 23, 2005.

Shukovsky, Paul. "FBI Cuts Agents Looking into Murder of Tom Wales." *Seattle Post-Intelligencer*, June 3, 2006.

Silvester, John. "'Mr Cruel' Filmed His Victims, Say Police." *The Age* (Melbourne, Australia), April 8, 2006.

Sixsmith, Martin. *The Litvinenko File: The Life and Death of a Russian Spy*. New York: St. Martin's Press, 2007.

Smith, Carlton. *Death of a Little Princess: The Tragic Story of the Murder of JonBenet Ramsey*. New York: St. Martin's Press, 1997.

Snookes, Harriet. "Rothschilds' Stolen Waddesdon Trinkets May Never Be Recovered, Police Fear." *Bucks Herald* (Aylesbury, England), December 17, 2009.

Spokane Daily Chronicle (Washington). "Pair Acquitted in Kidnapping," December 8, 1999.

Stephen, Andrew. *The Suzy Lamplugh Story*. London: Faber and Faber, 1988.

Stoler, Peter, Barry Kalb and Jonathan Beaty. "Italy: The Great Vatican Bank Mystery." *Time*, September 13, 1982.

Sullivan, Randall. "The Unsolved Mystery of the Notorious B.I.G." *Rolling Stone*, December 15, 2005.

Taylor, Troy. *Bloody Chicago*. Alton, IL: Whitechapel Productions Press, 2006.

Telzrow, Michael E. "The New Chinese Take-Out." *The New American*, August 20, 2007.

Time. "The Murder of Mehdi Ben Barka," December 29, 1975.

Time. "The Silkwood Mystery," January 20, 1975.

Time. "The Trouble with Harry," June 1, 1959.

Tomlinson, Gerald. *Fatal Tryst: Who Killed the Minister and the Choir Singer?* Lake Hopatcong, NJ: Home Run Press, 1999.

Turner, Colin. *In Search of Shergar*. London: New English Library, 1984.

Vaughan, Kevin. "No More Cuffs: Masters Free." *Rocky Mountain News* (Denver), January 23, 2008.

Villisca Review (Iowa). "8 People Murdered in their Beds in Villisca," June 13, 1912.

Williams, Paul L. *The Vatican Exposed: Money, Murder and the Mafia*. Amherst, NY: Promethus Books, 2003.

Wolfe, Donald H. *The Black Dahlia Files*. New York: Little, Brown Book Group, 2006.

Zacharias, Pat. "The Day Jimmy Hoffa Didn't Come Home." *Detroit News*, August 28, 1999.

Zoellner, Tom. "Amateurs Stir Embers of Notorious Zodiac Case." *San Francisco Chronicle*, October 2, 2000.

INDEX

PHOTO CREDITS